Praise for *The* ﹙

"Mark Jones brings a rare combination of talents to astrology. He is a professionally trained therapist in the UK, as well as a practicing astrologer. More that, Mark is an astrologer-priest, a seeker of soul, concerned with the spiritual aspirations of those he works with. In *The Soul Speaks*, he addresses the need to bring soul back into the consultation. He sees psychological astrology and therapy as natural allies in the exploration of the psyche. His empathy and willingness to go to places that others may shy away from shines through in the fine writing of this book. In addition, he makes a fundamental point: any astrological encounter has a therapeutic component whether this is the intention of the astrologer or not. He argues ᵛ that all kinds of astrology from horary to humanistic should include basic notions of counseling and transference." - Lynn Bell, author of *Planetary Threads*

"Mark Jones is a psychotherapist of rare ability and perception who uses astrology to get to the heart of a client's issues, life processes, and potentials. At a time when archaic approaches to astrology are being used for natal consultations, it's now more important than ever to have client-focused astrologers like Mark Jones who bring compassion and psychological insight to the consulting room. This book gives us an opportunity to see how he does what he does so well." - Frank C. Clifford, astrologer, lecturer and author of *Getting to the Heart of Your Chart*

"*The Soul Speaks* offers invaluable insights for astrologers who work directly with clients. Mark Jones details counseling concepts as well as translates astrological principles as facets of the therapeutic narrative. Through this, the reader comes to a greater understanding not only of why it is so important to honor the interpersonal dynamics that occur in a reading, but how to navigate them, so as to be of greater service to those seeking guidance." – Stephanie Gailing, MS, author of *Planetary Apothecary*

Praise for *Healing the Soul*

"This beautifully written, deeply insightful book, offers readers an evolutionary approach to astrology which is steeped in compassion and the desire to offer a depth healing tool. Accessible to both novice and more experienced astrologers, this book is also likely to appeal to non-astrological psychotherapists." - Margaret Gray MSW, D. Psych. Astrology, Member of ISAR board

"The author's open mind with regards to past-life experiences and their echoes in a person's current life is very much welcomed by a regression therapist like myself. I think *Healing the Soul* will be referred to as a seminal work for years to come. I highly recommend it." - Pimpernel, Amazon review

"Mark has presented astrologers and students of astrology with a beautifully useful text that outlines how to apply the Evolutionary Astrology paradigm to any chart. *Healing the Soul* is both poetic and simple at the same time. With ease and clarity Mark has written an intellectual yet hugely accessible work." - Lydia Trettis, Astrologer, Salt Lake City, UT

"Mark Jones, through his wisdom and experience as a psychosynthesis therapist and counselor, gives us a serious and well thought out, yet easy to read book, on evolutionary astrology that is useful to the casual reader and professional astrologer alike. As a student and practicing astrologer for more than thirty years, *Healing the Soul: Pluto, Uranus and the Lunar Nodes* immediately became a must-have book for me. This is far more than an astrology cookbook. For the past year, I found repeated new insight and wisdom from reading the same passages again while working on natal charts. For astrologers who use the book, take the time to digest Mark's words. You will benefit by deepening your own wisdom and perspective as an astrologer, and from that, offer a deeper meaning and understanding to your clients' needs." -Nicholas Theo, *ITA Professional*, Norfolk, VA

The Soul Speaks:

The Therapeutic Potential

of Astrology

Also by Mark Jones

Healing the Soul: Pluto, Uranus and the Lunar Nodes

Anthologies

Insights into Evolutionary Astrology

Astrology: The New Generation

Psychosynthesis: New Perspectives

The Soul Speaks

The Therapeutic Potential of Astrology

by Mark Jones

Raven Dreams Press
Portland, OR

Published in 2015 by Raven Dreams Press
1434 NE Prescott St.
Portland, OR 97211
www.ravendreamspdx.com

ISBN 978-0-9840474-4-4
LCCN: 2015944337

Cover Art: Clare Phillips
Book design and production: Tony Howard

Printed in the United States of America

Contents

ACKNOWLEDGMENTS

I owe a debt of gratitude to Laura Nalbandian and the Northwest Astrological Conference (NORWAC) community for the opportunity to present a number of lectures and workshops on psychology, spirituality and astrology over the past several years, in particular a keynote address and post-conference workshop in 2012, which led to the development of this work. Also thanks to Tony Howard for his ongoing support, and for hosting the workshop *Astrology and Soul Psychology* that I presented in Portland, Oregon in the fall of 2011. This workshop helped to solidify my thoughts on the subject and set in motion a chain of events that led to this book.

I need to thank Stephanie Gailing for her editorial responses and Patrick Graham for detailed copyediting of the initial draft. I thank Keith Hackwood for constant therapeutic focus as well as a magical journey inside Roberto Assagioli's world as well as Mary Ransdell for the ongoing conversation about astrological practice over the years that led to many of the central ideas in this book. I thank my partner, Clare for her ongoing love and support.

I would to like to thank my workshop participants and all of my students and clients for invaluable feedback and support, and for the healing experience of the shared influence of the *knowing field*.

INTRODUCTION

More and more people today are turning toward the healing arts, whether counseling, psychotherapy, astrology, hypnotherapy, Reiki, spiritual healing or one of the many emerging mind-body techniques. Astrology in particular holds a most interesting position within this individual and collective need. For astrology is one of the most derided arts/sciences within the modern intellectual paradigm. Many see astrology as the epitome of everything nonsensical about the "scientifically illiterate" or those "naïve New Age seekers." Paradoxically, in a world where we have turned away from an awareness of participatory meaning with everything around us, the astrological reading—this most derided of forms—can prove most transformative. When practiced well, astrology can remind us of our connection to the sky above, to the sensate world, and to the very cosmos.

In the early chapters of her 1982 book *Astrological Counselling*, Christina Rose makes some crucial points that seem just as pertinent now as they did some thirty years ago. She alludes to a shift she perceives happening among professional astrologers that she considers crucial to the efficacy of astrology. This shift involves taking in the *client's point of view* and moving away from a sole reliance on conveying a fixed set of delineations that we can apply to any chart as if it were a math equation.

She writes: "More recently has come the growing recognition that the act of interpreting a birth chart is only of limited value unless the client can be involved in that process as well as the astrologer and can be guided into possible ways of utilizing the information derived from the chart once it has been presented to him." [1]

Rose presents two key ideas: first, a core archetypal understanding of the twelve signs of the zodiac, emphasizing unity between humankind and the cosmos; and second, for this understanding to take hold, the astrologer must convey it in a manner that engages the client. This latter idea relates to one of the main intentions of this book.

She continues: "It is by the joint discovery of the interplay of these processes in the individual chart pattern, by the astrologer and client working *together* as a team, that the particular way the client manifests them in his life ... can achieve greater clarity." [2]

In the pages that follow, we will explore both a vision of the archetypes that seeks to establish humankind's unity with the cosmos as a co-creator of his or her experience and the interplay that occurs during the natal chart reading, with a focus on how best to serve the client's development and healing.

What Rose wrote so plainly in 1982 is far from being a generally accepted practice within the astrological community today. In particular, the understanding of the relationship between the astrologer and client still lacks consistent focus in the astrological mainstream.

As a Psychosynthesis therapist and hypnotherapist in private practice, as well as a practicing astrologer, I am in a unique position to explore the interface between counseling and astrology. Psychotherapy has a focus on the relationship between practitioner and client. Astrology is empowered by the multidimensional symbolic map of the horoscope. When the two goals are unified, the healing potential of the astrological reading is significantly increased.

The Origins of Psychological Astrology

Rose traces the origins of a therapeutically-focused movement among professional astrologers to the 1930s, with Dane Rudhyar's exploration of astrology, theosophy and psychology. It was during this critical period between the great world wars that Pluto was first discovered. And this archetype of power, depth and resistance colors Rudhyar's initial enterprise as well as many others from that time.

It was during the 1930s that Rudhyar first visited Florence and met Roberto Assagioli, a former student of Sigmund Freud, and friend and colleague of Carl Jung, whose work developing Psychosynthesis (what Jung had called the future of Psychoanalysis) had so enticed him.

Psychosynthesis was Assagioli's considered attempt to integrate depth psychology with spiritual truth and experience. This drew Rudhyar to seek him out, for he, too, was trying to integrate depth psychology with a pioneering vision of astrology, in part inspired by an unorthodox connection to theosophy.[3] This kind of thinking was out of step with its time, as evidenced by Benito Mussolini closing the Psychosynthesis center soon after Rudhyar's visit, claiming that it represented a pacifist threat to the National Fascist Party.

In 2012, I was privileged to visit the Psychosynthesis center in Florence where I was allowed temporary access to Assagioli's personal files. There I discovered that for the final half of his life (over forty years) he was a committed student and practitioner of astrology. In fact, for decades he routinely consulted his clients' birth charts as part of his work with them. I found these charts in files—hundreds of detailed hand-drawn charts in delicate ink, with detailed breakdowns of elemental balances and aspects—and was filled with awe.

This was a revelation: the founder of the first, explicitly spiritual vision of depth psychology integrated astrology as a necessary tool.

That astrology has so much to offer psychology is obvious to the committed modern astrologer. The traditional psychotherapist has to invest a great deal of time to get to know their clients well. Each therapist faces the new client as a complete unknown, without any guide to which of the myriad expressions of human potential are at play. The natal chart, then, is a profound counseling tool that can speed up and enhance this process—a map of the client's *specific* archetypal tendencies and soul potential. (My book *Healing the Soul: Pluto, Uranus and the Lunar Nodes* details a system for approaching the natal chart to discover this soul potential.)

In the current volume, I will explore the interface of counseling and astrology to underscore what a spiritual psychology can offer astrology and how, as astrologers, we can best reach our clients in order to maximize their potential—as well as our own—in this life.

-Mark Jones

1

Therapeutic Astrology

"If the astrologer thinks he merely gives bits of information and then is through with the whole thing, he is greatly mistaken. He has established a relationship." –Dane Rudhyar [1]

The Sanity Problem

Many famous thinkers have expressed the idea that one man's madness is another man's sanity. In a letter to Louise Dorothea of Meiningen, Voltaire wrote, "Men will always be mad, and those that think they can cure them are the maddest of them all."[2] Carl Jung said famously, "Show me a sane man and I will cure him for you."

The trouble lies in one's definition of sanity.

This problem of perspective was the great concern of Thomas Szasz, a psychiatrist who generated a profound critique of the psychiatry profession. His moral interrogation of a system in which one man could condemn another to a life of incarceration or electroconvulsive therapy on the basis of this elusive creature "sanity" rendered him a consistent and important voice against the prejudicial idea of the imperative to be "normal."

Szasz gave us these wise words: "If you talk to God, you are praying. If God talks to you, you have schizophrenia." But here we

2   THE SOUL SPEAKS

face a challenge—who determines which experiences of divine intervention are authentic and which are folly? This dilemma of judgment extends back as far back as we can trace, perhaps expressed most problematically during the Inquisition. It's a problem that still plagues us today.

And it's not easy, no matter which side of the equation we're on. If we're the ones hearing God talking back to us, we can find ourselves in just as much hot water whether we're a nun or a cab driver. The context may determine the judgment. For that reason, the cab driver is more likely to be prescribed lithium. But even for the nun, whose contextual reality includes the idea that the existence of God is unquestionable, the thought that she would be so special that God would deign to speak to her directly could just as easily be construed as "madness" by a psychiatric professional. Even a peer may view her inner voices as "the work of the devil."

So how can a sincere spiritual aspirant instigate an authentic connection with the divine and simultaneously keep one grounded foot on the earth?

It's not uncommon for a person undergoing a spiritual awakening or transformation to act "strangely" in the eyes of others. One may give up a "successful" job and lifestyle or walk out on a significant relationship commitment in pursuit of a profound calling. A person may make such a choice from an authentic need for an independent environment in which to follow her unfolding awakening. Or it's possible that the original awakening experience destabilizes her sense of identity to the point that she feels compelled to make drastic changes. The destabilization could even cause her to fear a breakdown.

More often than not, family members and those close to the situation perceive that such a person has "gone mad." Sometimes families attempt to restrain the individual or, in more dire situations, take steps to institutionalize them. There can be fights. Perhaps the family concludes that their loved one has been brainwashed by a cult. And perhaps they're right. The real truth is always complicated.

But navigating these murky waters is challenging for all parties concerned.

The question of what is normal and what is not normal, what is sane or insane, raises complex issues about model we use to predicate our analysis. In the 21st century, children as young as five years old are being prescribed antidepressants. In the not-too-distant past, anxious (or ill-informed) parents have given their children ECT treatments and even consented to the removal of parts of their prefrontal cortex because of perceived "bad" behavior on the part of the child. "Normal" in this analysis seems to indicate the boundary of a punishing line: a fascism of the self.

Furthermore, there is the question of what constitutes a "legitimate" experience of psyche (the interior life of the self). To the extent that the natural chaos of psyche is feared or elicits shame rather than excitement, some form of authority is sought to control the "destructive excess" perceived within. This becomes the basis for both internal and external forms of control. While some control is useful and healthy, the danger here is that, when taken as a shield to remedy a situation, controlling behavior can twist itself into an act of self-violence.

It's with the awareness of this troubling dynamic that we approach our clients, whether we are therapists or astrologers. So we must ask ourselves, how do *we* view the interior of the human psyche? Who defines what is "normal?" And does that definition serve someone who lives his life in an entirely different context than the person setting the limits on the very definition of the word?

These varying contexts can be thought of as containers. The containers themselves aren't bad or wrong. But we need to keep them in mind when we're interacting with each other. There are different containers that the therapist and client are in—the body (soma) holding psyche, the skull encasing the mind. We have the container that holds the societal-conditioned definition of what is normal. And those could be two different containers based on the various culture and subcultures to which each person belongs. We have the container of our own conditioning, dictated by the way we have done things in the past. And we have the container that comprises the entire set of assumptions within the given field of human experience—both internal and external—as to what is allowable. And that's just a start.

Determining a person's sanity involves more than identifying the contexts within which questionable experiences of psyche arise. But if we approach the question of mental soundness with the awareness that context can radically shift our perspective, we're at least making a good beginning.

The Origins of the Depth Psychology Movement

"What has happened to the language of psychology in a time of superb communication techniques and democratic education? Why has its language game departed from the soul's play? We no longer believe that psychology speaks for the soul."
-James Hillman [3]

The *Archetypal Psychology* movement has tried to address the loss of soul within psychological practice by returning to the primacy of the image—that is, the idea that the imagination itself and the images that arise within it have an inherent value and meaning through their relevance to psyche. The images within our psyches are not just an abstract set of choices, an accidental series of descriptions of something separate and "out there." They are not divorced from the one experiencing them. Instead, our mental images and the archetypes that comprise those images have value to the psyche of the individual, even to humanity itself. From Hillman's perspective, the images at the center of the story of our lives contain soul—for soul is what lies beneath the central motifs from which we construct the narrative of our individual, and then collective, lives.

This act of seeing what lies behind the images that make up our personal and collective history leads us into the core of our be-

Relate to Past Life Reg?
"Reason" for blowing change?

ing, and inside that core, into our deepest purpose and intention. If we understand the archetype in this way, we may then construct transformational narratives—a kind of "*healing fiction*," as Hillman suggested in his publication of the same name. [4]

This approach gels nicely with the twelve astrological arche-types. We can see the twelve main archetypes as revealing the soul's music: from Aries through Pisces we encounter a meta-narrative containing the entire range of human incarnational experience. From this perspective, astrology becomes a "music of the spheres" in which the endless combinations of notes (archetypes) express an *Fractals* ever more intricate portrait of the particular circumstances of an individual's life through her horoscope. Laurence Hillman, James Hillman's son, expressed this idea as explicitly relevant to astrology in his book *Planets in Play*.

Let's consider the narrative possibilities of the twelve astrologi-cal archetypes in such a way as to open them to the vision of the soul: that act of seeing with new eyes in order to reveal the rich potential of our inner life and impulse to meaning.

Alongside this exploration of astrological symbolism, we need a vision of psychology that returns soul to the center of our approach. Even the meaning of the word "psychology" reveals *soul* as truly cen-tral to the field.

Use

> "*The word psychology, properly translated, means 'logos (ac-count) of the soul.' The use of 'psyche' instead of 'soul' is a new import into scientific language, an artificial and abstract tech-nical term and is clearly inspired by the wish that arose during the 19th century to avoid the traditional word and to cleanse psychology from all the . . . metaphysical, religious overtones and feeling associations and implications of this word: to sterilize psychology.*"– Wolfgang Giegerich [5]

To understand how psychology suffered this loss of soul, we must return to the origins of the psychology movement. When we contemplate how important the psychological movement of the 20th century has been in contemporary thought and culture, and as part of the purpose of exploring its relevance to astrology, this short detour into the nature of its medical origins becomes crucial.

The Medical Model's Shadow

"The problem which set the background against which Psychoanalysis was developed was created by the breakdown of a context of meaning in European culture. Psychoanalysis as Freud constructed it undertook to solve the problem in medical terms. Experience with psychoanalysis of the past half century has increasingly shown, however, that one cannot reach an experience of meaning by following an approach of diagnostic analysis."
- Ira Progoff [6]

All the early psychoanalysts were also doctors: Sigmund Freud, Carl Jung, and even the explicitly spiritually-orientated Roberto Assagioli were all trained clinicians involved in crossing into the liminal territory between Psyche and Soma; between mind (a term that was meant to include emotions and memory) and body. Given the context of their clinical training, this step from the material world of the body and any dysfunction within it, into the interior world of the psyche, came from the same perspective—the search for pathology, to determine what was "wrong."

Progoff recognized this as problematic after enough time had elapsed to give some overview of the psychoanalytical project. It is only from this historical vantage point that many of the unconscious assumptions that motivated the original psychologists come to light. It is clear within a great deal of Freud's writing and work that, for a long time, he considered the key task to be identifying the hidden motivation behind an action, emotion or event. In exposing that unconscious mechanism of psyche, he believed, somehow everything would fall into its rightful place.

A sensitive reading of Freud reveals the disappointment he felt when this turned out not to be the case. One wonders if his prolonged returning to the "problematic" role of the superego or even the creation of *Thanatos* (the death instinct) was not part of his creative attempt to explain why analysis so often failed. Or maybe it was to ameliorate his personal disappointment that a merely intellectual explanation of complex underlying motivations did not seem to resolve the suffering associated with them.

We might observe a similar issue within certain expressions of astrological practice: that given this incredible diagnostic tool of seemingly endless subtlety and depth, disappointment can arise for the astrologer when the identification of core personality traits or motivations within the client does not produce more transformative results. So what is missing?

In a word: soul. Freud's work and the birth of the psychoanalytic movement emerged as the 19th century transitioned into the 20th century. And while depth psychology is a fundamentally modern movement, its roots lie firmly in the Victorian era. The late 19th century saw the publication of Charles Darwin's *On the Origin of Species* and a subsequent crisis of faith within the dominant Christian model of reality as the philosophical and scientific discourse that began in the Enlightenment era came to prominence. Freud saw the scientific paradigm as central to the success of psychology. His initial work took place in the lab dissecting the human brain, and while he shifted the focus of his study to the interior of the living psyche, he saw the biological, medical model as the central context for psychology. This is an important point in our current study.

The problem inherent in this medical-model approach to psychological healing is still a dark specter in the modern world. For it implies that our problems are all "mechanical" in nature, and so the cure is also assumed to be mechanical. Antidepressant medication is a multibillion dollar industry founded on, at best, dubious medical evidence of the efficacy of this class of drugs. [7] The popularity of this approach shows just how ingrained this limiting medical-model approach is. We'd rather take a pill to cure what ails us than to seek the true cause of our pain and heal it.

Consider this. In the United Kingdom, you can obtain six free sessions of counseling if you are in distress. The waiting list for this service is often one to two years. Besides frustrating, this delay can become tragic when those who would most benefit from immediate help are denied access to it. A client recently shared with me the story of a man who sought help after falling into a deep depression when his wife left him. After being told he'd have to wait 18 months to get help, he committed suicide.

What's more, the relative value placed on therapy versus pharmaceutical "cures" is evidenced here. To the extent that psychological therapy is even seen as useful, it is only paid for in the short-term. There is no recognition of or respect for the more serious psychological disturbance, and no plan for it beyond medication. In the medical culture, the "rational" approach reigns supreme.

At the same time, we can see that modern medicine and science are Apollonian/solar in nature, meaning that archetypally, they revel in the rational—the clear light of the Sun. Which is to say that, without a doubt, advances in science and modern medicine have had real value to humanity. They are an intrinsic part of the whole. It's the imbalance of an overly solar/medical/scientific approach that creates the problem. In such an imbalance, we become more aware of the shadow as expressed through the Moon, the Dionysian world of the emotions, the feminine, the psychological—the "irrational." It's time for us to reintegrate solar and lunar to attain balance. I suggest that we liberate psychotherapy from the purely cognitive approach and realign it, using astrology, with the lunar experience of psyche. In doing so, we'll create a truly holistic approach and a richer engagement with the process.

A major problem with the rational solar approach returns us to our earlier question about authority. Who determines what is "right" and who decides what constitutes the "rational?" This issue becomes especially problematic when the machinery of the state

gets involved. Szasz, who was a psychoanalyst as well as a psychiatrist, criticized the implicit coercion that occurs when the authority
of what he called the *"therapeutic state"* overturns the language and
needs of the emerging personal psyche:

"Freud had a very good idea which was very quickly abused.
Bertrand Russell said that Christianity is a wonderful idea—it's too
bad it's never been tried. That is my view of psychoanalysis. Freud
had a wonderful idea, namely, that he was going to have a completely
private, confidential, one-to-one conversation with another human
being about his or her life. There's no coercion. It's entirely contrac-
tual. The patient pays. But as soon as he developed this, he sacrificed
it ... It immediately became a thing where the premise was that the
therapist knows more about the patient than the patient himself.
There was a kind of manipulation, exploitation involved." [8]

Here we see the potential tyranny that arises when one individual decides what constitutes the state of mental health of another.
Certainly, I had my eyes opened to the problems of institutionaliza-
tion when I was 18. The summer before college, I worked as a cleaner
at a residential mental hospital. I was shocked to discover that some
women had been placed there as teenagers simply for becoming
pregnant outside of wedlock. An even greater tragedy than this injustice is that the institution itself damaged them. Over time their
psychological state deteriorated so much that, to my eyes, they were
indistinguishable from the patients who had been interred with genuine "issues." This speaks to the dire problems that can occur when
a mental health practitioner's world-view collides with a patient's.
History is full of similar examples and the casualties in the wake of
the shifting tides of public opinion. Consider British World War II
codebreaker Alan Turing's tragic end, the result of a widespread societal attitude towards homosexuality in the early and middle parts
of the 20th century, when it was viewed solely as a perversion to be
countered with aversion therapy.

As we delve into this particular shadow-side of human nature,
we see that it is not limited to the domain of psychoanalysts and

psychiatrists. The human urge to dominate, the tendency to place others in some kind of conscious or unconscious hierarchy (in which the *other* is either demeaned or perversely elevated), is prevalent throughout history and in every arena of life. It is important to repeat that the use of discriminating judgments can be healthy. That such judgment calls are open to abuse is almost too obvious to point out. But that this abuse can occur even within the "alternative" worlds of astrology or psychotherapy is not discussed enough. As we proceed, we must explicate this point and relate it ever more acutely to our therapeutic approach to astrology.

The Astrology Reading

When done with specific intention, the astrology reading can be an attempt to achieve what Szasz thought Freud had sold out on: to "have a completely private, confidential, one-to-one conversation with another human being about his or her life." However, even within this private, consensual, moonlit world of the astrology reading, unconscious power issues and expectations surface, indeed driving the very raison d'etre of the event from the beginning.

The suffering or searching client, and even the client with seemingly simple questions about his life purpose, may seek out the astrologer or therapist because he's seeking validation for, or awareness of, a potential that he can't attain on his own. This points to an important concept of which some in the astrological community seem to be only dimly aware: that the astrology reading is a *de facto* counseling dynamic.

It has been said often in the community that astrology has an advantage over traditional psychotherapy because, armed with the birth chart, one can rapidly get into deep territory with the client. But psychotherapy has an advantage over astrology to the extent that psychotherapists have spent more time contemplating the complex dynamics of the apparently obvious reality of two people in a room. In contrast, astrologers have spent more time with the abstract, looking for meaning and correlation within the birth chart.

By its nature, this special relationship of counselor/astrologer to client is loaded with subconscious power issues which must be acknowledged and taken seriously. And while the expectations on the part of the client to "get something" from the counselor are not shameful or inappropriate, they may very well unconsciously (or consciously) tilt the whole balance of the meeting in a skewed direction. So let's shine some light on this dynamic.

The Tyranny of the Should

Much of the stress that contributes to this imbalance is based on the belief that we have control over our lives, or that we *should*, when we feel that we do not. The paradox is that we either feel out of control, or troubled by our relative level of control, so we seek assistance. Even if, with outside help, we come to admit to ourselves that we are not fully in control, we will seek to regain the sense of being in control.

A problem can arise here if we're operating without awareness. Say a woman visits a psychotherapist or astrologer prompted by the desire to "regain control" of her life. A fruitful session may reveal the universal truth that we are never fully in control of our lives. But unconsciously she still has a need to maintain the illusion of control. So outwardly, she finds herself resisting any insight that counters her desire to maintain the illusion of control. She may stop listening, or even reject any help offered by her counselor. Here she becomes a slave to what I'll call the "tyranny of the should."

The inner dialogue that arises in this self-sabotaging state contains a paradox: "Because I am helped, that reveals that I needed help, and only an 'out of control' person needs help. Only a failure needs assistance, so I will sabotage the very help I need by not having wanted to be the kind of person who needed help in the first place!"

In *Neurosis and Human Growth*, Karen Horney calls this the voice of the "idealized self." The idealized self does not believe a

PARADOX

person should need help. Under the influence of the *tyranny of the should*, the person struggles to seek the help she needs because the very part of her that is wounded and needs the help does not believe she *should* need that help, and therefore should not receive it.

good pt.

Horney is unusual within the psychoanalytical community because she posits a real self for which self-realization is a natural and healthy goal (Freud essentially reduced the human psyche to a series of mechanisms or drives). She argues, however, that a person's attempt to evolve the self can create neurotic suffering. The trouble occurs when the person trying to heal begins to work with the *wrong* self—the *idealized* self instead of the *real* self.

Childhood wounding and narcissistic injury can lead to the formation of an idealized self, based more on what the person believes they should be than the reality of who they are. At the time it is formed, this idealized self can be a necessary creation of the imagination that protects one from basic anxiety and childhood shame. But eventually the idealized self can get in the way of our healing.

Even so, not everyone's idealized self will reject help. In some cases, the person develops an excessive attachment to the need for help and assistance. This can happen when fear or excessive alienation/isolation occurs in early childhood. The idealized self forms with the belief that in order to be lovable, constant validation from another is required. In extreme cases, the person may feel immobilized without constant help and reassurance. Such a person has no problem asking for assistance during a reading or counseling session. Instead, her problem takes the form of boundary issues around getting help. She might have trouble constructing a context in which she can address her problems by herself.

The mental defenses we form around emotional wounding express in a multitude of variations relative to our unique background. Whatever form they take, to the extent that they are a diversion from the vulnerability and energy of the real self, they become a source of neurotic suffering because we have lost touch with what is real within us.

The False Self

The *idealized* self is akin to what psychoanalyst Donald Winnicott calls the *"false* self." The false self develops as a protective façade against early intrusions into the child's innocence. As the child cannot bear the anxiety of parental failure, he instead preserves his real hurt in his imagination and presents an increasingly fictionalized self to the external environment in order to survive its disappointments.

Bringing this awareness to our counseling sessions, how can we be effective knowing that our client may be presenting a "false" or *HAPPENS* "idealized" self? What if the client whose suffering prompts her to *all the* seek the reading secretly despises the loss of control implicit in that *time* suffering—and by seeking help to relieve it, sabotages the reading's potential to meet that need?

And what about the astrologer, untrained in recognizing such dynamics and operating with her own unconscious drives and motivations? In the face of such complexity, we can see how easy it might be to slip into playing the safer role of "expert" and glossing over these problems inherent in the counseling dynamic.

Potentially, both client and astrologer can have an unconscious vested interest in making sure that nothing of great importance happens as a result of the reading. Everyone stays in their comfort zone. Everyone maintains control.

In fact, if we are honest with ourselves, the very impulse to learn astrology can arise out of a problematic desire to understand more about our potential so as to gain more control over our fate.

The Astrology Reading as Antidote to Fate

Our need for control (and even the fantasy we develop around that need) is one of the central ways we avoid responsibility for the nature of our experience. In fact, through our desperate attempts to avoid real pain, we can create ever more neurotic suffering for ourselves. We buy into the fantasy that we can control our fate because it makes us feel safer, but when things don't work out, we curse our fate, even though we may very well have a hand in it. If we don't accept responsibility for our actions, we're also likely to be unaware of limiting patterns that lead to self-limiting choices.

In the astrological community, we bemoan our "fate" with disdain towards our own astrological placements, such as, "My love life is rubbish because my Venus is in its fall and square Saturn." But all too quickly, this kind of limiting thinking saps our inner power and sense of autonomy; we have effectively surrendered to an abstraction around the nature of our birth chart.

Spiritually and existentially, this is delusional. All the great spiritual traditions of the world agree that there is a potential for freedom within life. This is not the same as saying that we can change every circumstance of our life; rather, that we can change the response that we have to such circumstances, and as such, shape our future. Can what we curse as fate in our weaker moments be elevated to our *destiny* through transformational insight and radical acceptance? I think so.

One of the critical steps in any therapeutic astrological reading is to be able to encourage others to take responsibility for their own lives. It is vital for the astrologer to allow self-compassion to emerge from *within* the client toward the inner wounded self that may have made poor choices or experienced suffering in the past. Without compassion for our past errors, we will continue to repeat the mistakes of the past for a complex set of reasons, including guilt—which then unconsciously requires punishment of the individual through continuation of the pattern—and/or lack of acceptance or fear in the present.

The person who doubts her ability to take a positive step forward may curse herself for not having taken that step beforehand. But if she is still so scared of facing the issue in the present, how could it have been any different in the past? In this sense, the past exists for the client as a potential boulder blocking the present path. Lack of acceptance for and blame of the past self (or the idealized/

false self) is most simply understood as a displaced anxiety about the present self.

As we review our past, a potential pitfall lies in getting caught in the loop of hypothetical excuses. We're all guilty of such reasoning, which usually begins with statements like, "If only I had not done this . . ." In cases of serious trauma, this can take on a persecutory intensity. But even within the relatively ordinary or trivial representation, this path represents an illusory conceit that divests the psyche of its energy, and therefore limits its potential to heal in the present.

So we can assume that the fundamental ground of a successful astrology reading is the complete acceptance of everything that has already occurred for the individual. All else is hypothetical and therefore unreal—a source of neurotic suffering. So we must accept that everything that happened in our past was on some level *meant* to happen, otherwise it would not have. Anything less than acceptance fails the client in that it lapses into justification for life's hurts instead of revealing the deeper currents of meaning that lie behind even the most severe of traumas. As psychiatrist Mark Epstein reminds us: "The willingness to face traumas—be they large, small, primitive or fresh—is the key to healing from them. They may never disappear in the way we think they should, but maybe they don't need to. Trauma is an ineradicable aspect of life. We are human as a result of it, not in spite of it."[9]

The Return of the Repressed

When you hold a ball under water and then quickly let go, it shoots rapidly back to the surface, seemingly with its own energy. The further below the surface of the water you take the ball, the harder it is to hold down. Likewise, repressed contents of consciousness take tremendous reserves of energy to hold down. One of the great sources of fatigue and burnout in our culture is not just generalized stress, but in particular, the psychic effort required to hold down the repressed contents of our consciousness. If we can successfully release this content, we can reclaim some of that vital life-force energy.

I'm calling this process the *return of the repressed*, because, like the ball under water, what is repressed must return to the surface.

To heal, we need access to enough psychic energy to overcome our fear and blocks. The necessary amount varies with the individual—but I am tempted to appropriate Winnicott's term for mothering, "good enough," as the amount required. My intuition says that for some high-energy people this might be as little as 50 or 60 percent of their psyche, while for others it might be more like 70 or 80 percent.

Through a variety of experiences in the early stages of life (particularly childhood), in the womb or in past lives, in which they were sufficiently conflicted, people leave parts of their psyche behind. Even Freud, with his vehement aversion to the "occult" phenomena that so interested Jung, called the contents of the unconscious "virtually immortal." [10] This is a most interesting term when one begins to open to the concept of a multidimensional self, or soul, which may carry memories of countless prior lives in addition to the current one. It's this concept that we hold when we approach an evolutionary astrology reading. (Refer to *Healing the Soul* for a deeper explication of this point.)

Like planets colliding, unresolved traumatic events and conflicts (past life or present) somehow dislodge parts of the overall psyche, leaving them as disjointed fragments stuck in some liminal zone defined by the past. How to recover these lost elements becomes a critical question when the client wishes to begin reintegration. On a practical level, we could liken a person's attempt at such an endeavor to clearing the weeds before the soil is ready for new life. He may need to release certain relationships with family, friends and intimates; leave a draining or demeaning work environment; or surrender outmoded habits or addictions before he can attain real growth.

This dynamic of the return of the repressed occurs on multiple levels. As we shift our view from the individual to the collective, we can see the dynamic at play in the way the general culture values and devalues astrology. Although astrology is well-accepted and practiced by millions of people, a prevailing world-view, often labeled as "scientific" or "skeptical," grants either no value to astrology, or a demeaned valuation of the astrological profession as "mere entertainment." To the extent that the very value of astrology is itself repressed within the collective consciousness, a core insecurity permeates that community. And it is out of this insecure collective position that the professional astrologer approaches her or his work.

For contrast, one may observe the opposite tendency (and the arrogance) within the medical community, which enjoys an elevated prominence: we project expertise onto our doctors, who we see as veritable gods consulted to repair broken psyches just as often as broken bones. This is the case even though the tools (medications) often do nothing to address the core issues, or worse, cause irreparable damage.

Any inherent insecurity within the profession of astrology creates the potential for collusion between the complex core anxiety and potential insecurity of the client, and its resulting compensatory drives within the astrologer or therapist. Inexperienced, or even psychologically naïve experienced astrologers, are compulsively led into pronouncements and commitments beyond their knowledge or certainty. Whether by their own accord, or driven by the unmet needs of the client, the astrologer may present an analysis which is not wholly justifiable or even true. It is from this place that any astrologer's assertion that the client "should" take this or that action becomes problematic.

The Astrology Reading as Reality Test

Since an astrology reading is often concerned with an unknown and idealized future, as the counselor it is important to keep one foot grounded in our client's reality. We can do this by checking in with our clients to make sure that any steps towards change we are co-creating are firmly rooted in the possible. Most clients will appreciate candor and realism over a rose-tinted approach that is unattainable.

 Those who resist frank appraisals of their circumstance often cling most tightly to the very painful patterns they profess to wish to explore or release. Positive change is always possible. But when the astrologer outlines the potential inherent in the birth chart, the advice may be experienced as unhelpful if the declaration is made without a realistic assessment of the client's circumstance and available support network. Prescribed goals that are too lofty can leave a client feeling disillusioned.

Some people go to astrologers precisely because they cannot face the commitment, expense and explicit expectations of psychotherapy. Such individuals subconsciously do not want to face how much work they need to do to heal. So they seek out an astrologer, expecting one session to provide the magic key that will unlock all their problems.

Both astrology and psychotherapy attract "wounded birds" by definition. It is not uncommon for one in need of healing to project fantastic expectations about breaking free from difficult circumstances onto their counselor. I am not for a moment suggesting that this is anything but appropriate. But our awareness of this dynamic necessitates that we work intentionally to counter it by outlining realistic expectations. As solutions come to mind, whether presented by you or your client, check in to evaluate whether they are possible. Does the client have the resources to make the change proposed? Do they already have the skill needed, or is it something they can realistically attain? Don't be afraid to ask questions that help the client determine the feasibility of any proposed solution.

It is our job to guide our clients towards the real and the possible if we want them to succeed, even if that means we are seemingly limiting the options on the table.

Astrology in a Materialist Society

The conscious and unconscious materialism of modernity heralded by Friedrich Nietzsche's proclamation and lament "God is dead" is the prevailing conditioning for all of us who live and work in the 21ˢᵗ century. That this might be a problem for astrologers, perhaps even more than other therapists or healers, relates to the origins of astrology within predominately animistic and polytheistic cultures in which there was no question at all that the world was anything other than infused with meaning. [11]

In a world of *things*, of meaningless random "stuff" ricocheting around the universe, the answer to Plotinus's great question from *The Six Enneads*: "Are the stars causes?" is a resounding No! [12] And what's more, they are not anything. His subtle elucidations on the relationship of the individual soul to the soul of the world—or in other words, that of Psyche to Cosmos—are rendered meaningless. The profundity and relevance of Plotinus's work, instead of inform- ing the practice of astrology, becomes instead a fascinating cultural diversion—a thesis topic for humanities students discussing ancient relics from civilizations long gone, mere antiques or curios. In this way, the transformational potential of a living astrology is sadly re- duced to the aesthetic value of an antique; ornamentation rather than implementation.

In the words of the celebrated modern philosopher of conscious- ness Daniel Dennett, astrology has been "relegated to the trash-heap of history," from where its psychedelic hues attract merely the intel- lectual magpie and the hippie. [13] From this context, it is completely understandable that many intelligent, relatively open-minded people today have little or no interest in astrology. In fact, compared with the overt breakthroughs within the sciences, medicine and engineer- ing, studying astrology can seem to the uniformed like rejecting a laptop in favor of an abacus.

Also writing about astrology, Patrick Curry, a doctor of the his- tory of science, suggests that despite the achievements of science and technology in the modern era, the system they comprise is as much a mythology as any other way of looking at the world:

"I came to realize that science itself depended on various assumptions that were not only highly questionable but themselves insusceptible to scientific validation. In other words, science was attended by as many mysteries and as much ultimate uncertainty as astrology, which rendered absurd pinning any hopes on clearing up those of the latter by resorting to the former." [14]

This insight is expanded beautifully by biologist Rupert Sheldrake in his book *The Science Delusion: Freeing the Spirit of Enquiry*. Sheldrake's title is a riposte to Richard Dawkins' fundamentalist *The God Delusion*. The irony with Sheldrake's book is that in exposing the limitations of science, it also serves as one of the most lucid introductions to the layman of what it does know. This is a compliment to the even-handedness of the Christian Sheldrake as opposed to the fundamentalism of atheist Dawkins (perhaps another irony).

Much of the problem with the science myth is the extrapolation of possible mechanical laws (physics) into the realm of ultimate meaning (metaphysics). The confusion of the two has rendered the extremely rigorous methodological world of science prone to real philosophical naivety. Most crucially is the tacit or implicit acceptance within the scientific community of a barely concealed primitive existentialism presented in the guise of "scientific materialism." In this picture, much as Jean-Paul Sartre imagined, the universe is conceived of as a meaningless array of matter from which we have no choice but to accept the absurdity, and our only choice is whether or not (through the use of our will) to create whatever meaning we can for ourselves. That the great edifice of modernity shares a core metaphysical parallel with the central character of *La Nausee* (Nausea) is itself perhaps a bit sickening.

Within this world of planets forming via meaningless collisions of dust, where genes replicate by their "selfish" impulses and evolution marches blindly on favoring the "fittest," we rise to apparent dominance, and through this elevated position dominate the world. [15] The way in which we survey the world from this vantage point (the world that we conquered) becomes ever more important for its (and our) survival.

For all our successful dominance over the world of things, the key insight Blaise Pascal raises, in his famous _Pensees_, remains that many of mankind's problems stem from the struggle of the individual to sit alone in a dark room and be at ease with him or herself. This discomfort is what many key psychoanalysts have called _basic anxiety_: "(the) feeling of being isolated and helpless in a world conceived as potentially hostile." [16] Much of mankind's compulsive drive to achievement is seen in a new light when we open our eyes to the extent of this core anxiety. The world becomes a plaything to distract us from our agitation. The more we can get from it, the more we shore our existentially vulnerable selves against life's vast mysteries.

Ultimately, the problem with _things_ is that they are not _people_— they are not sentient life—and equating the two leads to human violence and atrocity. _Things_ can be used up and thrown away. _Things_ can be taken to concentration camps and disposed of _en masse_. Some of the great crimes of human history have been committed by men who were great business managers, good accountants and efficient organizers: organizers of things, just "taking care of business."

When we use astrology to examine our life from within this damaging framework, the natal chart is used as a defense against the existential encounter of our _basic anxiety_ against the cliff face of reality. To this point, in my early twenties, when I first began studying astrology, I would toss and turn at night, wrestling with myself. Then, in the morning light, I would pore over my chart for signs that things would work out in my life ahead, or in worse moods, search for clues as to what might destroy me. What is the thing in which I invested such magical power? What is it other than myself?

I and Thou

Through his symbolically dense work _I and Thou_, Martin Buber has had a profound impact upon the humanistic psychology movement. In a parallel with opening the self to the mystery of the divine, Buber saw the true potential of relationship as that between the I and

Thou; the personal self alert to the transcendent meaning of the reality of the other. As a result of his work, many have responded powerfully to the elevation of the presence of the other as Thou and the implication of inner divinity—the Thou within.

We can contrast the inherent divinity of the I-Thou perspective with the technological salvation myth, or the medical fantasy where, in this privileged world, no one should be allowed to suffer; we can rest assured that clever technicians will create a new pill to ease our pain. The shadow of such a model falls far across the face of the therapeutic venture, turning a person into an "it" for which a mechanical tune-up will satisfy. But if you rob a person of the meaning of her suffering, you steal a portion of her soul, her deeper self. Suffering, depression and questions about the meaning of the individual (and collective) life deserve recognition as the valuable parts of the human experience they are.

Trained in the mechanical vision, harassed doctors cannot be expected to answer the needs of patients, the great majority of whom seek their aid because of emotional, psychological and intimately human dilemmas and fears. Instead, this becomes part of the remit of astrologers, psychotherapists and alternative healers: to offer a context that gives potential meaning to human suffering, or at the very least, allows for the existence of that suffering—without being in a hurry to make it disappear.

Poignantly, our compulsion to remove every trace of this suffering is just as much an indication of the prominence of basic anxiety as the needs of the suffering patients—it's merely more covert. Just as the medical profession expresses this anxiety to heal, or medicate away pain, so we as astrologers and therapists must be vigilant about this tendency in ourselves.

The first noble truth of the Buddha, that life fundamentally is suffering, doesn't mean that Buddhism is a pessimistic path, or that the Buddha was depressed. Rather, it is a fundamental recognition of the existential vulnerability of the human creature, caught "on the fly" between life and death, ever hopeful that the brief time allotted might afford some basic contentment, some semblance of dignity and meaning. This dignity is elucidated profoundly in Buber's maxim: "I and Thou."

The I-Thou bond, that sacred dyad of meaning in self heightened by the self in another, returning to add meaning to the self in me, which in turn, returns meaning to the other (ad infinitum) is the key to therapeutic meaning in the astrology reading. In this way, as astrologers, our best intention can be to overcome our techniques and intellectual positions and meet face-to-face the other—and to serve that being as best we can for the highest good of all.   *Use*

As we will explore further, the *Temenos*, or sacred space, of the reading should contain the potential to recognize the dignity of human beings and all they have had to traverse.

History of Crime

As we increasingly conquer the *outer world*, engaging in our mastery of *things*, we inadvertently make room for opening the doors of perception to the inner world. We discover that our inner experiences contain as many nightmares as they do dreams. This provides a context for the shocking increasing prevalence of mental health problems in the developed world. In *Reuters*, UK edition, September 4, 2011, we find the headline: "Nearly 40 percent of Europeans suffer mental illness." [17] Although people grappling with mental health problems don't necessarily harm anyone, often enough, personal and group psychology are implicated in extreme behavior.

Judging by its title, Colin Wilson's comprehensive *A Criminal History of Mankind* sounds like it would be a detailed forensic analysis of psychopathology akin to his book on serial killers. But it is actually an analysis of the violent history of human civilization: the brutal excesses of the early empire builders, the Romans, the Khans of Asia, and the shadows of religious and ethnic genocide.

Viewed through Wilson's lens, one could argue that our collective history is a history of crime. Consider some "highlights" from this bleak look at the "evolution" of human action on the Earth. In the 12th century, if an entire city did not surrender unconditionally to Genghis Kahn, if residents did not leave the doors to their homes open to his instantaneous plunder, if they fought only for a day before being crushed by the might of his army, he would slaughter every single man, woman and child and pile their corpses into pyramids for his amusement and vindication: tens of thousands of bodies as trophies of his displeasure.

In the 20th century, such megalomaniacal narcissism accounted for the deaths of over a hundred million individuals. We only need mention a few names to evoke mass events of such cruelty that they seem like a dark poem of mourning: Hitler, Stalin, Mao, Pol Pot ...

Today, in the developed Western world, we encourage relative peace with our immediate neighbors and take our aggression instead into the political, economic and sporting arenas. As we create more stability and sublimate our aggression and hostility, we increasingly, whether we wish to or not, open the doorway to Psyche, which recalls the past in layers that Jung saw as opening to the *collective unconscious.*

What Jung perceived in the deepest layer of the psyche was a repository of all the archetypes and forms of human experience. From this perspective, history is the collective unconscious of humanity itself playing out in space and time as events on the world stage. This collective layer of the psyche may also be seen as a karmic dimension in which all the events from our prior-life selves, alongside the prior-life selves of every other person, still resonate. History has a lasting impact on these subtle levels of our inner selves.

As we experience the relative peace of the developed world in the 21st century, sufficient spaciousness emerges for many of us to experience the reverberations of those past conflicts and struggles. From this radical perspective, one of the core reasons for the validity of Pascal's observations on our struggle to be at peace with ourselves comes from the unresolved prior karmic memories and unconscious patterns bubbling up from within.

The Outer Planets as Transpersonal Symbols

We can see, then, that history is on one level an experiential repre-sentation of the collective conscious and unconscious of humanity. It is a literal record, a painting on the canvas of space and time, of the predominant motivations, compulsions, fears and aspirations of humanity as a collective body.

[Humanity understood as a collective is a transpersonal issue] It is literally beyond (trans) the personal. The outer planets represent this transpersonal context of the birth chart. A transpersonal context is one that operates from beyond the boundary of the personal self.

The personal self is symbolized by the inner planets; [*Saturn repre-sents the boundary of the personal self, and the outer planets symbolize the transpersonal self.*]

The transpersonal realm involves the collective, as society and larger socioeconomic forces, and the larger philosophical and cul-tural milieu, just as it represents the collective dimension as it has played out through history. Jung saw the collective unconscious as the well from which humanity draws the archetypes, or templates, of its core potential experiences that can be seen through myth, history and stories.

There are only so many stories, so many character types, that then take on infinite variations through their unique and specific occurrences in human life. Similarly, there are only twelve core ar-chetypes in the zodiac which play out through endless variations to create an inexhaustible set of possible meanings or applications. This is astrology's music of the spheres; that we can, as an act of soul, use as a tool to perceive the karmic dramas contained in the greater meta-narrative.

Through the *perennial philosophy*, the core spiritual teachings of the ages, we discover a pervasive teaching as to the transcendent origins of man's being that has existed as a consistent narrative throughout multiple world religions and mythologies. [18] This inte-grative approach recognizes parallels in the mystic teachings of all

major religions and the origin myths of multiple peoples. While the
individual forms of these teachings and the unique beauty and wisdom they bring in their specificity are to be respected, the perennial
philosophy refers to core metaphysical truths that interpenetrate the
essential teachings of these varied traditions.

These core truths include the recognition of the sacred; the inherent divinity of life, and that within every person, there is an essential point of contact with the sacred dimension of life. This could
be likened to a jewel inside our hearts. In ordinary or unawakened
states of consciousness, this jewel is concealed within layers of conditioning, negative thoughts and emotions. If awareness, itself a
manifestation of the sacred quality of life, and therefore a kind of
love in action, is brought to this jewel, it can become clearer, eventually shining forth with royal light. This is the meaning of *raja yoga* as
the royal path; the inner jewel has inherent nobility. The recognition
of this essential inner foundation of our being irradiates our lives
with the light of love and wisdom.

From the perspective of the perennial philosophy, we can see
that the karma of the individual and the collective karma of nations
and all of humanity are contained within the transpersonal realm.
Karma is a complex issue worth exploring further.

Karma

"Ye shall know them by their fruits." - Matthew 7:16

Karma, a word originally from the Sanskrit language, is translated as
"action or deed." The essence of one's deeds was seen to have subtle
impact on the fabric of reality. A kind act literally developed a light;
a cruel one, darkness on the face of things.

We can use the word karma to refer to the impact of one's
thoughts, desires, emotions, fantasies and actions on reality and the
quality of one's being. If this were not a powerful enough concept in
and of itself, when applied to systems of thought, such as Hindu and

Buddhist lineages, in which reincarnation plays a central role, karma is seen to extend through time to include all of one's incarnate selves.

Karma then implies that we are witnessed in our entirety by Cosmos. The infinite field of reality, the totality of all that is, knows us both inside and out. From Luke 12:7: "even the very hairs of your head are all numbered." From this mystical perspective, there is no question whether one is alone: every life is witnessed and every being matters. Karma is more than the dualistic idea it has come to mean in many quarters, where it is seen as a more Saturnian mechanism of punishment or reward. This diminishes the potentially profound spiritual teaching of karma, reducing it to a concept more related to the idea of sin.

The concept of sin undergoes a remarkable transformation between the Old and New Testaments of the Bible, as it moves from an original crime scene in the garden of Eden to something that requires exacting punishments and great lists of what not to do in order to avoid it (the Old Testament book of Leviticus, for example). And then into a potential we all have that God's all-forgiving love can alleviate ("He that is without sin among you, let him cast the first stone," John 8:7). This is the *good news* and it represents a shift away from the all-too-human records of a desert people (majority of the Old Testament) to the profound spiritual power of Christ's teaching.

The parallel notions of sin and karma have arisen simultaneously in such different traditions because the essential nature of reality contains a transpersonal justice that both concepts attempt to symbolize. But the nature of ultimate reality is beyond concepts, and therefore beyond the capacity of language to describe.

This limitation of language, and the very nature of thought, is symbolized in Dante's *Comedia* (Divine Comedy), in which the Latin epic poet Virgil is his guide through the *Inferno* and *Purgatorio*. And yet Virgil, as the symbol of wise intellect, cannot journey into the heavenly spheres of Paradiso. Instead, Dante is met by his love, Beatrice, who leads him into heaven. Language can only point the

Reveals & conceals

way to ultimate truth—and even then, most powerfully in poetry. Poetic imagery offers the potential for perceiving the truth that is beyond words, "the love that moves the sun and the other stars," as Dante so sublimely put it.

Karma operates as a universal law from this nonlinear dimension of ultimate truth. *It symbolizes the way the totality of all that is recognizes what occurs within our very being. All that we are, all we have ever done or dreamed of doing or being, becomes a part of the inner magnetism of our core self. That core self is then made buoyant within the infinite field of reality as an expression of that magnetism, the real nature of our being.*

From the *spiritual* understanding of karma, there is no fate—there is only the expression of who you are (the accumulation of everything that you have been). From the origin of that which is, was and ever shall be, our transcendent being becomes clothed in the deeds (karma) of our lives. And this karmic raiment represents the subtle dimension of our conditioning.

To expand: while our birth may seem accidental, and the conditions of our childhood beyond our control, when approached from the expanded vantage point of karma as spiritual law, our origins actually represent the perfect set of conditions for our evolution. Our origins are the expression of our magnetism as it sits within the field of reality. While in our personal experience, Martin Heidegger's existential idea of our being *thrown* into life has validity, from the perspective of karma, the trajectory is an expression of our *true self* (selves) coming into manifestation.

The Astrology of Karma

The above understanding of karma is the source of Sri Yukteswar's words to his disciple Paramahansa Yogananda: "A child is born on that day and at that hour when the celestial rays are in mathematical harmony with his individual karma." [19]

Spiritually speaking, to develop the implications of the teaching around karma is to recognize the power of intention; that life itself notices our true feelings, that life itself cares about the difference between the accidental and deliberate hurt. Life itself then is witness into the heart of the human being. Thus, in following archetypal psychology into the primacy of the image, as the essence of the twelve archetypes of astrology, we are attempting to emulate life itself, to peer into the essence of the human being—the deep self or *soul* of the individual.

In terms of a therapeutic and *evolutionary* astrology, we can identify the psychological and emotional aspect of the soul as signified by Pluto, and the mental aspect, by Uranus. Karma is contained within the Pluto archetype as our core emotional and psychological orientation, and in Uranus, as our long-term memory, including events of significance, traumatic or otherwise. This emotional and psychological orientation is the karmic inheritance of Pluto, Scorpio and the 8th house, and the subtle mind through Uranus, Aquarius and the 11th house. In their different ways, both point to the memory of intense events in this and other lives.

Pluto operates in terms of intensity. The deepest and most significant emotional and psychological events in the soul's history are the primary significance of Pluto, and therefore, the most direct route to a depth awareness of the soul as perceived through the natal chart.

Uranus operates through subtle conceptual significance, events that left their trace on the mind-stream, that unconscious aspect of the mind that—through hypnosis and certain altered states—can witness experiences beyond the normal range of awareness of the conscious self.

Another way of stating this relationship is that:

Uranus, Aquarius and the 11th house symbolize the subtle, far-ranging quality of the mind that remembers all the experiences that the person has had: be they in early childhood; intrauterine; bardo or prior-life states or memories.

⊙ (Pluto,) Scorpio and the 8th house symbolize how the psyche has selected the most significant of those events and interpreted that significance through ascribing emotional and psychological meaning to what occurred.

⊙ (Neptune,) Pisces and the 12th house symbolize on the ultimate level— the nature of the infinite field of consciousness itself, including both the collective unconscious (the repository of all archetypes) and the essence of consciousness itself: the luminous quality of emptiness characterized as dharmakaya by the Buddhists; the Holy Spirit of the mystic Christians; the ocean of divine love of the Sufis; the Ain Soph Aur (limitless light from the great mystery) of the Kabbalists.

From the perspective of Neptune, all is one and the same, arising from the same basic ground—a non-dual (literally not two) consciousness, inherently divine and blissful, which is then stepped down through all the infinite possible variations of human experience, states of mind and feeling.

Surrender to this ultimate consciousness, and individual karma begins to dissolve into the ocean of bliss and emptiness from which all creation emerges as potential becoming actual, endlessly, without end. From the clusters of star-forming nebulae to the soft ears of a baby deer, to my tired hands writing this chapter on a warm May evening.

Insight is Just the Beginning

To hear of enlightenment is an opportunity, but it does not make one enlightened! So it is with the insights offered by the natal chart. Even if an astrology reading comes close to describing the core potential within a birth chart, that insight alone will not be enough to fully transform the client's life.

Yet, the astrologer can be careful to fulfill the criteria that give the greatest opportunity for transformation—a process that on one level operates by a kind of grace that we cannot, and ought not, aspire to control. That, after all, would just be another way of succumbing to our *basic anxiety*.

Insight is the beginning of a journey towards wholeness; indeed, *use* without insight one cannot even begin. But it is the way in which insight is received, digested and metabolized into an individual's life that is the real key to transformation.

2

Counseling Skills for Astrologers

The field of psychotherapy utilizes a specialized skill set and language that enables therapists to explore the core reality of their clients. In this chapter, we will explore some of these psychotherapeutic concepts with an eye on what can be usefully applied to an astrology reading.

Let's start by exploring some of the personal assumptions that are common within the healing professions in general. One of the most witty and honest analyses was put forward by Jungian analyst James Hollis in his exploration of what he conceived as the chief fantasy of therapy:

> "The chief fantasy of therapy . . . is the notion of progress through goodwill and insight. The general public believes three things of therapy and therapists. One, that therapists know secrets, and that, for a fee and a certain ritual, they will reveal them. Alas, generally speaking, therapists are ordinary people who know no secrets. One may more easily find the secret to losing weight, or finding romance, or improving self-esteem, in almost any popular magazine. Therapists have little to offer on these fronts.
>
> Secondly, it is expected that the therapist will be a good or bad parent to the client. This is a more unconscious notion, to be sure, but it arises from the parent-child paradigm, which is stirred by any supplicant coming before an empow-

ered Other. We have all been there before and will play out the familiar relationships by over-identification with, hostility toward, or dependence upon, the parent surrogate evoked in the therapeutic relationship. As long as this transference remains unanalyzed, the client stays stuck in all the developmental tasks, which have brought him or her to the current impasse.

Thirdly, the public expects magic, that some shaman will venture into their psychic space, exorcise troublesome personal demons, and heal them instantaneously.

Were therapists required by 'truth in advertising' legislation to tell their reality, then virtually no-one would enter therapy. The therapist would be obliged to say at least three things in return to the suffering supplicant:

First, you will have to deal with this core issue the rest of your life, and at best you will manage to win a few skirmishes in your long uncivil war with yourself. Decades from now you will be fighting on these familiar fronts, though the terrain may have shifted so much that you may have difficulty recognizing the same old same old.

Second, you will be obliged to disassemble the many forces you have gathered to defend against your wound. At this late date it is your defenses, not your wound, that cause the problem and arrest your journey. But removing these defenses will oblige you to feel all the pain of that wound again.

And third, you will not be spared pain, vouchsafed wisdom or granted exemption from future suffering. In fact, genuine disclosure would require a therapist to reveal the shabby sham of managed care as a fraud, and make a much more modest claim for long-term depth therapy or analysis.

Yet, however modest that claim, it is, I believe, true. Therapy will not heal you, make your problems go away or make your life work out. It will, quite simply, make your life more interesting. You will come to more and more complex riddles wrapped within yourself and your relationships. This claim seems small potatoes to the anxious consumer world, but it is an immense gift, a stupendous contribution. Think of it: your own life might become more interesting to you!

Consciousness is the gift, and that is the best it gets."[1]

This remarkably wise and funny passage raises a number of critical points, many of which we will explore here. However, let us first address the significance of the central idea of the supplicant other seeking out an authority of potentially magical power. This is so relevant to the astrological world and the intimacy of the astrology reading that I raise it again now for us to understand the stakes of what we are exploring.

Examining and acknowledging the nature of one's defenses is critical to healing. As Hollis suggests, our *defenses* present our biggest roadblock to healing, not our wounds. Without some awareness about our defenses, the transformational potential of an astrology reading is limited.

Reasons Why People Defend Themselves

Let's contemplate the reasons why we create these defenses in the first place. While our young selves are finding ways to grow during earlier developmental stages we rarely have the support or freedom that we enjoy in maturity. The parents we have, the schools we attend and our social groups are fixtures in our lives over which we have little control. Defenses become crucial ways of protecting our nascent identity from excessive damage by outside forces. We may split off from sensitive parts of ourselves to protect them from emotionally brutal situations.

Tragically, we often have difficulty finding our way back to those split-off parts of our identities, even later on when our lives are potentially more conducive and receptive to their gifts. Our sincere attempts to protect those sensitive parts causes us to lose out on fundamental experiences of inner beauty and joy.

Now, while it becomes extremely important in any process of transformation to question and overcome these kinds of defenses, we should bear in mind that we had very good reasons for forming them in the first place. Jung was clear about the need to respect the resistance that people put up when faced with the prospect of changing themselves and the defenses that underpin such resistance:

> "There is good reason and ample justification for these resistances and they should never, under any circumstances, be ridden over roughshod or otherwise argued out of existence. Neither should they be belittled, disparaged, or made ridiculous; on the contrary, they should be taken with the utmost seriousness as a vitally important defense mechanism against overpowering contents which are often difficult to control. The general rule should be that the weakness of the conscious attitude is proportional to the strength of the resistance. When, therefore, there are strong resistances, the conscious rapport with the patient must be carefully watched, and ... his conscious attitude must be supported ...
>
> Nor is it beside the point to add that consistent support of the conscious attitude has in itself a high therapeutic value and not infrequently serves to bring about satisfactory results."[2]

Jung is saying that when the defenses are strongest, the conscious capacity of the individual is weak and needs extra support. Furthermore, he suggests that the act of simply supporting someone in remaining conscious, while their unconscious defenses are threatening to take over, can itself produce therapeutic results. That is to say, the very support of the conscious self may allow the individual to break past the defense—something of which we should be aware during the super-charged power of a birth chart reading.

People come to readings expecting *something* to happen, expect-

broach

ing some information or understanding that can ignite momentum for positive change in their lives. So, as astrologers, we can accept that and run with it, using the inherent power of the reading to support the conscious desire of the person to transform his life. By exploring and understanding the resistance he is experiencing, his blocks and defenses, and in revealing them, he can gain clarity. And so empowered, he can start to move beyond them.

The Importance of Trust

Despite the fact that we must respect the origins of our defenses, their toll on us can be heavy. By walling off these parts of our earlier selves, we may live only a fraction of our potential in the present. We may maintain the barrier even decades after the reasons for erecting a wall have passed. And when we remove it, we may very well re-experience some of the pain we were trying to wall-off from.

We can imagine that some clients will not be prepared to engage this process. Therefore, we must approach such territory carefully and with skill. We must be commensurately subtle and gentle, or we risk the client's retreat and the further fortification of her defenses. However, some risk is unavoidable. Just as there is no such thing as risk-free territory when approaching one's partners or family member's defensive behavior, escaping any tension in a client consultation may also be unrealistic. Still, there are costs in not questioning these things just as there might be in doing so.

Again, unless an individual is being actively traumatized in her current life, it is the protective defenses she has formed in the past that are still wounding her.

An important aside: if an individual is being actively traumatized in the present, the only appropriate therapeutic response is to focus the reading on how that can stop, how she can achieve a safe space and heal. Know your own limitations here, and be ready to refer out for professional help. The subtleties of the client's natal chart are secondary to the primary need to achieve safety. Active encouragement towards and construction of a plan to seek a safety zone away from any active trauma in the current environment should be the main priority in this kind of situation.

In most cases, though, individuals are frequently haunted by the specters of events long past. And what holds this in place is the scaffolding they erected at the time of the original trauma which *well put* they have yet failed to dismantle. Someone contemplating removing these barriers may fear that if he does, uncontrollable emotion will burst forth like floodwaters from a breached dam.[Long after the causes of the defense have passed from our lives, we can desperately cling to the defensive structure with surprising vigor.]

To ride roughshod over these defenses is neither appropriate nor effective, but to politely move on despite them is hardly ideal either. This is the great dilemma of Therapeutic Astrology—the issue of discerning the right time to move in on this level. There is no right answer, and yet, if we employ certain principles, we increase our chances of competently—and sometimes masterfully—facilitating movement. The key principle to develop is core trust.

In a one-off astrology reading, our capacity to develop deep trust with a client is limited, but this does not mean that identifying defensive issues is impossible—far from it.[That people are open to hear the powerful potential inherent in their charts also opens them to the possibility of change.]Just how much can be made of that opportunity depends on a fusion between their capacities and ours.

The defensive structures we will now explore can only really be held and understood within a relationship that is built on trust—even as some of the defenses will actively challenge that.

Types of Defense Systems

To promote self-awareness and contemplative insight for the astrologer or student of astrology, I will now offer an overview of common types of psychological defense systems. Since astrologers are not immune to these defense systems themselves, it is crucial to spend time doing our own personal growth work. By understanding how we use these defenses in our own lives, we can better support our clients in addressing them.

None of us enjoys having an assumed authority tell us about our defenses. People are much more open if they feel they are having a shared discussion with someone who also *knows what it is like* to struggle with defenses. A shared vantage point validates the reality that we all have problems. And from that foundation, a truly co-creative attitude towards the reading will facilitate expressing the chart's full potential.

Reaction Formation

To understand this kind of defense, we start by looking at the psychoanalytic insights of ego, id and superego. The **ego** is the *conscious self-awareness*, the **id** is the animal instincts and passions, and the **superego** is the set of *codes internalized from parents and authority figures* regarding the most appropriate way for the conscious self to act. The ego takes hold of certain impulses from the id and turns them into a more acceptable expression (in keeping with the demands of the superego) that is often the actual opposite of the way the individual is really feeling.

One common *reaction formation* is the redirecting of aggressive impulses from the id into a conscious expression of being extra nice and insistently helpful—a process which takes the unacceptable energy (aggression) and uses it in service of an ego ideal. But there are several problems with this disguise. Primarily, in glossing over what is really going on, the defense type avoids authentic feelings and therefore corresponds to the *false self* (which we explored in the first chapter)—the adaptive part of the identity that will only act in ways that fit the survival strategies of the identity.

In lacking authenticity, the false self creates a split in the individual between her conscious stance and true feelings. With this split active in an astrology reading, whatever she hears from the as-

V. Imp.

trologer will be filtered through the distance she has between her own awareness and her deeper feelings. The reading will then only reach a superficial level.

Another problem with this defense type is its acceptability. The whole point of *reaction formation* is to help the person avoid unacceptable feelings that are intruding into self-awareness. One of the problems in breaking through this defense is that the splitting-off from negative emotions (aggression, in our example) is not necessarily easy or desirous for the astrologer to feel or face, either.

For example, let's say we show up late for the reading. If we have a client who is overly nice and accommodating about our mistake, we might automatically accept such a response, as it serves our own interests. This is one example of why the reaction formation is often such a successful defense strategy: we may not be invested in exploring someone's authentic feelings if those feelings are difficult or more socially challenging than the mask he wears. The pleasant mask hides the reality within, making both parties "feel" more comfortable on the surface.

Another common expression of reaction formation occurs when people channel anxiety into socially pleasing behavior. In a reading, you may become aware of this in your client within the early stages of your appointment. Once, at the start of a reading, a client said to me, while smiling, that when anxious she always smiles. She went on to explain that she engaged in this mannerism to the extent that her face often aches because of smiling so much. This process was exacerbated in the naturally socially dynamic conference setting in which we were working. So I asked her if that might be happening even now, as we were about to start her reading. She said that it was. And since we had begun the reading by employing immediacy, exploring what she was anxious about in the moment and acknowledging the "real time" pattern of behavior, the reading was initiated on a foundation from which she could then imagine real change. Had that reaction formation been overlooked, the reading might have unfolded with her fixed in a habitual posture and expending energy on maintaining her subconscious defensive structures. Instead, those very defenses were clearly articulated as a part of the larger issues that she was hoping to grow beyond, which was ultimately the main purpose behind her seeking the reading.

This brings us to another crucial point: the defensive structures of the psyche, the false self and all its adaptive postures, require tremendous amounts of psychic energy. If we let our defenses run the show, we drain ourselves of life energy to such an extent that there is none left to engage in a process of creative transformation. In many cases, no healing or change is possible until the defenses have been minimized, simply because the person does not have sufficient energy while they are maintaining them. Through overcoming a primary defensive structure in the psyche, transformation will precipitate simply because of the tremendous liberation of energy it releases. This is an inspirational phenomenon to witness and facilitate in a client, and makes it well worth the effort and awareness to undertake.

Projection

In psychological terms, *projection* refers to the externalization of psychic content onto a situation, or another individual. A person who employs this kind of defense typically does so because the content projected makes her uncomfortable. By focusing it externally, she is able to release it. In many cases, the content projected is so uncomfortable that the person is in denial that it exists at all, except when seen in other people. In this manner, the mechanism of projection allows an individual to experience what he is really feeling; by denying the feeling in himself, he is only able to see it through the process of externalization, painting the world the color that he feels.

Difficult feelings that are commonly projected include hostility, grief, self-hate and criticism. But all extreme emotions or states of mind can become the basis for projection. Recently, a client who had been extremely depressed and vulnerable for several weeks went out to a club. Because she felt so distressed, she had been conflicted about going out at all and had discussed canceling with the friend who had invited her out. She finally decided to go. Upon her arrival, the girlfriend of her friend greeted her with, "Oh, you made it then." This statement, she realized only much later, was just an acknowledgement of her arrival, a simple greeting. Yet, my client projected onto this woman a complex set of motives in which that statement thinly concealed that she was being criticized for being a *prima donna*—that by coming, she had shown that her previous distress had not been severe after all, and as a result, there was no good reason to have wavered about coming out in the first place!

With projection in full swing, our inner storytelling apparatus goes overboard. A simple greeting becomes an indictment of one's (defective) nature. Here, the girlfriend of a friend is seen externally as enacting the inner critique from which my client was consciously detached, and which was ultimately the foundational component of the distress she was feeling in the first place.

So, projection as a defense strategy co-opts the other to externally enact the emotions that the individual struggles to contain or deal with herself. As such, projection is as common in a one-off astrology reading as it is in a longer-term therapeutic relationship (except that the long-term situation provides greater duration and more opportunity). Unlike *transference*, which we will explore in the next section, projection does not require a great deal of time to develop. In actuality, the fact that the person does not know the astrologer very well is, if anything, likely to increase the chances of projection, as the unfamiliar face of the astrologer provides a blank canvas on which to paint.

A common projection is that of criticism. Those who express this defense strategy are often compelled by a strong inner issue that cannot be contained; they see the reading (or therapy session) as a critique of them instead of a supportive experience. Those who suffer from a tyrannical superego, expressed as a critical inner voice of authority (often parental), are particularly susceptible to this projection as the inner voice becomes unbearable and demands externalization.

To work proactively with this kind of projection, the astrologer can start by recognizing that a client's criticism could be an external expression of his attempt to process uncontainable levels of inner criticism and negativity. If this is the case, he will need support. It can be therapeutic to help these clients safely express their anger or frustration, even when directed at the astrologer. This will require that the astrologer maintain both a degree of emotional detachment from the client's projections, as well as heart-centered, compassionate inner space. When done successfully, this can liberate a hidden energetic potential within the field. If the astrologer is secure enough not to become defensive herself, the client may experience genuine healing.

Some astrological concepts can themselves play into these kinds of negative inner voices, such as when someone links his inner shame to the notion that he has a *"bad"* chart. Inherently limiting terms, such as planets being in their "fall" or "detriment," as well as an underlying sense that there can even be *bad* aspects, can provide fodder for the inner critic to feel justified in lashing out. I do not believe that there is such a thing as a bad chart. A perfectly lovely person could have the same chart as Adolf Hitler and become a successful painter (as he failed and yet aspired to do) and live a respectable life. *It is the consciousness of the individual that creates the moral ground for her life*, not the birth chart.

While traditional astrological techniques can offer real insight, in modern practice we should take care to reframe them using all of the psychological and cultural understanding that we've gained. In some cases we may need to explain this to our clients, especially if we hear them use one of these loaded terms. With a client who is expressing the critical form of projection, it's important to convey this in a way that doesn't shame him, but supports him in opening up his limited definitions. We might present him with an example of someone admirable, for instance, who has the same so-called malefic natal placement he has. We can repeat this with "negative" transit aspects. As the client opens to the possibility that something good could actually come from his more challenging placements and transits, the inner critic naturally begins to soften.

Another common form of projection is *anger*. If conditioning and powerful messages early in life conveyed that anger is bad and should not be expressed, anger that arises naturally in the present becomes problematic and often leads to suppression. Eventually, everyone around the person suppressing her rage seems to her to be angry, as if evoking the hidden emotion buried within. She becomes energetically invested in projecting outward that which is so uncomfortable on the inside. Seemingly innocuous events become triggers. Someone makes a mistake, or a child spills some milk, and suddenly she is consumed by rage.

Continuous suppression of this sort of anger can lead to a sense of hopelessness and disempowerment about life. The individual can then internalize the feeling as self-hatred, feeling that "life is unfair," feeling that she is too blame. Carrying this internally, she will then project onto others that same hatred directed back at her—even when it isn't there. For instance, she may see a complete stranger on the street "looking at her strangely" and craft a story inside that the stranger doesn't like her. This projection confirms her inner narrative that she is "hateful and a failure."

It is this combination of suppressed anger and self-hatred that can lead to the sadomasochistic cycle of domestic abuse. For example, the husband who has been beaten down all day at work comes home and beats his wife. Maybe he is too afraid to face his tyrannical boss. So, his more vulnerable wife, whom ironically he "trusts" more, is the recipient of his pent up feelings about himself. The thing that actually triggers his rage is often meaningless—maybe she did not "fix his drink right," or his meal has gone a little cold (even though it is *he* who is later than he said he would be). He is desperate to project the unbearable feeling inside himself outward onto another.

Learning to recognize projection is important both for our own peace of mind and as a potential tool for our clients' healing.

Transference

Transference is really an extension of *projection*. With transference, what is projected (transferred) is the content or patterns of early significant relationships. The early psychodynamic models of psychotherapy, stemming from Freud's work in psychoanalysis, stress the importance of transference to the therapeutic project. This is why in Freudian psychoanalysis the patient would lie on a couch and the analyst sat behind him: in order to remain as much of a blank screen as possible for the projection that is transference to unfold.

Most forms of psychotherapy now find this posturing extreme and instead emphasize the therapeutic relationship of deep contact that thinkers like Jung and Assagioli put forward. Jung was famously a large man and he would sit knee to knee with his patients, looking them right in the eye. This was such an intense experience that the young James Hillman—who would go on to become director of the Jungian training center in Zurich and found the archetypal psychology movement—ceased working with him because he didn't want to feel too overpowered. As an astrological aside, Hillman sought out another, less charismatic Jungian analyst who did not eclipse his Sun-Moon Aries need to develop his own strength rather than soak in the power of Jung's!

Projection takes uncontained feelings and places them outside the psyche. Transference does this too, but in a very specific way; transference takes unresolved childhood feelings about specific figures, such as one's parents, and transfers those feelings onto figures of significance in one's current life. This is why transference tends to develop more over the duration of long-term work rather than in short-term relationships. Yet, I have found that transference is frequently present and can be recognized right from the beginning of therapeutic work, and is therefore relevant even in a one-time significant encounter such as an astrology reading.

So let's learn how to identify two forms of transference that psychoanalyst Heinz Kohut illuminated in *Self Psychology*.

Mirror Transference

This form of transference arises from a core "empathic resonance" stemming from the basic need infants have for mirroring via the mother's nurturing gaze and appreciation. Author and psychologist Mario Jacoby describes the expression of this need as: "If nobody in the whole world is taking joy in the fact that I exist, if there is nobody who understands, appreciates and loves what I am and what I do, then there is hardly any chance of keeping . . . a realistic sense of self-esteem." [3]

Individuals whose basic trust has been compromised due to material, emotional and social deprivation in their early life may exhibit the need for strong *mirror transference,* which usually expresses as a very low tolerance for the other person's reality. So, a client with this kind of transference may not respond well to astrologers who use long examples culled from their own life to make their point. Instead, the client needs to be virtually the sole focus of the reading and of the astrologer's attention, which will provide a platform for his unmet needs to be met. If mirror transference is the client's dominant issue, any part of the reading not addressing this need will literally escape his attention. *All About SELF*

Recording the reading can partly ameliorate this issue. The therapeutically aware astrologer, however, may adapt to this prominent unconscious need and offer a "holding environment" in which the potential of the birth chart is explored in a way that serves the need for mirror transference. The astrologer can accomplish this simply by maintaining a culturally appropriate, attentive gaze. This gives her client permission for the needed self-focus and space for personal sharing without implicitly judging that by trying to force the reading into a predefined format. With mirror transference, less is more. The astrologer will find greater success by allowing her client's own process and sharing to lead the reading. She can shepherd the journey using salient points taken from the chart as guideposts.

Idealizing Transference

Kohut developed his understanding of *idealizing transference* from the dual need of the infant to find within the parent both a mirror and an ideal, which the child then models. This form of transference develops from the need for an all-powerful or all-knowing figure that the child can both admire and aspire to be.

To the extent that this process has failed within the early environment, either through an absent parent or a disappointing one, the client will hold an unmet need to find another to fit their ideal and to be able to model through the protection of that idealized other. Kohut describes this as a natural and essential part of development and makes the claim that it is healthy for a person who has developmentally missed or only partially fulfilled this infant need to find it through another. The challenge for the astrologer facing this kind of transference is to hold space for the process in a balanced fashion, especially if he finds the prospect of being held in such high regard enticing.

Clients with idealizing transference commonly have histories of disappointment or disillusionment with those they place in this parental role when their surrogate does not live up to the ideal. Since the ideal has an aspirational quality to it—the infant seeing the desired quality in the parent so that she can learn to become it—any failure by the parent can be experienced as self-failure, which may then be internalized as shame. This shame then becomes associated with a fear of punishment or loss of the parental safety—which is explicitly linked to fears of death in the dependent life of the infant. When idealizing transference is a dominant unconscious factor in the client, dealing with the disappointment of the ideal is a crucial component of healing.

This kind of transference might show up in a reading as pressure not to "fail" the client or to hold space for the disappointment of the ideal in the client's past. The complexity of this process is explored below in *The Problem of Positive Projection or Transference.*

In the following example, I share a client's story to demonstrate transference. Hers was significant throughout long-term work, but also present from the beginning, so it will make clear how transference can be an issue even in the first session of an astrology reading.

Antiope

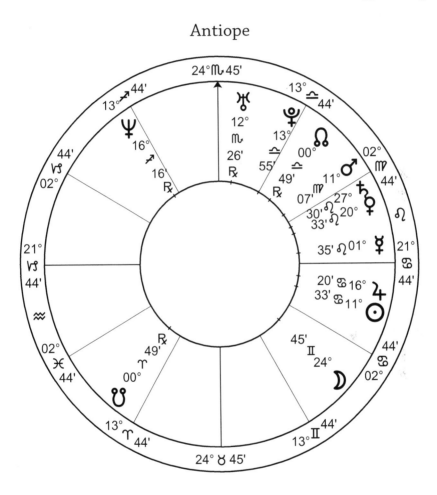

b. July 3, 1978, 10:00 p.m., Tavistock, England

If we focus on the nodes of the Moon and their rulers, we can understand the developmental path that Antiope was seeking in life. The south node of the Moon is in Aries in the 2nd house. Its ruler

Mars in Virgo in the 8th house is square Neptune in Sagittarius in the 11th house. The Moon in late Gemini is square the nodal axis of the Moon.

The past as revealed by the south node and its ruler speaks of loss (Mars square Neptune), including loss of life (south node in the 2nd house relating to biological survival) and loss of her family (Moon square the south node in the 2nd house). With the Aries south node in the 2nd house, Antiope's past has been characterized by operating in survival mode (2nd house under stress) with an emotional fallout from the family (Moon square the nodes) informing a crisis in her will (Mars in Virgo) in which she is seeking to heal (Mars in the 8th house square Neptune) through a new commitment (8th house) to herself.

Antiope had lost her father twice in her early life: first as a little girl when her parents separated, and second, when he died of alcohol-related health problems. She had only met him twice as an adult. She was haunted by a vision of herself lying face down in a stream, unable to move, an echo of his submersion in substances (she completely avoided substance use). Her father had been replaced by a stepfather whom, although a more stable influence than her biological father, she experienced as stern and at times bullying. The combination of her stepfather's strict rule of the house and her biological father being associated with decadence and loss left Antiope with a rigid posture and attitude.

The chair in my client room has a slight recline to it, and most people just sit back into it as it is very comfortable. But some people never do. One man with long-term issues bordering on the autistic spectrum always sits perched on the front of the chair leaning forward (actually quite difficult to do). While not as extreme as his posture, Antiope always sat demurely on the point of balance with hands folded on her lap, as if, perhaps, in a job interview.

The crux of my work with Antiope centered on her fear of coming to therapy, which was present from the very first session. I speculated that when she no longer felt sick about attending, that would signal the end of the process. It proved accurate. Her fear of coming for counseling stemmed from the powerful transference constellated from the first session, which only faded partially by the end of our work. This transference took the form of her placing her complex of unresolved feelings about masculine authority squarely on my shoulders. The important takeaway is that this kind of transference may be present even in a one-time astrological reading.

We can see from the balsamic (applying) conjunction between Saturn and her north node ruler Venus that her issue of facing the significant father figures in her life was critical to her maturation and development. The north node in Libra in the 8th describes the importance of therapy: to have a relationship (Libra) that allowed for in-depth exploration of her feelings (north node in the 8th house), which included how to express her gifts (Venus in Leo) with authority (Venus-Saturn), instead of repressing them in the face of bullying and excessive control. So, the fact that Antiope felt physically sick before attending our sessions was a critical part of our work. Now, obviously, I do not want people feeling sick about coming to see me, but way beyond that, I was aware of the important childhood feelings that this transference allowed to emerge.

To begin to heal her idealizing transference, Antiope needed to work with someone in whom she believed enough to be able to express her disappointment at her original loss of the paternal ideal. This would be finely balanced with her need for someone who could also maintain the basic "empathic resonance" of the mirror transference so that, within a safe holding environment, she could express her disappointment, anger and hurt. The empathic safety of the mirror transference was essential to offset the childhood fear that accompanied her own shame at the loss of the ideal: fear that this would lead to the severance of parental love, the equivalent of death in the mind of the infant. It was this complex of emotions— essentially, fear that her inner shame would lead to punishment and death—that led to her feelings of physical sickness.

Her case of transference was so strong that within the limited time we had (for financial reasons as well as her obvious discomfort), Antiope could not always come weekly, so I had to get creative. In one session I insisted we swap seats. Another time we went into the garden, using movement to elicit more than the survival response of concealment and decorum.

Once, we used a laptop screen cleaner in the shape of a frog to throw back and forth at each other while shouting the letters of the alphabet to allow her the possibility of expressing anger at me and to recover the possibility of play. After some initial resistance, Antiope really got into throwing this soft toy at me. In fact, this exercise proved so successful that "Froggy," as he was known from that day, has remained in the client room and adopted many guises for other clients.

Such an exercise served a dual purpose: to break the transference enough to allow play to enter the space, and, to the extent that the transference was maintained, to deconstruct its meaning, whereby the father could be someone with whom Antiope could express herself. This is the best tactic in the short-term that I have found. Not throwing toys! But moving the transference away from the therapist enough to communicate, and then, in the communication, shifting the energy in a way that educates the client that the past could have been experienced differently. Here the therapeutic alliance creates a reparative relationship: going with the client into the territory where it all went wrong in the past to create a new outcome together.

This process is possible in more subtle ways, even in an astrology reading. The first step is the capacity to recognize the projection or transference. The second step is to not get defensive about it. This is harder than it might sound, primarily because of the issue discussed in the following section.

Counter-transference

A crucial issue with transference is the response it tends to elicit from the person upon whom the energy is transferred: the *coun-*

ter-transference. We have seen how transference is a super-charged projection which can channel the unhealed emotional energy from the past into the present and onto the therapist or astrologer. The response that this process then sets in motion in the therapist, the recipient of the transference, is something that seems to be largely misunderstood or totally unacknowledged.

Counter-transference refers to the specific way that the energy of transference evokes, or at least, seeks to evoke, a response in the person who received the transference. This seems to be something innate to the nature of transference itself: because it was formed in a dyadic relationship (usually the child with the parent), the pattern of energy created naturally seeks a correlative response. This can be very disarming.

Projection differs from transference in that it is not so charged by the early childhood need for the parent. And the response or reaction from the therapist is genuinely in line with what is being expressed.

For instance, if a client projects onto me that I am being critical (when I am not), this might be understood as a projection arising out of his own struggle with inner criticism. This projection may elicit a response from me that is actually critical, which is how many people create self-fulfilling prophecies from their own subconscious fear and negativity. Still, my response is addressed at what I feel in response to the expressed projection. Of course it can be irritating when someone misunderstands my intention and insists on believing I have been intentionally critical of him when I have not. But this is something we can work out through dialogue.

The challenge with counter-transference is that the counselor's evoked responses are not necessarily innately hers. Counter-transference can actually create feelings in the counselor that she previously did not have!

It should be clear now that counter-transference can derail a therapeutic endeavor or an astrology reading. If this process is powerful enough to create a new emotional dynamic between two people—out of nothing in the present—it can easily tilt the direction of an astrology reading, if not skew it completely.

I'll share another example from my work with Antiope. My attitude to the sickness this young woman faced each time she visited me was essentially that of a concerned professional who would regularly contemplate and explore the ways in which this struggle inside her might cease. Sometimes I would be so concerned by the severity of her experience that I would work creatively to find ways around it, such as the use of "Froggy" outlined above. In that urge to be creative, to overcome the frustrating situation that she faced, I was already creating a subtle susceptibility to counter-transference, because in my empathy, I too experienced the stuckness and the emotions it evoked.

Now, one day we had made a breakthrough, and she was beginning to communicate more freely when the old defense re-emerged, shutting her down completely in the middle of sharing how she was beginning to transform. The temptation in me to tell her off, to shout at her to try harder, to push past it arose in me. I did not react; I just watched this feeling arise in me, sweep across my emotional field, and then, as I did not resist or express it, I watched it pass. All the while, she just sat there transfixed. We both seemed to be aware that something powerful had just taken place in the silence.

What I had experienced was a surge of counter-transference. I had been taken off guard, as had she, by the progress we were making. When her defense overpowered her again, its energy was so extreme that she was silenced and, in my connection to her, I was open to the sudden power of the defense too. That took the form of a very strong wave of emotion that produced in me the urge to verbally abuse or punish her for her "failure" to stay with the unfolding process of coming out of herself.

This was not a feeling that I had before towards her. In the early months of her struggle, I had experienced much compassion for her. Now that she was starting to change, this feeling had morphed into a hopeful creative impulse on her behalf. I like it when transformation is attainable for my clients. It is part of why I love to do what I do! This feeling was evoked in me by her transference defense as she went silent, assuming her rigid stance in response to past loss, control and verbal abuse. Through the counter-transference dynamic, I was energetically invited to play the part of her bullying stepfather—to criticize or verbally abuse her. Though I did not enact this, the energetic feeling of that process still played out silently as we sat in the room.

This brings me to an important aside. Sometimes silence is the most powerful healing space. Making good use of silence can be especially important when powerful emotions are emerging. As an astrology reading is a high-cost and short-duration event, long silences would represent a serious failure to deliver value to one's clients. But to never include room for silence, to never allow the moment to just be there in the space between you, is to minimize the transformational power available when two or more are gathered. Short silences to digest powerful insights or to allow powerful waves of emotion are therapeutically valid, even essential at times, whether in a phone reading or an intense one-hour live reading.

As professional astrologers, I suggest that we begin to shift our approach to one of quality over quantity. People can only take in so many insights in one reading. *It is more effective on many levels to deeply understand and convey a small number of critical insights than to try to convey everything we can possibly see in the chart into one session.*

In the example I shared here, in spite of the powerful energy, and perhaps because of the explicitly punitive aspect of the counter-transference, which ran so counter to my nature, it was relatively easy for me to let it go. I knew clearly that the feelings were not my own, and the energy passed through me and left as quickly as it had come on. But counter-transference can also operate on far more subtle levels that are more difficult to identify. It takes skill, practice, much self-awareness, and the ability to cultivate internal objectivity.

Finally, counter-transference can also take on more seductive forms, such as feelings that are positive or congratulatory. Even greater diligence and awareness are required in such instances.

The Problem of Positive Transference or Projection

Everyone projects or experiences transference. There is no need to pathologize these processes; they are a natural part of life and human relationship. As one begins to study and work with these issues, a strange realization begins to emerge: Negative transference is more of a gift than you would think, and conversely, *positive projection* or *transference* is more difficult than you would expect.

To continue with our example, sickening though it was (literally) for Antiope, her negative transference gave our work complete clarity. It granted us a clear vision of the direction for the work. In contrast, positive transference energies can indicate a trickier situation. Remember, transference is specifically the projection of the significant relationships from the past onto a figure in the present; whereas *projection* is the *externalization* of a variety of feeling states from inside the psyche onto the outside world through a situation or another person.

Positive projection or transference is normal to some extent. Without a certain degree of positive projection or transference, an individual would not be drawn to a specific astrologer for a reading. In choosing who to work with, the client most often bases his decision on positive attraction: perhaps he is drawn to something on your website, or inspired to call you based on a friend's gushing review. Either way, positive projection is implicit. It could not be any other way.

This level of positive projection is healthy and natural. It can be constructively used by the therapeutically sensitive astrologer to create a space in which, from the very beginning, whatever transformational possibility is sensed from the chart can be on the table as a potential for growth encouraged in the client. For most people, the choice to invest in a reading represents a significant decision. It is appropriate to be aware of that significance and to use it in service of the client and her potential for self-development and fulfillment.

This means navigating any idealizing transference or positive projection and not becoming unconsciously complicit in maintaining it at the cost of the truth: the capacity of the reading to make a genuine transformative statement or impact on the client. There are significant traps for the astrologer hidden within positive transference from their clients. One I have already addressed, is that it can tempt the astrologer into statements beyond his knowledge, especially when influenced by a client who is desperately seeking some kind of salvation.

I have met people at astrology conferences who feel dazed, upset and confused by the conflicting messages offered them by well-meaning astrologers who have overstepped their mark or who, unaware, bought into the client's desire to project savior onto them. To some extent this is unavoidable. As astrologers, we cannot control how our clients ultimately digest and act upon the information we discuss with them. Add to this the popular assumption that the cosmos is "speaking through us" and we have a bit of an uphill battle on this front.

However, by holding awareness of projection and transference, we can learn how to qualify what we say and more importantly, continually affirm the client's empowerment and freedom of choice. Although the allure can be powerful, we should resist the temptation to accept the role of the "all-knowing astrologer" whose prescriptions promise "happiness and total fulfillment." In the end, that kind of imbalanced relationship can only leave the client disempowered, no matter our motives. Let us instead cultivate an I-Thou dynamic of mutual respect in which true healing can emerge between two equals with positive intentions.

Congruence

Congruence is a term referring to the right fit between the real thoughts, feelings and expressions of both the counselor and the client Congruence can only exist when there is a living potential for an authentic self to be expressed; congruence is, in fact, the alignment of speech, emotional expressions and deeds with the real self. Lack of congruence is the space in which all defenses thrive.

To be her authentic self during an astrology reading, the client must be allowed her full range of expression, from positive to negative. This includes the full use of her critical faculties and even direct criticism of what she is being offered by the astrologer. If we cannot bear criticism from our clients, and steer the reading away from any sort of "negative" contribution from them, we deny them their full selves and may limit the readings' potential.

Holding space for the client to say things we may not like is tricky territory indeed. But allowing this kind of dynamic free play may greatly enhance the potential for healing to occur. After all, we practitioners would be unrealistic to expect solely positive remarks from clients about how they experience us. When they share negative feedback, we will naturally weigh how much their defenses have been triggered and how much of their feedback is legitimately our responsibility (and the seemingly endless shades of gray in between). The key (especially while in the session) is to remain as objective and non-defensive as possible.

By inviting this kind of feedback when it seems necessary to the client's authentic self-expression, we may well heighten the potential for dynamics such as projection, transference and counter-transference to run riot. Yet, to avoid this territory altogether is just a form of repression.

In allowing the I-Thou contact in which the real presence in both self and other meaningfully intertwine, we can imagine an alchemical process in which the information we read in the natal chart becomes a living possibility for the client.

> *"To learn who rules over you, simply find out who you are not allowed to criticize."*
> -Insight commonly attributed to Voltaire.

The Survival System of the Psyche

In times of great trauma or stress, our systems seem to innately construct defenses that protect us from greater harm. Jungian psychoanalyst Donald Kalsched shares his insight about this process:

> "In the self-defense system the caretaking side is typically personified by an inner figure who swings between being protective and being persecutory. The protector may take the form of an angel, a wise old man, a fairy friend or a great good mother who accompanies the child and gives him strength, but because this inner figure will do whatever it has to do in order to prevent a repeat of the original, unbearable experience it can just as easily morph into an axe-man, an evil angel, a devil, a rigid, cold stone statue, an extra-terrestrial or a terrorist with an AK47."[4]

Kalsched points out that these self-protecting inner forces can be agents of our undoing in a therapeutic context, including an astrology reading. For while the positive aspect of the inner caregiver may be mobilized on behalf of an individual's healing, the persecutory aspect of the survival defense system can just as easily be triggered and stunt the healing process. The greater the degree of the original trauma (or of the susceptibility of the individual to existing trauma), the greater the likelihood that complex protective forces within the client will shut down any conversation about transformation or progress. The protective system tries to maintain homeostasis at all costs, and perceives any change, positive or negative, as potentially harmful.

Kalsched writes: "Being an unmediated, unintegrated, magical system, once the archetypal self-defences have been mobilised the system ossifies into a closed, rigid paradigm which is shut off from human influence. The system resists being educated. This leads to tragedy: because the system is stuck at the original trauma it doesn't take account of the fact that as the child grows, other defences be-come available, and so the innocent, creative, relational, essence of the child is locked away in a prison for safe-keeping for ever." [5]

The sobering therapeutic reality is that when trauma reaches a high degree of impact within an individual life (especially when there is significant boundary invasion or abuse within childhood), defenses of "shutting down" and an almost magical imprisonment are unavoidable. This is because these defenses are crucial to the very survival of the developing psyche. When the client is ready, and hopefully within a professionally mediated healing relationship, these defenses can be addressed.

This process can be respected, named and referred to directly without necessarily going into the specific historical material or at-tempting to deactivate the defense system—which would not be ap-propriate in a one-off astrology reading. In this way, the astrologer can, without unnecessary incursions directly into the traumatic ma-terial, frame a realistic discussion regarding the importance of a goal for healing alongside a realistic assessment of what it might take to get there.

To recognize this pattern requires, not astrological understand-ing, but an understanding of psychological processes and the acqui-sition of counseling skills. For the astrologer without such training, it is sufficient to notice that the client is exhibiting a false self. This can manifest as: withdrawal, spacing out, changing of topic, hyper-vigilance (a thinness or veneer to his or her relational quality), or as the client describing a dysfunctional life pattern, such as withdrawal and social isolation, or powerful, but elusive, negative feelings toward the family of origin.

For the purposes of this book, *it is recommended that the astrolo-ger not attempt to diagnose a defensive structure*, but simply consider this pattern as a possibility and have at hand the name of at least one quality therapist to whom one may refer clients.

Parallel Process

Parallel process occurs when the material brought to the reading by the client happens to directly trigger an unresolved issue within the counselor or astrologer. This can take the form of a significant event, such as the loss of a parent, for example. Say a client comes to the reading in grief over the loss of his father and you have also just lost yours. Or a client describes how his mother shamed him as a child, and his description captures exactly how your mother used to do this.

Parallel process can increase empathy and insight and give you a capacity to mirror your clients' experiences with finesse and appropriate sympathetic resonance. But we have to be careful. Just as easily, one could think one was offering appropriate sympathy and yet, through unresolved emotional material around the issue, actually start to unconsciously take over the session or steer its content towards what best fits one's own unmet needs!

This illustrates the importance of working on oneself when employed in the helping professions. This is critical. While you can help another with an issue that you have not yet resolved yourself, it takes serious effort to remain objective and to watch for your own gaps in understanding. Fundamentally, your ability to guide other people comes from your own capacity to evolve, to follow the guidance of your inner self or spiritual essence. If you do not make an effort to follow your own healing path, your clients will expose so many struggles and blind spots within yourself that the effort required to work with people will become unsustainable. In this way the universe is self-regulating.

Vicarious Trauma

The term *vicarious trauma* refers to a situation in which despite one's best intentions for personal care and processing the issues that arise from working with the suffering of others, one experiences personal burnout. This is most common for people working in front-line positions with high levels of trauma. This is unlikely to be a major concern for most astrologers responsible enough to work within the limits of their abilities and energy levels. It may only become more of an issue if these sensible limits are exceeded, or if the astrologer has high levels of traumatic experience that remain unresolved in her personal life. In such cases it may be helpful to seek out mentors to speak with, or to schedule some sessions with a counselor for yourself.

Alchemical Potential

The alchemy of the reading is that two people are potentially transformed by becoming non-defensive and willing to go beyond their adaptive or narrow ego self. As Richard Rohr writes in *Immortal Diamond*, "The ego self is the self before death; the soul is real only after we have walked through the death of our ever fading False Self and come out larger and brighter on the other side." [6] The next chapter will explore the seeds of this process through the twelve astrological archetypes, as each archetype leads us closer to union with the indwelling presence of life.

3

The Signs: Twelve Steps to Healing

In this section we'll explore the twelve astrological signs as a therapeutic narrative and their potential to transform individual lives in the context of a counseling session. The core astrological archetypes can be approached in many ways. Let's explore what the twelve signs can teach us when seen as guideposts for exploring the deepest potential for an astrological reading.

Aries

Aries teaches us to start by acknowledging the courage it takes for a client to come to the first reading. Courage is the cornerstone required when one takes the first step on such a vulnerable exploratory journey of one's life. In the consciousness scale employed by David R. Hawkins, the critical breaking point at which one's experience becomes life-affirming rather than life-negating is initiated with intentional *courage*. At this level, he describes courage as: "... an intuitive acceptance of the truth of accountability as a spiritual and social reality .. . Truth is now seen as an ally not an enemy.. . The dictum 'what gains a man to win the world but lose his soul?' now becomes an axiom that guides decisions and choices of options." [1] Courage is what we need to muster when we start looking at the truth.

Consider the following two core applications of courage in the context of a reading:

1. *The courage to admit the truth of a given situation (both internal and external), which is a fundamental requirement to gain clarity over what is therapeutically necessary for healing.*

2. *The courage, once the truth is seen, to take the first steps towards transformation and empowerment necessary to respond fully to the call of that truth.*

But courage isn't all bravado and fearlessness. Dr. Brené Brown defines the true measurement of courage as one's capacity to be vulnerable. [2] Often our experience of courage starts with a fear or *basic anxiety* that we then choose to overcome. If it was not so, if every step we took was guaranteed success, there would be no need for courage.

In his wonderful book *Callings: Finding and Following an Authentic Life*, Gregg Levoy writes, "It can be more heroic to be willing to act in the absence of certainty than to refuse to act without absolute certainty." [3]

We see then that the initiatory quality of an astrology reading is a powerful thing. The client has taken a risk in seeking out the astrologer. And that risk could backfire—plenty of people have been disappointed by astrology readings. But the hope is that the reading could be the starting point of a transformational journey, of which the first step was taken by summoning the courage to see the astrologer in the first place.

As the first sign, Aries corresponds to the first steps taken towards healing: a pioneering moment in the evolutionary journey of the soul. If successful at this level, an astrology reading can profoundly change someone's experience of her reality and set her firmly on their path.

Exploring the second application of courage, we see the client's responsibility to be honest about whatever life situations—inner or outer experiences—appear to be holding her back from expressing their true potential. Without taking the risk to share her authenticity, the potential of the reading is limited.

The degree to which the astrologer can be present to this fundamental encounter will be directly proportional to his capacity to bring willingness and integrity to the process of his client's transformation. This is when the sensitive astrologer realizes that there is also a risk for him in every real encounter: that he can also be changed by the reading.

Taurus

With Taurus, we become aware of the issue of value, and especially inner value. In the counseling space, this relates to the need to guide the client towards affirming her value.

To the extent that it symbolizes our self-worth, the Taurus archetype reveals our need to be affirmed in life for just showing up. In World War II, men like my grandfather received service medals, not only for bravery or any particular incident, but *just for having survived* a stint in the North Africa campaign, or the fighting in northern Europe. In a very real sense, we could say that every human being deserves a medal just for having shown up.

This insight applies especially in cases of extreme adversity or abuse, where there can be great benefit from the simple value of having survived thus far. This needs to be affirmed if it has not been. In some cases of serious abuse, acknowledging one's survival is in itself miraculous, and the counseling room might be the first place this issue makes itself known to the client.

In fact, this exposes a critical therapeutic issue that can be summarized in the immortal lines of that most mortal of heroes, Hamlet: "To be or not to be—that is the question." Many people have not yet truly committed to showing up for life at all. As a result, such people cover their core inner disempowerment, shame, apathy and disappointment with fantasy material. Fantasies can vary in scope from those of suicide or escape, all the way to heroic or romantic fulfillment that they idealize as far removed from their actual life experience. Such fantasy material allows people to conveniently sidestep the issues they face simply by being alive—the *basic anxiety* that living reveals within them.

Such ambivalence is therapeutically critical to acknowledge—even in a one-off astrology reading. Unexamined, it will dominate every area of the individual life to some extent.

Taurus also points to the basic tools of survival. In his seminal book *The Denial of Death*, Ernest Becker makes the consistent point that in anxiously grasping for survival, we risk missing a crucial aspect of our own existence. He quotes Jose Ortega, whose central image is one of the "the shipwrecked":

> "The man with the clear head is the man who frees himself from those fantastic 'ideas' (the characterological lie about reality) and looks life in the face, realizes that everything is problematic, and feels himself lost. And this is the simple truth – that to live is to feel oneself lost – he who accepts it has already begun to find himself, to be on firm ground.

> Instinctively, as do the shipwrecked, he will look round for something to which to cling, and that tragic ruthless glance, absolutely sincere, because it is a question of his salvation, will cause him to bring order to the chaos of his life. These are the only genuine ideas; the ideas of the shipwrecked. All the rest is rhetoric, posturing farce. He who does not really find himself lost . . . he never finds himself, never comes up against his own reality.[4]

Contextualizing the existential position: *To become shipwrecked is to lose the swift momentum of the adaptive ego self (the ship) and therefore to experience the vastness of the ocean for the first time.*

Our vulnerability and anxiety in the face of the mystery of being (the ocean) are the precursors to authentic participation. Some existential thinkers, Sartre for example, argue that the courage to live with the apparent meaningless of the self in the face of the everything is all that we can manage. I see Sartre's point as an initiation experience into real presence. The scale of the ocean does alter the experience of the personality. You cannot be buffered by your own pretensions and ego ideals if you want to experience the truth of your own depths and potential. However, there is an experience of self that begins as one surrenders the prior limitations of one's sense of self to include the part of the vastness, the drop of the ocean that lives within you.

Taurean survival anxieties (perhaps tied in to prior and present-life traumatic memory) tend to create a buffer against the threat of the encroaching ocean of consciousness, to which one might have to voluntarily surrender to allow a greater experience of reality to unfold. I have witnessed that people do, time and time again, bravely look over the parapet wall and take those first steps, acknowledging their value, and affirming the gift of having made it thus far.

To admit that one is shipwrecked is a crucial step towards healing. Otherwise, it is possible to remain on the wrong course, which no amount of clever sailing can alter.

Gemini

Gemini's contribution to a powerful astrology reading centers around the issue of communication: we raise a number of core intellectual issues within the reading with the goal of finding a shared language in which a meaningful dialogue may exist.

As we endeavor to find a shared language and create a fruitful dialogue, it helps to keep this insight in mind: if in doubt about something, *ask the client*. Do not feel compelled to impress or second-guess him or create suggestions, if you're unclear about what he actually needs. Just ask him. No one knows more about the client's world than the client does, and our desire to wow others with our knowledge can stand in the way of true healing. [5]

Another key issue in discovering a shared language is raised by the very context of astrology itself:

1. *Does the client already know some astrology? If she is a student or has an interest or knowledge in the subject, does she want you to explain the astrology to her as you look at her birth chart?*

2. *If she knows nothing at all about astrology beyond her interest in having the reading, are you prepared to convey the multidimensional potential of the birth chart in a language she can relate to?*

Answering these questions will help you meet the client where she is. You might start by having a physical chart to give the client. I have found that even clients for whom astrology is a completely foreign language still appreciate looking at the physical chart and having a copy of it to keep. Some find insight through identifying the visual elements of the natal chart during the reading. Geometric patterns can convey meaning that visual learners will readily see: a stellium, a loaded eastern hemisphere, a see-saw opposition shape, squares to the nodal axis as impediments to the pathway of the nodes, etc.

Realistically, most people will leave an astrology reading with, at most, a handful of key points forefront in their minds. Providing the service of recording the reading affords the client time to review what was discussed and recall the key points. In many cases, there is often just *one critical reason* for the client to be compelled to get a reading, and to identify and serve that need is critical for the reading to be of greatest therapeutic value.

The birth chart is a multidimensional map that changes over time as a person lives his life and (hopefully) evolves. It is useful to drop the fantasy that one could possibly convey all, or even the great majority, of the information contained in the chart in one reading. The approach I teach is to focus first, in the broadest evolutionary terms, on the information that the chart reveals about her deeper self. From there, you can explore the specifics around what may be pinpointed as the leading or cutting edge of the person's current evolution.

Finally, we can make the rather obvious observation that we will get along more easily with some clients than with others. We will find a shared language that just clicks more with people who share our interests, outlooks and common references than with those who do not. (While I do not commonly take the time to indulge myself in consulting synastry charts between myself and my clients, they can reveal important dynamics.) With some very shut-down people, we may struggle to find a meaningful aspirational language, as they do not really have one, or even know what one might sound like. An excellent book, *Fierce Conversations* by Susan Scott, explores the issue of authentic communication in depth.

I once counseled a very socially isolated young man who worked the Walmart night shift and played online role-playing games. He achieved such success in one of these games that he could have sold his characters for a considerable sum: a virtual life dreamed into being from the bedroom of his parents' house. In discovering we had a shared language in the form of *Star Trek: the Next Generation*, we were able to discover a way of conceptualizing his process and the role in life to which he might aspire. From that place of common ground, and through his admiration for the *Star Trek* character Number One, I was able to recommend the book *Manhood* by Steve Biddulph—that rare gem, an authentic therapeutic work in extremely readable form. This young man found the book remarkably useful. It was the only book (article or essay even) he had read in his adult life, though he was 30 years old.

There is a fundamental limit to the mind, and the recognition that our thoughts can only label reality—not construct or even reconstruct it—carries implications for the astrology reading. At its best, the natal chart is still just a map, and as a map its efficacy is found in allying the map's symbolism to the consciousness of the individual. Anything else is fallacious. We realize that reality transcends our thinking about it—even our most clever thoughts.

Cancer

In the Cancer archetype, we uncover the need to create a safe and secure personal space in which to conduct the reading. To foster the *creative vulnerability* of the encounter, the astrology reading needs to boundary a *Temenos*, or sacred space. In her popular 2010 *Ted Talk*, Dr. Brené Brown called vulnerability the "birthplace of innovation, creativity and change" as well as "our most accurate measurement of courage." [6]

The key to creating a sacred space is to start with good internal intention and integrity. In an ideal world, every reading would take place in a private room with comfortable chairs and a desk or table for a computer and recording device. Indeed, this is often the case. I have, however, played my part in readings that have proven to be transformational even in more uncomfortable environments. For instance, sequestered in a hotel restaurant just after checkout with my bags piled up at the side of the booth, my laptop on lap, or while sitting on the floor huddled in the corner of a crowded conference room.

Creating the personal space most facilitative of the client's capacity to safely share his personal reality is easier in a private space set aside for the work. And yet it is possible outside of that comfort zone based on a couple of key factors. Foremost amongst these is the intensity of the client's need or the degree of power of his motivation for having the reading. The client who is so eager to discuss his issue with me that he would do this in the corner of a conference space during lunch hour is already indicating a serious intention, a substantial commitment to the potential for what might occur within the space. This commitment becomes part of a bridge to step over the limitations of the physical space.

The second part of the bridge is *the astrologer's inner commitment* to serve the highest good of the client. This is the baseline my professional practice (akin to a spiritual discipline) is based upon. I urge any practicing astrologers or therapists reading this to consider this phrase: serving the highest good. This does not mean to "be good," which is a *tyranny of the should* and is modeled on the *idealized self* that we have already seen can be intensely problematic. To serve the *highest* good as an intention is an act of inner commitment to the truth and to the sacred potential of life. It is not a conceptual stance, it does not take a judgmental position on what is right or wrong, good or bad for the client; rather it is an ongoing openness to the potential of life to manifest meaning, and to endeavor to serve that potential with all of one's being.

I approach the client's reality with a truly open mind; then I intentionally and energetically create safe space in which the person might have the best chance of feeling heard and discovering for herself a sense of meaning and purpose, a potential for empowered choice within her life.

It is not the *outer space* that facilitates the necessary safety for the client to be vulnerable (and therefore creative). The outer space certainly can help or hinder, but it is the *commitment of both the client and the astrologer*, allied to their inner attitude or integrity, alongside the capacity and experience of the astrologer, that creates the space in which the reading can become a meaningful encounter.

There is a core insecurity in the Cancer archetype, encapsulated by the Aries square to Cancer—I can pioneer (Aries), yet that causes separation anxiety (Cancer), because being instinctively myself (Aries) differentiates me from my family or tribe (Cancer). This kind of insecurity can be experienced both by the client, in his process, and the astrologer, who also must "risk" herself in the encounter. But the fact is that no amount of astrological knowledge or preparation for a reading can compensate for or remove *basic anxiety*.

One good indication that your practice may be subtly influenced negatively by anxiety is if you find yourself preparing a reading for considerably longer than normal. It is amazing how much time can be consumed doing what we rationalize as intellectual preparation, but which is actually not a thinking process at all—rather a hamster wheel of imagined possible futures pertaining to the reading and the insecurity that can emerge when confronted with the *frisson* of the encounter with the client.

Here we have an issue that needs further exploration, since much of its potential use as a tool for one's continuing professional development and personal growth is sidestepped by a failure to recognize the issue in the first place. What becomes an internal dialogue about one's approach to astrology, a dialogue within our community about the many varied methodologies, conceals the *basic anxiety* about the encounter with the client. The tendency is for rationalization concealing anxiety (astrology as symbolized by Aquarius, the detached air sign) instead of recognizing the value of anxiety: its potential to build rapport with the client, or with our rivals or peers within the astrology community. For anxiety is innate in the human form prior to enlightenment. Simply through having and identifying with an ego we are, by definition, anxious because the ego has no inherent existence. Therefore, we are on shaky ground from the start.

Over-preparation can be a compensatory drive, a way to manage anxiety. On a purely practical level, if one wishes to practice astrology professionally, the issue of preparation becomes central. It is simply impractical financially and in terms of efficiency to spend most of a day, or even a whole day, preparing a chart (though the latter is not an uncommon practice, especially among beginners). By over-preparing, we minimize the amount of assistance we can offer by making the very act of helping so laborious that it cannot be sustained.

Again, the reader must take care to do his self-work here. The astrologer or therapist who is caught in a pattern of self-shame, perhaps as the result of an internalized childhood conflict about a parent who was critical or did not believe in the person (a voice that may now be internalized), could find himself sabotaging his own potential by making the quest of the *idealized self* to give the perfect reading such hard work that it will never happen—or that it is so tiring as to be unsustainable in the long term.

Leo

With Leo, we encounter the need for validation. If in doubt, validate. Validate the person's experience up to and including the experience of the reading. This validation is crucial for a number of reasons:

1. *This leading edge of the individual's personal process could be the critical reason for her seeking a reading in the first place.*

2. *Affirming the client's experience is sometimes the central purpose of the reading.*

3. *When we existentially, philosophically and spiritually affirm the purpose of life, we recognize that everything is, was and ever shall be the way that it was meant to be.*

4. *To validate the client's experience (as well as one's own) is then, ultimately, true in the sense that, by definition, what is, is what was meant to be.*

The last two points rest on the answer Einstein gave to the question: what is the most important question? To which he replied, "I think that the most important question facing humanity is, 'Is the universe a friendly place?'" In much of his writing, Freud expressed a vision of life as hostile. In his *oeuvre*, Jung described life as a chessboard comprised of equal light and dark. In contrast, Roberto Assagioli affirmed a fundamental goodness and meaning in the universe. If we can accept Assagioli's approach (perhaps the ultimate validation of life), then we can see that in essence, everything that is was meant to exist in that way—a spiritual understanding of reality that grants an unambiguous affirmation to life.

Why would God—i.e., the infinite impersonal sacred field of life infusing all creation with a living mystery, the limitless luminous presence—want any creature to suffer? What would be the point of that? The creation of a God invested in human life in that way is an anthropomorphic distortion: the projection of the fearful parental image onto a city in the sky and a bearded Wizard running the show.

The Sun (Leo) is the creative center of the solar system, its beating heart. In the natal chart, the Sun represents the core energy of the current life. To validate it is to touch the heart. To allow a *joie de vivre* within the energetic space of the reading is to touch upon the creative joyful potential of the individual and lights the way forward in ways that may outlast the reading considerably.

The paradox of the wounded healer archetype is that one can affirm the creative joy and potential for self-actualization within the other even on days when one is struggling to find that light clearly in oneself. How is this possible?

To return to Aries, the natural trine from Leo, we may discover our answer in part through the courage and integrity to stand by the vision of truth even when the personal connection to that truth is not at its strongest. To look across to the opposition point of Aquarius, we can see that a certain impersonal quality of understanding arises when life is seen as an infinite field of potential. Such detachment allows for a perspective that is not just mired in the myopia of the personal self.

Most crucially, when doing healing work with others, one becomes protected and elevated through the healer archetype; one is raised up to some extent beyond one's frailties through the examples of the great healers and teachers who have walked the way before us. I am not talking about inflation, about forgetting that we have *basic anxiety* or core issues and narcissistic avoidance of them. I am speaking of a space for which I have been subtly witness to time and time again, of my own empathy for my own insecurity and suffering being increased through my empathy and openness to the process of my client. It is as if there is a positive feedback loop.

In my serving something of value in the client, even on a personal bad day, it is as if I am led back to that thing of beauty in myself. The work elevates me; in being open to the transformational encounter of the astrology reading, I am open to becoming a better person.

To the soul within us, the only reasonable response to the mystery, the presence of divinity within the infinite field of life, is love and gratitude. When one experiences the field, if only for a moment, if merely the slightest whisper of the truth reaches the inner ear or the heart, then all one wants to do is say "thank you" and aspire to live within the power of that infinite love forever:

> *Center of all centers, core of cores,*
> *almond self-enclosed, and growing sweet--*
> *all this universe, to the furthest stars*
> *all beyond them, is your flesh, your fruit.*
>
> *Now you feel how nothing clings to you;*
> *your vast shell reaches into endless space,*
> *and there the rich, thick fluids rise and flow.*
> *Illuminated in your infinite peace,*
>
> *a billion stars go spinning through the night,*
> *blazing high above your head.*
> *But in you is the presence that*
> *will be, when all the stars are dead.*
> *Buddha in Glory,*
> -Rainer Maria Rilke.

Leo, the Sun and the 5th house all express the potential of the child and most crucially, *the innate innocence of the child*. Despite all our past karma and despite all the difficult experiences awaiting the young being, every one of us is born innocent. To hold nurturing space for that innocence for the client as real and inviolate no matter what past experience has taught them is to serve a powerful spiritual truth:

"Can our lack of fidelity cancel God's fidelity? That would be absurd. God will always be true, even though everyone is false."
-Romans 3:3-4 [7]

Despite everything that has happened to an individual, the divine child is still alive in them. This is metaphorically referred to in the German concept of infant schooling; *kindergarten*—literally the garden of children; as if they are like flowers of differing kinds growing in different ways. Or in the age-old saying "we are all God's children," we can see ourselves free of judgment, and that places us in the context of Matthew Fox's concept of *Original Blessing*, where all is transformed. So many hurt from perceived slights or inner flaws; the innocence of the child will shine through these pale ghosts into a brave new world.

Affirming the innocence of the child within the client is a very powerful therapeutic tool to bring into the astrology reading. This is especially important when natal chart dynamics reveal stresses in the early home-life and the client confirms having grown up in a dysfunctional family environment. For then the child has been starved of love and gratitude for her presence. In her innocence, the child does not understand why the parent does not find more joy in her company. She is not capable of understanding her parent's mental health issue or problems; instead she tends to internalize a sense of failure or shame that she could not evoke a more positive response from her caregivers. To reaffirm the innocence of the child is to build new pathways for her return to love and affirmation of life.

Virgo

With Virgo, we encounter the question "How can I serve?" To set the intention of service as the underlying imprint of the reading, I always begin by asking my client, "How can I help today?" Alongside the general alignment with the principle of service, this has a practical value: it allows the client to ask his questions to set or articulate his intentions, if he was or is uncertain of them. This opportunity increases the chances of assisting the client from the beginning.

When Parsifal initially encounters the Fisher King, the keeper of the Grail, he falls silent in his presence and is unceremoniously escorted from the castle housing the Grail. His mission as a knight in tatters, he journeys through many hardships and many long years. Finally, he encounters the Fisher King again and is able to ask the wounded King and man, "What ails thee?" This is the release, the point at which the knight is able to serve and to access the redemptive power of the Grail cup. It is the question—and all that it implies about the knight's intention—that liberates. This is the question that we need to make our own when we face the client as a servant of her highest good.

Whenever I am about to work with people, either publicly or privately, I will pray to serve the people I am teaching or giving readings with and for. I set the intention to serve the highest good of my clients or any and all of those attending my classes or talks. In so doing, I am both ameliorating my own *basic anxiety* that (no matter how well one knows one's subject matter) can arise fiercely when about to address a room of a hundred people and I am beginning to get out of my own way. This means that I am withdrawing my energy from the fantasy of control—that I can somehow take care of everything. And instead I open to the possibility of what will be. I affirm that I might be transformed by the day of readings just as my clients might, that I might learn from my students just as they might from me. I am including the possibility, then, that others may surprise, enliven and inspire me, or, through their own inspiration, see me take, appropriately, the back seat.

This capacity for surprise is critical for the spontaneity and integrity of an attitude of service. It is rigid, arrogant and delusional to assume that I will know what this service will mean or entail. And in staying open to the surprise of the encounter, I undermine any mock humility, or spiritual sub-personality (an aspect of my *idealized* or *false self*) that sees me as a spiritual type of person who ought to express in a prescribed kind of way.

To remain truly open to the encounter with the intention of serving the highest good is a radical existential state. It involves the risk of expressing my real self, the spontaneity and unselfconscious expression of my identity free from the filter of roles: the psychotherapist, the evolutionary astrologer.

The highest good is an expression of the multidimensional potential of the infinite field of reality which can take infinite forms within its expression in the individual life of the client, and within the relational space of the astrology reading itself. Real transformation has a grace to it, a flowering of a certain potential in the moment, that emotional suffering or karma did not previously allow. I cannot control that. Grace is the expression of the divinity of life breaking through previous barriers. What I *can* do is my utmost not to be that barrier myself.

This grace is an expression of Pisces, opposite to Virgo, the reality of the love present within creation. The Tibetan Buddhist concept of *bodhicitta* has both a relative and an absolute form. In its relative form, it finds expression in the serving of others' happiness with the same dedication as if it were your own happiness. In its ultimate form, *bodhicitta* is found through the realization of *sunyata,* or the luminosity of emptiness in which there is a realization that all beings are part of your happiness, because truth is non-dual and there are not two of you—just the one life in which all live. [8]

In the Tantric traditions of Buddhism, the Vajrayana path, this *bodhicitta* is seen as a white drop above the crown of the head that grows in power the more you serve the truth of the other as equal to you (relative insight) or as not other than you in the first place (absolute truth through non-dual realization). There is a parallel in the Christian mystic tradition of painting halos above Christ and the saints, in some traditions very painstakingly differentiating certain states of realization through halos of varying size and brightness.

In my limited experience, this halo, or white drop, is an energetic truth, a literal pattern in the subtle bodies of the energy field at the crown. When one connects with this *bodhicitta,* or white light at the crown, one realizes that service is not humility in the sense of powerlessness or a servile attitude. Instead, it is humility in order to contain the vast power of certain forces without destabilizing the identity. It is an occult law; *one requires humility to be able to experience the power of divinity as it manifests through the energy body and the relative world.*

On a final practical level, Virgo as an earth sign, and ruled by Mercury, represents discrimination: of all the information we take in (Mercury-Gemini), what is the most useful to the current purpose (Mercury-Virgo)? The question of discrimination arises within the astrology reading as: within the limited time available to us today, how can this be of the most use to the client? That is why I start with "how can I help?" and the natural constellation of the client's vested interest or purpose in undertaking the reading. It pays to consistently touch base with that purpose during the reading, what therapists call *the presenting issue,* to make sure that the experience is working and useful for the client. I suspect many an astrologer has felt he gave an extraordinary performance of the power of his particular method of this ancient art while the client has left befuddled and more confused than when she arrived!

The process of meeting the client's expectations is collaborative. It is not only determined by the client. Plenty of people will have unrealistic expectations of the reading, and some not enough expectation. Yet it is important to remember the client in the realization of one's full potential as a proponent of one's methodology.

A problem can arise when a traumatized psyche attempts to defend itself against challenging situations (whether triggered by an outside threat or not). The psyche tries to root out the thoughts and emotions associated with those states and eject them. This can lead to hypervigilance in which every situation is experienced as "about to become traumatic." Then, the internalized aspect of the trauma leads to a pattern of continuing the trauma:

"Most contemporary analytic writers are inclined to see this attacking figure as an internalized version of the actual perpetrator of the trauma, who has 'possessed' the inner world of the trauma victim. But this popularized view is only half correct. The diabolical inner figure is often far more sadistic and brutal than any outer perpetrator, indicating that we are dealing here with a *psychological* factor set loose in the inner world by trauma—an archetypal traumatogenic agency within the psyche itself . . . It functions, if we can imagine its inner rationale, as a kind of inner 'Jewish Defense League' (whose slogan, after the Holocaust, reads 'Never Again!'). 'Never again,' says our tyrannical caretaker, 'will the traumatized personal spirit of this child suffer this badly! Never again will it be this helpless in the face of cruel reality . . . before this happens I will disperse it into fragments (disassociation), or encapsulate it and soothe it with fantasy (schizoid withdrawal), or numb it with intoxicating substances (addiction), or persecute it to keep it from hoping for life in this world (depression) . . . In this way I will preserve what is left of this prematurely amputated childhood—of an innocence that has suffered too much too soon!'" - Donald Kalsched [9]

Kalsched relates how the introjected aspect of trauma can create its own internal weather system in the psyche of the individual and dominate his life experience. With the Virgo archetype we need, at times, to be sensitive to our client possibly feeling inferior or lacking in some essential way. If this fundamental lack is present, it can manifest as an internal shame response in which the individual feels that difficult life experiences are his own fault. Children often mistakenly assume responsibility for childhood disappointments or difficult experiences such as divorce or the loss of a parent. If we grow up and don't transform this pattern, we find that as adults, the hurt inner child continues to take the blame, even when it isn't due.

In worst-case scenarios, people with this pattern walk around in a perpetual state of shame. In the inner world, they are caught in a trap of treating themselves as if they have done something terribly wrong. The triggering event in the present is often revealed to be a minor social infringement or personal falling-out. And yet, the inner self responds as if the person has murdered someone. Their childhood traumatic states and/or prior-life traumatic memories are introjected as core shame.

Paradoxically, while most people understandably want to avoid feelings of core shame, the nature of healing is such that it must be acknowledged if it is to be surrendered or healed. And Virgo guides us to attend to the healing one step at a time, day by day, and to keep working at it until we heal the pattern.

Libra

With Libra, we encounter the importance of the *relational field*, which is comprised of three components: the client, the astrologer and the relationship itself. In a reading, this dynamic is made up of three charts: the natal charts of the client and the astrologer, and their composite chart.

The composite chart is an expression of the relational field between two or more people. The meaning of the relationship as illuminated in the composite chart is also the key to understanding synastry dynamics. Synastry analysis (looking at the relationships between two natal charts) is next to meaningless without a clear understanding of the two natal charts in addition to composite analysis, which reveals the evolutionary purpose of the relationship. Synastry without the composite chart is like understanding the style of the two dancers without knowing which dance they are attempting together; or even more fundamentally, why they are dancing in the first place.

As I stress repeatedly, the highest intention in our interpersonal relationships is to aim for the *I-Thou* dynamic. *I-Thou* is a sacred bond of respect and equal footing in contrast to the imbalanced *I-It* relationship. The high message of Libra suggests that if we approach our clients (and any other relationship) from the *I-It* perspective, the astrologer and the client become trapped in roles, potentially imprisoned in empty gestures and safe words that conceal their *basic anxiety*, rather than revealing and potentially transforming it. Shifting our perspective to *I-Thou* can in itself be enough to facilitate healing and deeper connection.

The relationship subtext between astrologer and client will unconsciously mirror or evoke the relationships that the client has with family and intimates. So too will the *relationship in the counseling room* potentially evoke from the astrologer issues with relationships within *her* family and with significant others. Libra compels our awareness towards these complex relationship dynamics, nudging us to become more aware of the other in a way that shifts the dynamic towards one of equality.

A reading is a collaborative effort in which both parties bring their relative expertise to the table. The client brings his expertise of himself and his biography, the astrologer her knowledge of the natal chart and counseling dynamics. This is an equal collaboration. The client's experience, memory, self-worth and core psychological/energetic state are key to the process. As I've already suggested, the profession of astrology can only benefit from a shift away from the rigid old stasis approach to readings in which the passive client comes to the intellectually knowledgeable astrologer for relevant titbits of that knowledge.

As we approach a reading, Libra reminds us that we're about to undertake a *shared process*. The astrologer is a guide and both parties will be asked to participate. That shared effort can be tremendous fun even as it is hard work. To be a guide is to be a pathfinder, a forerunner of routes that the client had no idea existed. Sometimes it is to bond through the commonality of shared humanity, both resting and breaking bread together at the summit of their journey. At other times, as the guide we nurse the wounded client, encouraging him to continue when appropriate, and pointing out when to stop and seek further treatment.

In his presentation on "Transformation and Transition," Remy Aquarone, the head of the Pottergate Centre and specialist in Dissociative Identity Disorder, discussed the importance of the parental image in the relationship between healer and client. [10] Relating to the natural t-square relationship between Cancer/Capricorn and Libra, this has to do with the way the mother and father archetypes meet in the relationship. In infancy, maternal-type love (Cancer) involves a totally open empathic bond with the child. While Aquarone advocated this core empathy, he argued that expressing maternal-type love between a counselor/healer and a client who has experienced complex trauma and abuse is actually *contraindicated*. He suggested that it can be damaging for the counselor to identify too closely with the kinds of dissociative states that result from post-traumatic stress. Instead, he pointed towards a greater emphasis on Capricorn: with the healthy father (Capricorn) archetypally carrying the mother's love (Cancer) in a more dis-identified and yet encouraging fashion. Interestingly, he suggested, this expression is more appropriate both for the preservation of the therapeutic relationship and also for the mental health of the healer: Cancer-Capricorn resolving through Libra.

So in order to function in our best capacity, it's important to think about what kind of guides we wish to be, and to understand the consequences of that choice. While motherly empathy is an important part of any healing equation, overidentifying with a client's pain may do us more harm than good, and limit our capacity as useful guides. We need to maintain a balance of Capricorn-Cancer energy that allows us to carry space for our clients with compassion for their pain while maintaining the ability to see a way forward and out. We can aim towards being empathic of the client's suffering without extending such empathy into actually suffering with them, which vicariously extends the suffering, serving neither party.

As we combine this insight with the Libra archetype, we find the need to hold space for the complex relationship dynamics in the room, to honor our real nature, with its relative strengths and weaknesses, to be co-present with that the client—ready to step in and also step back when needed. This is a powerful self-discipline to practice. It requires appropriate self-care as a professional combined with the fatherly quality Aquarone suggests: warm and encouraging rather than overidentified.

And this healing relationship dynamic can have ripple effects. The mutual respect for the soul's evolutionary journey becomes a blueprint for respect, integrity and honesty in all relationships. Just as in grade school the positive regard from a single good teacher can ameliorate the struggle with disinterested or controlling teachers, so, too, maintaining an attitude of respect for the client can have an impact far beyond the reading itself. People may forget all the clever astrological points made in their reading from five years ago, but they will never forget the overall impression of the reading, the energetic space it occurred in, and the way they were left feeling.

To expand on this point, many studies of therapeutic efficacy have discovered that the approach or training of the therapist or healer is secondary in importance to the *quality of the relationship* between healer and client. Consistently, studies find that the technique (presumably a really important issue to the practitioner, the therapist or astrologer) is of less importance to the client, who finds the quality of attention and care received to be of far greater magnitude.

Scorpio

The Scorpio archetype corresponds to the purpose of the deeper self as it seeks (impersonally it seems) to move us beyond our pre-existing limitations, to transform us.

The word transformation comes from the Latin *transformare*: the linking of *trans* (beyond, across) with *formare* (the verb, to form). This has two levels of meaning: first, of changing form, moving across (*trans*) from one form to another (metamorphosis); and second, of moving beyond (*trans*) form. Most astrologers use the term *trans*personal to describe the nature of the outer planets (Uranus, Neptune and Pluto). Scorpio relates to the idea that the deeper self seeks to risk powerlessness in the search of empowerment through the changing of state (linear movement from one form to another), and the outer planets move us beyond form altogether into the formless and nonlinear.

The greatest potential of the astrology reading is that it can transform someone's life for the better. To achieve this potential, there must be explicit permission, a readiness within the field of the encounter to enter the world of depth, Scorpio's terrain.

My first therapy office space was in a rental house. After I moved out, the new tenants (a friend and a couple) shared that they all had a special love for that room. Even visitors to the house would comment on how good the room felt. I remember my friend's sadness when, after a few months, the "aura" of the room had shifted after its function became the couple's television room. It seemed as if the unique quality in the space had evaporated.

While I was working there, I regularly did ritual energetic cleansing of the room to support the health of the vessel for my working life. I did depth work with clients there every week for three years. My friend had enjoyed the subtle energetic quality left behind from this life-affirming and positive energy that came from creating a safe container in which people could enter the depth of work promised by the Scorpio archetype.

This therapeutic and astrological work also created a reverent quality *within me* through an ongoing commitment to transformation and the possibility of intimate human relationship.

To be able to enter a transformative space, people first need to feel a level of trust in which to share personal things they may normally hide even from themselves. A certain percentage of my work involves people sharing things they may not have ever told to another living soul. Although this isn't surprising given my work as a therapist, many astrologers report a similar dynamic, and it is something you should be prepared to encounter.

As astrologers we need to prepare by asking ourselves on what level we wish to work. Think about how deep you'd feel comfortable going with a client and set an intention beforehand for that. Be aware of what energy you hold as you enter the reading, and keep your intentions clear. Knowledge is shared within the subtle field of the reading space which is conveyed unconsciously (from client to astrologer and vice versa) through the energy body, physical gestures, body language and even tone of voice. Many clients will know instinctively from these nonverbal cues if they are safe to share and at what level. And with practice, you will be able to pick up the same from them.

A great intention to start with is to offer yourself as a route-finder in potential, a soulful GPS for the client. When material arises in the session that you aren't willing (or able) to work with, be prepared to refer the client to someone with the skills to do so. Have a list on hand of licensed, trained professionals whom you trust. The astrological chart is only a map, a symbolic potential. The motivated client looks to embody that potential in her life. The dedicated astrologer looks to support this embodiment with multiple referrals at his or her disposal.

I have referred clients to other astrologers, therapists, regression therapists, equine-facilitated therapists, psychics, chiropractors and mental health services. Inevitably, issues will arise that are beyond the scope of the astrology reading. It is ethically sound to have contact information on hand for a good licensed psychotherapist and other healers of different modalities that can help the client make best use of her potential. Don't feel like it's your job to take on everything that arises, especially matters outside your comfort zone or area of expertise.

It is a part of one's professional responsibility to know one's strengths and weaknesses and to be clear about them. It is also important to clarify with whom one likes to work and in what way. Once you have your focus set, let that inform your marketing materials, and state your intentions clearly with your clients. Like many astrologers, you may ultimately choose to limit your approach to only sharing astrological information (without dialogue from the client or exchange). This can be done with integrity, but make sure you explain what you can and cannot offer beforehand, so expectations are in line on both sides.

Scorpio relates to the energetic exchange and power dynamics that arise naturally in the counseling room. The method of astrology I teach has the potential to lead people into areas of exploration that frighten them, bringing them face-to-face with their own resistance to change and transformation. That brings us to the issue of trust, a critical Scorpio focal point.

Many people have conscious memories of being betrayed by others in this life, partly-conscious memories of betrayal from early childhood, and/or predominantly unconscious memories of prior-life betrayal. Such people will consciously (or unconsciously) scan their space for cues as to whether such a betrayal could occur again. In preparation for a rich encounter with this type of client, ask yourself if you're energetically prepared for that kind of scrutiny, especially if your client has a strong Scorpio signature. Are you operating at full integrity? Have you spent time looking at your own response to betrayal, disappointment, and withdrawal?

The more time you've spent looking at these issues, the easier they will be to face with a client, and you'll set the tone for deeper healing and transformation to take place. You'll also energetically convey to the Scorpionic client that you are trustworthy and will set that part of them at ease, allowing the work to go deeper.

Finally, at the start of every counseling-based reading, it is important to share your guidelines about anonymity and confidentiality. The Scorpio-oriented client will appreciate knowing that what is shared in the counseling room will remain private. If you don't already have a confidentiality policy, spend some time creating one. You might even post it on your site, so that this type of client will feel comfortable contacting you in the first place. If you present charts publicly, or discuss them with friends, always ask for permission from your clients before sharing any information publicly. The more you operate in full integrity, the more you will attract and facilitate deep connection with others.

Sagittarius

"A child is born on that day and on that hour when the celestial rays are in mathematical harmony with his individual karma. His horoscope is a challenging portrait, revealing his unalterable past and its probable future results . . . Superstitious awe of astrology makes one an automaton, slavishly dependent on mechanical guidance. The wise man defeats his planets—which is to say, his past—by transferring his allegiance from the creation to the Creator. The more he realizes his unity with Spirit, the less he is dominated by matter. The soul is ever free; it is deathless because birthless. It cannot be regimented by stars." -*Paramahansa Yogananda, quoting his guru Sri Yukteswar.* [11]

The natal chart is a multidimensional map of an individual's karmic potential as expressed through correspondence with the cosmic alignment of the universe at the moment and place of birth. The chart is therefore a window to a *broad vision of meaning and possibility*. To ignore the bigger picture is to fail the potential contained in the chart and the healing that might result by unlocking this vision. This is the domain of the Sagittarius archetype.

Many are drawn to astrology because of a nascent sense of higher meaning in life, whether conscious or not. As a result, we need to make this a part of our training as astrologers: to contemplate our world-view and understand how that informs our particular vision of healing and big-picture potential for our clients.

To the extent that we, the astrologers, are still searching for our own understanding, or struggling to orientate to our own thoughts about the *meaning of life*, we may find it hard to serve our clients on that level. Doubt is the companion of faith. We do not need to have resolved *all* our existential or metaphysical questions to work with our clients at the level of meaning. But we do need to always be engaged in a thoughtful process with these big questions.

Let's consider the modern existential perspective that life is a random series of events without order or meaning. If life is not meaningful, how could astrology's multidimensional map of consciousness, the natal chart, exist? Are astrological correlations and meaningful synchronicities just random cosmic accidents like many scientists claim? When contemplating the glory of a sunset or the night sky, the existential philosophy seems ludicrous. If we can accept that clues about the very nature of the deep self are embedded within the natal chart, then it is simply irrational to believe that life is meaningless.

And this is one of astrology's greatest contributions to the current age—a natural antidote to the angst fostered by a void-of-meaning, existentialist scientific perspective on the universe. As Richard Tarnas so beautifully illuminates this point in his magnum opus, *Cosmos and Psyche: Intimations of a New World View*, astrology can help us reclaim some of the greater values of pre-enlightenment, pre-eighteenth century, civilization: that of the harmony of psyche and cosmos.

To study astrology is to open oneself to eternally-relevant metaphysical teachings from pre-Greek times through the Neo-Platonists into a countercultural stream within Western civilization. In books such as *Reality* and *In the Dark Places of Wisdom*, classicist Peter Kingsley has illuminated the spiritual origins of Western culture through his translation of recently discovered pre-Socratic texts. These origins have been largely forgotten or re-interpreted into a more materialist form in the West.

We can appreciate the gains Western society has made in its overemphasis of the solar principle, especially within the material realm. As William Scammell writes, "The tendency to equate civilization with repression . . . might be countered by quoting Chekov's observation that there is more love for humanity in electricity and a hygienic water supply than in any amount of spiritual breast feeding." [12]

Yet, to some extent we have thrown the baby out with the bath water. Though we have successfully exiled many of the limiting superstitions of our past, we have also let go of too much of our core philosophical and spiritual heritage. The modern tendency towards meaninglessness, depression and anxiety disorders results, at least in part, from the loss of this depth. Astrology can play its part in recovering it. Understanding this and making it a mission could be a self-validating component of how we serve humanity (Sagittarius applying through the natural square to Virgo).

On some level, the astrology reading is dealing with the meaning of the client's life whether we want it to or not. The more we are able to understand this consciously and seek to support the client's emergent potential for meaning, the more we empower him.

Another core practical application of the Sagittarius archetype in a counseling dynamic is the principle of honesty. In traditional psychoanalysis, the analyst hid behind the client, who was lying down on the couch. The analyst deliberately withheld any form of sharing with the client so that she might be like a blank sheet of paper onto which the client could draw his projections, which could then be analyzed. This is one extreme. Another is the therapist who spends much of the session talking about herself, having identified with the first question raised by the client. She may spend the bulk of a session giving advice culminating from the story of her own life and her responses to such issues, while time for the client's own process bleeds away. The best approach lies between these two.

To find that middle ground, it is important to spend time predetermining how to respond to various situations with clients. Again, self-awareness of one's core issues is key to becoming a skilled counselor. If you have an unmet need for conversation and connection, it is better to meet that need outside the counseling room. A client who is desperate to feel a connection or to ameliorate her shame around some burning issue may probe for feedback and validation by soliciting our response. How much do we wish to share? When is it useful for the client to hear one of our own stories in order to take in the universal truth that she is not alone and when is it better to compassionately validate her experience and leave space for silence?

Whatever approach you take, the Sagittarian archetype reminds us that authenticity is the key. Self-disclosure is a therapeutic tool in which one engages for a purpose. It is important to be selective about how much to share and when. Shadow Sagittarius reminds us that going off on a tangent at length to fulfill one's unmet needs for being on a soapbox with our own world views is not the most mindful or useful approach with clients.

When you choose to share, be honest and clear; otherwise, the false note will ring out energetically. Develop enough self-awareness to recognize when sharing something will take you on a detour into your own "stuff." If you are at all uncertain about whether a specific story or piece of advice might overwhelm the client, err on the side of not sharing.

Capricorn

With Capricorn, the keyword to remember during astrological counseling is responsibility: the ability to take responsibility for one's personal emotional experience, the nature of one's relationships and a spiritual stance based on personal autonomy. Psychologically, Capricorn corresponds to the *maturation process*. At this critical juncture, people move beyond the psychological dualism of victim/perpetrator in response to their parenting and intimate relationships, as well as in their career or self-expression in the world.

Many people struggle to take responsibility for their lives and actions. They may feel as if others have let them down. Perhaps they experience their family or key relationships as having "failed them" and therefore see others as the "cause" of their unhappiness. That this is fallacious is the key insight of the mature adult, who understands that usually, other people do not *cause* our individual suffering. They simply behave the way they do due to their own psychological make-up and personal problems.

A problematic relationship becomes a choice for us. For instance, we might decide to approach a problematic relationship that is still based on an authentic loving bond with the intention of working on it for a period of time to see it might get better. If that doesn't seem possible, we face a choice: to stay in that relationship and accept the consequences of its limitations or leave the relationship. That this can be a rational process is easy to see from the outside. But *inside* difficult relationships, many people experience terrible suffering and nightmarish fears about being alone or unable to cope in the world if those relationships disintegrate. Yet others experience crippling guilt for desiring to leave, even if the relationship has descended into a ritual of duty rather than devotion.

These kinds of relationship experiences often have roots in early home-life dynamics, especially in parent-child relationships. One of the two main causes of unconscious personal pain within relationships (Capricorn square to Libra) is displaced childhood emotions (the Cancer polarity to Capricorn); the other main cause is prior-life traumas.

When we are infants, the need for attachment, for bonding with a primary caregiver, is essential for survival. It is within the mammalian world that an extended experience *in utero* and the prolonged need for early infant maternal care came to prominence. The maternal love that guides this process is a more sustainable template for love than much of what is called by that name under the guise of romance.

To the child within, abandonment and separation are real concerns; one really can die if abandoned as an infant. Unresolved emotions from early infancy complicate adult relationships; seemingly out of nowhere, previously "sane" adults can behave erratically due to overwhelming fear of the failure of an adult bond. This points to an acute form of neurotic suffering caused by not completing the natural maturation process into adulthood, signified by the Capricorn archetype. Although we know the adult responding poorly in such circumstances will not actually die because of a separation, he does feel as though he will. At some level, we are on our own here. Those trapped in an infantile attachment to external nurturing will need to take a crucial step into adult self-awareness *of their own volition,* accepting personal responsibility for their actions, and ultimately entering (and exiting) relationships as fully-actualized beings.

As Erica Jong astutely writes, "The truth is simple, you do not die from love. You only wish you did." [13] You feel like you will die to the extent that you have identified your primal need for attachment with the figure of the partner. Helping a client gain this insight can be an event of central significance.

We can expand this perspective to other life topics—relationships, family, career, finances, creativity, joy or need for down time. Is there some area of this client's life in which there is an emerging need for him to take responsibility in order to further mature and grow? And if so, to what extent does apathy, shame, guilt, fear of judgment or ridicule prevent him from taking that critical next step? These questions will shine light on Capricornian shadows.

The sad truth is that many of us experience arrested development. At any critical stage in our developmental process, our response to adversity can freeze part of ourselves so that it never really matures. We see then the potential for discrepancy between a person's biological and psychological ages. An individual may be 70 years old but still behave as if he was a surly teenager routinely threatening rage if he does not get what he wants.

Remy Aquarone teaches that the appropriate parental archetype for the healer to emulate when dealing with complex trauma or disassociation (of which arrested development is a form) is *the archetypal father*. Adopting a detached but loving presence is a key to facilitating maturation. (Note: both genders can express the high father archetype.)

Along the Cancer-Capricorn axis, we find the need for balance between parental authority and parental nurturing. Many people who have a freeze in development have experienced parental authority wielded without love. Such experiences can prompt some individuals to fearfully retreat from their own power and self-worth. They may internalize threatening, controlling or abusive parental figures.

To increase the healing potential with these types of issues, we must project *loving* authority. Consider the way you hold oneself, the tone of your voice, and how you actually feel about the client. This inner alignment facilitates a fruitful encounter with the wounded inner figure of the developmentally frozen client. Ultimately, the goal is to rightfully place the authority back in the hands of the client, through loving guidance and support.

Aquarius

Aquarius introduces the potential to *deeply witness* the client. To truly witness another's reality through her story and presence is to offer an antidote for all the previous times that she was *not* witnessed. To be truly seen can be a healing event in itself. Many people carry parts of their personal stories as shameful burdens or disassociated states that have broken off due to trauma. To witness these in the powerful space of the *I-Thou* connection is to form a potential bridge that allows for integration of the split-off material that inhibits their day-to-day functional self.

In cases where trauma is still active, special skills are needed. In such situations, I have risked the balance of the reading to address a still-present harmful core issue. I then extend the period of deep listening to witness the process and energetically hold a safe space for healing in the individual's life. At best, this can create a clearing ground from which to begin the work of reconstruction.

I recall one client for whom this witnessing had been the primary function of our initial reading. At a subsequent meeting, she expressed frustration that she hadn't received more of my perspective on other dynamics in her chart. I conceded that some of those possibilities had been sacrificed with the intention of heart-centered witnessing that might create a healthy boundary to quell the retraumatizing events still occurring in her life. She then shared that her insights gleaned from that initial reading regarding the domestic abuse she'd experienced had led her to change her life and leave that relationship. This in itself marked a victory. Although other potential avenues of chart exploration had been limited, the power of the path we did follow was undeniable. In the end, you will have to make judgment calls in the moment, based on your own intuition, skill level and intention.

My understanding of Uranus/Aquarius as a trauma signature is explored in depth in *Healing the Soul*. The Saturn/Uranus joint rulership of Aquarius symbolizes the structural difficulty of working with trauma in that, when the source of what is stressing the individual is still active, the priority is to remove the individual from that problematic influence or experience. No amount of intellectual awareness or emotional rapport can compensate for that primary need. If trauma is still occurring in the person's life, look to where there might be a safe retreat space. Ask what support, friendship or community they might have that could help to ameliorate such influences.

Aquarius corresponds to traumatic events contained within the long-term memory. This archetype also relates to the impulse towards *individuation* held within the subtle mind of the individual. On this level, Aquarius can be likened to the idea of morphogenetic fields that the biologist Rupert Sheldrake finds existing around all forms, with the true form that they will grow towards being encoded within. This electromagnetism is envisioned as a subtle transformational template held as potential within the mental body as we grow towards our own unique potential.

While individuation as explored by Jung follows certain core archetypal forms (encounter with the shadow, the realization of the anima/animus—the inner opposite gender within, and the encounter with a teacher figure symbolic of the Self) we can take a general view of the term as the quest towards the unique treasure within.

As Paulo Coelho's popular modern fairy tale *The Alchemist makes clear, this treasure might* prompt one to journey far, only to discover that it was buried at home (within) all along. Quoting Isabel Allende, Veronica Goodchild writes, "Perhaps we are in this world to search for love, find it and lose it, again and again. With each love, we are born anew, and with each love that ends we collect a new wound. I am covered with proud scars." [14]

A key part of the individuation process involves consistently coming back to the newness of an experience (working with another in an intimate space). I have done so many thousands of times, as a reminder to never become stuck in just one way of looking at an astrological signature, one perspective on human relationships or even on the nature of depression, for example. One is then always open to the reality that there are as many different types of archetypal experience as there are different people in the world. Paradoxically, our shared humanity comes into perspective most clearly within the precision of our uniqueness. Unity is experienced through diversity rather than through conformity or the delusion of there being just one way.

This applies to that other Aquarian topic—community and friendship ideals. Many see astrology itself as ruled by Aquarius. How is the potential of unity in diversity within the astrological community? Can we remain respectful of our peers even as they engage in forms of astrology that do not interest us or that we consider a waste of time? How do we react when people do not treat us the way we would like? One potential response is traumatic defense, shutting down or even attacking those before they attack us. Another is to develop the necessary (healthy Aquarian) detachment that allows us to see that people behave the way they do *because of their own processes* and the nature of their consciousness. It's truly "nothing personal."

From the Uranian perspective, everything is impersonal and arises from the field of energy within which we all participate. In fact, anger, for example, arises from *identification* within that field. Anger is not actually *my* (or your) anger, but an impersonal energy that, through stress, someone has mistaken as her true nature. While aggression can be in service of self, it is far from a complete expression of one's true potential in the moment. We can mistake our true nature for the temporary rush of anger and the compensatory behaviors that it then justifies.

Detachment, then, a quality of Uranus/Aquarius, is the precursor to the capacity to self-witness. In self-witnessing we can notice the subtle identifications, justifications and self-pity in which we indulge, often just prior to our emotional identification with a particular event. As the astrologer and client look at the client's life together, the shared space can naturally create a healing perspective of healthy, detached witnessing. The intention is key.

Jung shines light on this process. He writes: "Since (the Self) stands for the essence of individuation, and individuation is impossible without a relationship to one's environment, it is found among those of like mind with whom individual relations can be established . . . like every archetype, the Self cannot be localized in an individual ego-consciousness, but acts like a circumambient atmosphere to which no definite limits can be set, wither in space or time. (Hence the synchronistic phenomena often associated with activated archetypes)."[15]

Pisces

The last sign of the zodiac symbolizes the ultimate nature of reality. Pisces also refers to all the dreams and aspirations of humankind through the ages as they attempt to express or integrate their vision of that ultimate truth. So in addition to symbolizing the ultimate, it also symbolizes all the delusions and disillusionments in humanity's attempts to respond to the ultimate. Pisces is about the *nature of essence* as well as about *everything that could obscure essence*, within the dream of separation from life that every human self can create.

In the supplements to *A Course in Miracles,* we find that: "Psychotherapy is a process that changes the view of the self. At best this 'new' self is a more beneficent self-concept, but psychotherapy can hardly be expected to establish reality. That is not its function. If it can make way for reality, it has achieved its ultimate success. Its whole function, in the end, is to help the patient deal with one fundamental error: the belief that anger brings him something he really wants, and that by justifying attack he is protecting himself." [16]

We can easily replace the word "psychotherapy" with "astrology," or indeed any other healing modality. In addition, let's substitute the word "client" for "patient" because of aforementioned problems with the medical model.

With that in mind, we can understand this passage to suggest that, as counselors, we are aiding clients with the process of surrendering identification with our defenses that can, in turn, prevent us from experiencing our true nature. The great Piscean insight here is that once the clouds of misjudged self-concepts evaporate, our true nature shines forth like the sun.

One of the core mistakes here is thinking that rearranging the patterns of the clouds is a true creative enterprise in and of itself. Real creativity emerges when we can *watch those clouds disappear through the progressive realizations that deep surrender brings*. As an approach to healing, astrology can either serve the blue sky or it can spend endless hours rearranging the clouds. Both fall under the realm of Pisces/Neptune/12th house. The latter can be entertaining, and may indeed entrance people for lifetimes. But the former serves the nature of what is was and ever shall be.

The truth of our nature, the inherent divinity of life in which we are participants, exists as both birthless and deathless, inviolate and whole; therefore, there is no need to do anything other than to *be* within that truth. From that place, truly spontaneous life emerges at the crux of the formless meeting form.

It is only our separation from life, from a lived experience within our one life, that needs to be surrendered. If we are honest with ourselves, from the vantage point of the non-dual nature of truth, *this surrendering is a joint process*—a sharing within the field of reality in which the idea that there is one authority figure doling out wisdom to a supplicant other is revealed to be fantasy. No healer heals. No astrologer transforms. There are not two, there is no other.

In his book *Radical Forgiveness*, Colin Tipping presents the idea that a shift in perspective allows the fallacy of being a victim of life to evaporate when one realizes that there is no separate self to be a victim.

The more time I spend in the consulting room, the more I experience the existence of the *knowing field*: an energetic resonance with the infinite field of life which contains a direct knowing about the client or the material that is surfacing in the moment. This awareness is validated each time an intuition about the client's karmic history helps to recontextualize something previously unconscious in the client.

When such a resonance is particularly deep for the client, I often experience a series of shivers in my crown and down the back of my head and neck that corroborate the experience. I have come to understand this physical experience as the field itself confirming the soulful direction that the reading has taken and validation to follow that course into more depth. As an individual with a strong academic background, in a culture that values a primarily rational and linear understanding of reality, coming to trust this communication from the field has been a process. But the wisdom of Pisces suggests that to trust the *knowing field* is to open to the nonlinear.

The *knowing field* can be perceived in the space between two people, and it is also always there within a group. The *knowing field* is present any time the personal boundaries of the self expand (becoming porous) to include information from outside the "normal" parameters of knowledge. In the next chapter we'll explore the scientific and philosophical knowledge that underlies this idea of a larger field of information that can communicate with, or otherwise influence, our personal experience. What I have found is that becoming consciously open to this non-linear field of information allows me to access intuitive information that would not be possible if I only conceived of myself as an isolated entity.

At times, the *knowing field* can reveal surprising information. At other times it seems to use the element of surprise to get the information across. I'll share an uncomfortable personal example during which the *knowing field* overtook my conscious mind altogether. While presenting a lecture at an astrology conference in Sedona, Arizona, my mind went completely blank. I often speak without notes, endeavoring to always stay fresh with the material, which is close to my heart and relies on a depth of experience both personally and with clients and students. Not working with notes, however, does mean there is nothing to fall back on. In that moment on stage, I suddenly could not remember much more than my own name. Quite a shock!

After a moment of dry-mouthed panic, a kindly soul brought me a cup of water. I turned to the audience and asked, "Does anyone have any questions?" And I added a spontaneous proviso: "Any questions about the whole conference, not just this presentation?" In hindsight, I see that this is what the collective field had wanted from me, and in fact, had forcibly evoked from me. Because what poured forth from the audience were so many questions that an administrator of the conference had to step in to end my presentation.

A more rational person might describe my close-call and successful turnaround as "just luck." But evaluated in the context of many more presentations before and since, this was the one and only time I have ever blanked out completely. I propose an alternative view: that *the field itself* evoked the circumstances for this exchange. This can happen if the participant is willing. In my case, I opened to this possibility by setting an intention for the highest good of all present prior to the speaking engagement. The overt rise in the collective energy of the space when people were granted the opportunity to ask questions was confirmation that I was in sync with the *knowing field*.

While giving readings, we can take this lesson to heart in moments when we are called to surrender our prepared material to whatever arises spontaneously. If we're attuned to the field and the client, and both seem to be steering the reading in another direction from the one we originally intended, the best path is often to surrender to what is.

Through Pisces, we can observe that, in fact, there is a fundamental limit to the capacity of the rational mind. Even at the absolute peak of its genius, the best the mind can do is to describe reality accurately and analyze the constituent parts that make up a whole event, experience or thing. *The mind cannot directly know the true nature of reality.* Only by surrendering linear understanding, and even the seemingly sequential nature of time, can the full essence of life become approachable.

Piscean wisdom teaches that even the other is only *seemingly* the other. Only through the eye of the heart can direct involvement with the "other" transcend the subject/object split. Only love can bridge the apparent separation between our self and the rest of life. Note the words "seemingly" and "apparent." Those separations only exist within the linear realm; they are not transcended per se in the nonlinear realm, rather surrendered—they just do not appear to exist in the same way. This insight applies to the counseling dynamic as much as any other relationship dynamic in our lives.

The ideal healing relationship is a shared enterprise to open to the truth within a shared experience of the field.

4

Saturn: Guardian of Our True Potential

Continuing our exploration of the therapeutic potential of astrology, we'll now turn to the Saturn archetype. Saturn is fundamental in the formation of a unique personality, an ego, or sense of separate self. In highlighting crucial turning points in the developmental process of the personal self, we'll look at many of the key counseling dynamics possible within an astrology reading. To understand Saturn is to understand the fundamental boundaries of the personal self and therefore what is both *approved of* and what is *pushed out of* awareness. It is crucial to initiating successful therapeutic dialogue to create a safe space in which the client can explore this interior material that has been denied, shamed or pushed aside.

Freud was both fascinated and vexed by the principle of limitation that seemed to capture people's sense of identity; rather as if the "wind had changed" after their childhood years, and they were left with a static personality for both good and ill. Jung spoke of the cost of creating a personal self—pushing into the shadows everything excluded from one's experience, rather like the dark side of the Moon.

In its opposition to the Moon/Cancer archetype, Saturn/Capricorn acts as the principle boundary that allows the personality to form as a distinct and separate entity. The personality is symbolized astrologically by the conditioned self (the Moon) as a focal point expressing the personal planets. It is then fashioned by the structural principle of Saturn.

Saturn symbolizes the principle of structure. This can refer to a family, a society or civilization, and to the very way that we structure our own consciousness.

Saturn bridges the experiences of the personal self and the transpersonal self. The personal self is expressed through the inner planets within the layers of the unconscious and epitomized through the conditioned self, the "I" (the Moon). The transpersonal self is held in potential by the outer planets. Saturn is a critical factor in determining the structure of our consciousness and the strength of the self, as Saturn is the mediator between personal and transpersonal worlds.

The Nature of the Boundary

The nature of boundary is critical to understanding the role of Saturn. To a disempowered self that has not yet opened up to the riches of the unconscious, and of the self as supportive parent to the "I," the apparent boundaries of the personal self can seem all too concrete and fixed. The relationship of the personal self to the collective can appear to be set in stone until one achieves greater awareness.

Conversely, from the perspective of the outer planets—the power of the deep self, operating through the unconscious and the developing I/Self relationship—what is seemingly rigid and unmoving in fact represents an increasingly flexible and interactive opportunity. This point is developed elegantly in Ken Wilber's book *No Boundary*, which describes multiple states of consciousness embedded as layers within the human psyche. Each layer is experienced as progressively reaching towards the realizations expressed most clearly by the Buddhists as the emptiness of the "ultimate identity." This ultimate identity is actually a luminous formless awareness from which certain states arise. If we identify with those states, they appear to have boundaries and phases of expression; yet, underlying all of them is a primordial awareness within which there is no boundary.

Saturn's Shadow

Donald Winnicott once defined maturity as the capacity to handle paradox.[1] To the immature psyche, life appears to be black or white. However, the increasing capacity to integrate experience reveals that life really exists in all shades of all colors. Misunderstood or un-integrated, Saturn can cast a pallid shadow over the individual life with the belief "I am right and everyone else is wrong."

I have had clients stuck in a negative Saturn fantasy who fear that they are abnormal, doomed, a train wreck; one whom everyone else has overlooked. In this fantasy, everyone else is "normal," while they believe they exist alone under a dark cloud of "wrong, sick and hopeless."

One client, in her early thirties, had the belief that life had already passed her by. She was born with Saturn in Leo retrograde on the I.C., t-square to Jupiter and Uranus. Some people with Saturn in Leo tend toward total identification with the extremes of what they perceive as good or bad. In this polarization, life can feel amazing: the person feels especially creative and things are moving in a positive direction. And then, when there is even a slight criticism, the self-identification (Saturn/structure combined with Leo/self) with that criticism is so strong that the person experiences it as a direct attack on her self-identity, and she falls into a downward spiral of despair and often self-deprecation.

Some may take an even more drastic version of the split, believing that they are light and only other people are shadowy. One client's father with this pattern actually refers to himself as "perfect" and this is a moniker used frequently within the family, without irony. In his work *Madness Explained*, clinical psychologist Richard P. Bentall shares evidence from statistical clinical surveys showing that depressed people score more highly on certain self-reflective exercises than do people who are not depressed! Bentall makes the point that the healthy individual tends towards a subtly inflated self-image. This inflation can become extreme self-delusion when one denies one's shadow; that one can make mistakes is in evidence. A mature expression of the Saturn archetype includes an acceptance that one is not perfect, no matter how hard one tries.

The Saturn function reveals that our suffering and failings have a place in our journey towards wholeness—that in themselves, they contain the seeds of real self-knowledge. Bentall's work acknowledges that in "depressing" our ego inflation, Saturn reveals a difficult but more accurate truth. Without the capacity to face the difficult awareness of our limitations, we may become prey to the perfection delusion of the sort held by my client's father. The cost of this denial of our humanity is high. His family tries to live up to an impossible myth of following the "perfect" lead of an imperfect man. This led to alcoholism in the case of my client's sibling. My client moved to the other end of the continent in order to gain perspective and avoid a similar fate.

Blaming Fate Instead of Owning Saturn Material

"The roles and expectations, the shadow of Saturn, rest heavily on us all. We can continue to blame 'them' – those who mysteriously invented and institutionalized all of this – but then nothing will change. We can no longer wait for something to change 'out there'... we must change ourselves. All change starts within ... but we ... often have trouble internalizing our experience. So the task is difficult, but it is far preferable to living forever under Saturn's shadow." – James Hollis [2]

Hollis' point of how we attempt to offload our undeveloped Saturn function is universal. Jung observed that what we are unable to own within our conscious self will come back via our unconscious self in the form of "fate," events in the outer world, or embodied in others.

One classic stance of the young idealist is to blame all the world's woes on the "Man," that shadowy, often corporate Wizard of Oz who manipulates the machinery of state. Now, this problem is a complex one, because as the old adage says, just because you are paranoid does not mean that they are not out to get you! So let's hold that in mind as we look at the bigger picture. Like many other figures, Timothy Leary really was tailed by the FBI for years. What many thought was simply his "stoner paranoia" was, in fact, real. In 2012, the realization that the world's banking system is rigged and that the world is run on "casino economics," as Morris Berman suggests, is genuine. [3] But to project *all* the unresolved issues in the world onto the bankers is psychologically naïve.

When we're caught in Saturn's shadow, we are unable to see our own complicity, or accept our own role in whatever plagues us. It's much easier to point outside, to blame an enemy. But there is no one all-powerful enemy, no "Man" per se—just a lot of men and women operating within the parameters that they have set within their lives. *Saturn is about taking personal responsibility.* Certainly, there are difficult issues in the world that individuals and governments need to approach with integrity, letting people's needs guide their mandates and actions. That's part of the Saturn process—working with structures, and creating systems that offer positive support (as opposed to negative or fear-based support). But people drain energy from their personal centers of power when they blame others for the limiting conditions of their lives rather than accepting a fair share of responsibility for their lot.

Saturn in the Family

Saturn is often present in our formative experiences—childhood messages from family and schooling shape the nascent identity through our response to imposed structure and feedback, whether encouraging or problematic. In youth, we yearn for a positive expression of the Saturn archetype via parents, teachers and role models who embody authority mediated by love. Many young people search a long time for this rare quality, with potentially lifelong consequences if the need is not met.

In a healthy and supportive family, the child naturally wishes to stand out, to shine and experience the glow of appreciation from an appreciative audience (Leo/Sun). A friend's 3-year-old child has, since age 2, wanted everything to be pink; she has a wardrobe of princess dresses and slip-on shoes. Her mother dresses soberly and cannot abide pink, but she supports her daughter's self-expression. The joy in this little girl when she shows an assembled company her favorite princess outfit, tiara and all, is something to behold.

In an abusive dysfunctional family, to stand out is to become a potential target (Aquarius/Uranus opposite Leo/Sun). When being noticed results in verbal, emotional, physical or sexual abuse, there is an additional survival advantage in remaining unseen. Instead of naturally developing gifts or talents to be shared, some abused young people become masters of invisibility to minimize the survival threat from the abusive parental authority.

We can note two main types of family trauma: the intense impact event (physical violence or sexual molestation), or trauma that develops through duration or repetition. In the latter, seemingly mild verbal commentary can be harmful when reinforced over time. For example, slightly negative words about a child's weight or intelligence, or the often-repeated family story "you got the brains while your sister got the looks." Repetition causes the child to assume validity of the harmful message. In a worse-case scenario, both forms of trauma are combined in the form of intense impact events that are repeated routinely, which can lead to very complex and deep-seated traumatic wounding.

The tipping point for a dysfunctional family is linked to the degree of narcissistic injury present in the parent. This is based not only on the kinds of difficult childhood experience that the parents may have suffered, but also the degree to which they have been able to ameliorate that suffering through their adult relations, critically with the other parent. Much pain is inflicted on children through the failure of the parental relationship to establish and maintain a loving or even simply supportive foundation. For more insight on this dynamic, see John Bradshaw's *Bradshaw On: The Family*.

Narcissistic Injury and the Impossible Dilemma

The term "narcissistic injury" refers to the level at which we have experienced a failure of care or healthy mirroring in our early childhood. Each of us has some degree of narcissistic injury from experiences when our primary caregivers failed to understand us or support our true nature. This is inevitable in even the most loving of families, and indeed, provides very useful evolutionary lessons to the developing psyche, since many environments later in life will be more hostile than the basically supportive and loving family home.

This gray area can turn into clear dysfunction when we move from unwitting failure to mirror or support the needs of a child, to a profound lack of connection with that child. Donald Winnicott used the term "good enough" for the kind of parenting that maintains enough contact with the fundamental part of the child's identity to avoid dysfunction. When such contact is *not* good enough, the child is left with a near-impossible dilemma: either the parent is failing the child (which in early infancy can even lead to death since the parent at this stage is key to survival), or the child is failing to elicit the right responses from the parent.

Many children opt for internalizing the problem as "their fault" so as not to face the unbearable anxiety of the devastating parental failure.

This complex is instrumental in the creation of the *idealized* or *false self*, in which the child makes increasingly acrobatic attempts to generate the desired parental response—all the while having to deny the increasingly evident lack within the parent's capacity to care.

The Core Saturn Wound

The failure of parental care can, in and of itself, lead to what we could term *the child's individuation crisis*. The developing child must recognize that to grow as an individual, she will have to symbolically (and sometimes literally) step over the parent's body on her path. At this stage, "all progress is accompanied by guilt," writes Bert Hellinger, the originator of Family Constellation work. This shadow is cast by the unresolved Saturn principle within the family. The parent is unable to balance authority with love and so the child faces a struggle, much of which remains unconscious, to claim her own power in a fashion mediated by love or basic compassion.

It is no surprise, then, to find that the child who is a bully at school is bullied at home. These imbalances between authority and love, the core Saturn wound, can remain operational within family systems for generations.

Even as an adult, an individual may struggle to emerge from under the shadow cast by the parent. To identify that shadow is the first step of integrating the dark side of the Saturn archetype. Key components involve shame about what was not acceptable in the parental reality and then guilt in seeking to overcome that reality. To finally emerge victorious from the influence of the parental shadow is the first real step toward individuation.

The Great Betrayal

"Not being seen for what we truly are has led to a betrayal of this preciousness that is our essential core. We come to understand that we became false because the people in our early environment not only did not see and support our true self, but wanted us to be something else. They conditioned us to fit their idea of what we are or what we should be. The feeling of betrayal that accompanies our realization of this development is one of the ways in which we experience the narcissistic wound. We may experience the betrayal whenever we feel not seen or appreciated for who and what we are." - A.H. Almaas [4]

Almaas is articulating the powerful way that the pain we feel when let down by another resonates profoundly with the earliest failures in our familial relationship. If we have not done work around these issues, their symptoms can take us by surprise. A simple disconnect with someone not making eye contact while we're talking to them could provoke a "bigger than appropriate" reaction if underlying hurts are still needing our attention.

In my therapy training I was given an exercise in which I was acting as the counselor to a colleague in a real session, with the only rule being that I was not allowed to make eye contact. My partner soon became frustrated and angry with me and refused to share any more. Even though she was fully aware of the requirements of the exercise, she could not contain her frustration, it was so triggering. Such a simple exercise, and yet so revealing.

Almaas brings a powerful spiritual insight to his analysis of the psychodynamic processes of early childhood; he observes that even within the most loving and supportive of families, there is a failure to understand the *essence* or spiritual core of the child. As a result, disillusionment may occur even in the most wonderful home setting when the profound depths of one's own being are inevitably unacknowledged or sidestepped.

> *"We became what they wanted us to be, what they paid attention to in us . . . Through this process of accommodation, we abandoned and rejected what they could not see, the parts of us they did not relate to. Since our essence was the element they recognized or understood least, our essence was the central element we disowned. We ended up abandoning and hiding our most precious nature. We hid it finally from ourselves, most of us eventually forget it all together."* [5]

Furthermore, Almaas recognizes that any deep therapeutic or spiritual work requires us to re-experience those developmental failures and the hurt of the loss of relationship implicit within them, if we wish to connect with our true selves, now.

This is the struggle that we all face when we grow up—to remember our essence, our true nature, and then have the courage and integrity to live that nature; to truly *be*.

Saturn and the Super-ego

Saturn recycles pain to the extent that it conditions us through the repression function, with particular emphasis on the libido, the sexuality, Eros or life-joy. The threat of shame is present if these essential creative functions are expressed in a way deemed inappropriate by the "authorities" around us.

> *". . . many of the highly valued assets of our civilization were acquired at the cost of sexuality and by the restriction of sexual motive forces."* - Sigmund Freud [6]

Freud notes the harnessing of repression as a crucial component of empire building (the shadow of Imperialism that underpins two world wars) only a few pages after dreaming of a world where children are allowed more free play. To place such ideas in their context, we may consider the words of Jacques Barzun in *From Dawn to Decadence*. Here he writes on the 19th-century relationship to sexuality and repression:

"It is . . . a mistake to think that 'the Victorians' in their pursuit of a purified life became blind to sexual realities. To ignore does not mean to be ignorant of; on the contrary the effort heightens awareness. Hence the verbal absurdities of 19th-century moralism that were devised to conceal facts and drive away wrong thoughts. The body and its parts must not be mentioned; even a piano was debarred from having legs. The parallels today are the words used to conceal bodily and mental infirmities and spare their victims; it has been held that 'hard of hearing' is an offensive phrase." [7]

Putting Freud in this cultural context in which he matured, we see a world of *double entendres*, of hidden meanings concealing truths of a sexual nature. On this level, Freud's opus is a guidebook to translating and revealing the era's conventions of language and behavior to reintroduce the missing sexual components. It is no wonder that Freud appeared to be so radical when we take into account these restrictive social mores.

We can see then that this quality of policing piano legs, language, and even in principle our very private thoughts, forms the material of Freud's super-ego. This controlling principle is at best the voice of conscience, at worst the inner dictator of consciousness given to creating a potentially punishing regimen for the ego. The Moon is astrologically opposite the voice of authority in Saturn, the Super-ego.

Crime and Punishment

Saturn relates to the societal forces that are punitive. In a pure Saturnian framework, the punishment suits the crime. Justice is "an eye for an eye." Of course, in reality, punishment for wrongdoing is more complex. Let's look at a story of crime and punishment that took place 400 years ago:

"It is Tuesday, 10 March 1612 . . . a routine criminal case. An unmarried man and woman have been arrested . . . they are accused of having had sex together. The woman confesses. The man denies it. It does not take long to decide their fate. They are put on trial before a jury of men, interrogated and found guilty. Their punishment reflects the heinousness of their crime: not only did they have sex, they have brought into the world a bastard child. For this Susan Perry and Robert Watson are to be cut off from their homes, their friends, their families, their livelihoods – to be forever expelled from the society from which they live. The Judges order them to be taken directly 'to the prison of the Gatehouse; and both of them to be stripped naked from the waist upwards; and so tied to the cart's tail and to be whipped from the Gatehouse in Westminster unto Temple Bar; and then and there to be presently banished from the city.' What happened to their baby is not recorded." - Faramerz Dabhoiwala [8]

Apart from the brutality—the sadistically intimate punishment and complete abandonment forced upon these two poor beings (with seemingly no care for the life their "terrible" act has produced)—

what stands out most from this description and court transcripts is the routine nature of the proceedings. This is just "another day at the office" for the judges and jury.

Although we've evolved since then, this kind of injustice still takes place in our world. In present-day Afghanistan, a couple were recently publicly beheaded for having eloped together: in effect brutally killed for being in love. In Britain there are routine cases of "honor killings"—a recent example being a young Muslim woman raped by an uncle and then murdered by her father and brother for the "stain" her loss of virginity had brought upon the family.

Of course, the original crime lying behind many of these events is the religious one: hence, the excessive value placed on virginity as a symbol of the unblemished soul. In Christian cultures, the original crime is that of Eve's in the garden. We are "suitably" punished then as carriers of the original sin.

These events symbolize the *externally punitive* impact of the distorted Saturn principle. They concern us because they carry such weight within the collective unconscious. In terms of the life of the psyche, the brutal and routine events of 400 years ago are still recent memories. We can carry imprints of such events through reincarnational memory within the deepest emotional aspect of the psyche (Pluto). These imprints can also be left on the subtle mind (Uranus). We carry them as aspects of the collective unconscious (Neptune) that we emotionally (Pluto) and mentally (Uranus) identify within our core selves.

Inner Tyranny

In *An Outline of Psychoanalysis*, Freud writes, "It is a remarkable thing that the super-ego often displays a severity for which no model has been provided by the real parents, and moreover that it calls the ego to account not only for its deeds but equally for its thoughts and unexecuted intentions, of which the super-ego seems to have knowledge." [9]

Freud wrote this in his early eighties while in the final stages of a painful throat cancer (exacerbated by his beloved cigars) during his exile in England. His words articulate his troubled sense of the power of the internal super-ego function to outdo the punitive behavior of the actual parental imprint. The passage's inclusion near the end of Freud's last book indicates the significance he ascribed to this observation.

Certainly I have experienced this question during a session: what is the *source* of the ferocity that my client feels toward himself? A basically good person, who would not treat any other living soul with such malice, can justify treating himself badly because of a deeply internalized dynamic of shame and guilt. It is as if he has created an inner being just to attack himself. But why?

In *The Inner World of Trauma: Archetypal Defenses of the Personal Spirit*, Donald Kalsched shows us how, in the name of self-defense, traumatized aspects of the psyche can develop into self-traumatizing monsters. This happens when energy that is supposed to be directed towards *defending* against future trauma instead begins to attack the self that was being protected. In the psyche, the very nature of this protective inner army is to fight, and if we don't dismantle it after an appropriate battle, it can turn its energy inwardly, waging battle on the self. Kalsched writes, "Trauma doesn't end with the cessation of outer violation, but continues unabated in the inner world of the trauma victim, whose dreams are often haunted by persecutory inner figures." [10]

He also makes the point that those subject to psychological trauma often find themselves encountering those same kinds of traumatic life situations again and again. Even when a traumatized person makes an effort to change and better her outward circumstances, there seems to be some inner process that simultaneously undermines her efforts. He writes, "It is as though the persecutory inner world somehow finds its outer mirror in repeated self-defeating 're-enactments'—almost as if the individual were *possessed* by some diabolical power or pursued by a malignant fate." [11]

We might identify this as misdirected persecutory Saturn energy. The energy wants to go somewhere but isn't being properly directed. What's more, the source of these traumas and the inner tyranny that arises in response can stem from past-life experience, making it even harder to identify and treat. These show up in the present life as unresolved karmic complexes around power, personal self-expression (including sexual expression) and experiences of familial and societal punishment. In *Understanding Karmic Complexes*, Patricia Walsh describes past-life regressions that show specific prior-life traumas underpinning current-life psychological blocks or phobias as the weight of personal and collective memories of punishment.

When it comes to healing and finding the right time to change these kinds of patterns, there is no easy recipe. I have witnessed clients who show up ready for change. The change then manifests within our conscientiously held space, created just for that purpose, and is an unfolding of what was already poised to unfold. All that was needed was the right intentional space in which to allow the process.

For others, years of committed work will produce only limited results. Of course, we must respect that the damage some people are healing from is very severe. So *patience*, a high-functioning Saturnian energy, also applies here. Knowing that as an astrologer, you may only see your client once, it would be useful to learn how to recognize this pattern and at the end of the session, if appropriate, suggest the client consider ongoing counseling to help dismantle the inner tyrant.

Still, even in the presence of clients who have endured the most difficult circumstances, we can create a healing context in which the inner tyranny abates almost miraculously. This teaches us that at the heart of the therapeutic project, there is a mysterious grace that none of us can own or control. The lesson here is to set the stage appropriately, make a concerted effort, have patience when required, and trust grace to show up when the time is right.

Moving Past Judgments

Within the mysterious rhythm of healing, we can observe a general principle that applies equally to the one-time astrological reading and to long-term therapeutic work:

To the extent that the client is undermined by a punitive Saturnian superego, the counselor, as his guide, needs to facilitate a compassionate space in which the client's hypercritical voice can be sufficiently quieted to enable him to explore the nature of his true potential free of internal tyranny.

The key to a fruitful therapeutic encounter is to provide a safe enough space for the superego's punishing voice to subside sufficiently for the individual to contemplate her life without the imprisoning "should" and "not good enough" that otherwise cloud the inner sky so much as to obscure the light of the radiant inner Sun.

All client work, whether astrological or psychotherapeutic, must pay homage to Saturn. If this initial requirement is not met and the client does not feel safe enough, the danger is that the whole encounter is filtered through her pre-existing negativity. During a one-time natal chart reading, this concern is heightened and especially important to notice. If not properly addressed, a client's negative super-ego may block her from taking in healing messages from the reading so effectively that she is prevented from gaining the benefit that she needs in order to grow. Even the best-intentioned messages on the part of the counselor can fall on deaf ears because the client's state of mind is so shadowed, her attention so unconsciously preoccupied, that the impact of the reading is all but squandered.

If you are unable to soften the client's punitive inner Saturn during the reading, it helps to know that recording the reading can alleviate this issue in some cases, when repeated listening over time can help the client eventually receive the needed information.

When a client has the potential for this kind of Saturnian inner dynamic, it's important to choose our words wisely. A pattern of self-judgment is more likely to be constellated if we present information with phrases like "you should" or "you ought to." Even classical astrological terminology such as "detriment" or "exaltation" plays into this Saturnian shadow. To be on the safe side, if you use these words, think about whether they are truly useful with a client who has no interest in learning astrology. You might try to find ways of avoiding the terms altogether. If you do decide to use them, make sure to qualify them with descriptions of what the words mean to you. If a client has Venus in Scorpio (classically termed "in detriment"), describe the evolutionary potential of such a placement. Give the client some constructive information to work with. Explain how a detrimental trait can be turned into an asset.

At times we need to make a judgment call about whether the client is expressing her real self or some *false self* or *idealized self* that is responding to an inner *tyranny of should* (the distorted Saturn shadow). The easiest way to make this judgment call is to analyze the quality of the client's inner prompting or motivation. The aspirations that have been co-opted by the inner tyranny will always have a punitive or unrealistic edge—pushing her, waiting with eager self-punishing judgment if she fails to make the self-imposed grade. In contrast, the aspiration of the *real self*, while acknowledging the effort that may be required, will include a healthy realism and acceptance about how change might play out. If the real self is running the show, you should be able to sense the humanity of the individual, the self-care involved.

In such moments we proceed with caution, but do not back off. Empathy and experience are your best assets here, and they combine to form the gentle power to stand for the individual's true self-expression even while risking an apparent conflict with her current expression of herself.

The Core Dilemma of the Healer

In any modality that involves primary interaction with the conscious self, the healer will face the following paradox in the intention expressed towards her client:

You are perfect just the way that you are and I love and accept you within that inherent value. Alongside: *I wish to help you feel better, minimize unnecessary suffering and enable your further potential—so there is something in you that needs to change and grow.*

The Buddha conceived of a "Middle Path" existing between the illusion of eternalism (perfection, or heaven in a fixed, unchanging form) and the illusion of nihilism (all is change, so there is no ultimate meaning). The Buddha's Middle Path provides a model the healer can apply to the above dilemma. On the one hand, difficulty arises when we admit that we are not perfect (eternalism). On the other, we can feel that we are a failure or worthless (nihilism). In a reading, a client may get stuck at either side of this equation. The perfection problem can take the form of identification with a happy childhood: that everything in the family experience was "just great." Then, as the reading unfolds, it becomes clear that this was not really the case. The danger then, when the client has an identification with a fragile fantasy of perfection, is that when that illusion breaks he can quickly descend into anger or despair. He may then swing to the side of nihilism. Our job is to point him towards the middle ground, to find healing balance between the two positions, and also something closer to the truth.

We can be most useful to our clients if we convey that she *is already* perfect as she is and simultaneously act as a powerful advocate for her desire to transform and change. We can start by stating that *every chart is perfect as it is*, arising as it does out of the divine and intimately connected to the perfection of the cosmos. We can explain that our chart describes the *unique potential* each of us is charged with fulfilling—and that to achieve that, we need to *identify areas in which change could be useful.*

5

The Outer Planets

As mentioned in Chapter 1, the transpersonal dimension signified by the outer planets (Neptune, Pluto and Uranus) relates to the collective dimension of experience. Since the Outer planets are slow moving, they define generations by their positions. However, in terms of the therapeutic potential of astrology, what most interests us is that aspect of the transpersonal which concerns the inflow—from the Soul—of meaning and empowerment into the individual's immediate experience.

Guiding a client to consciously experience the transpersonal dimension of the psyche can facilitate enormous transformation, but usually requires that the client already has a religious or spiritual framework or at least an unusual degree of open-mindedness. However, soulful healing can still be achieved even if the client isn't fully conscious of the forces at play.

Sometimes when clients experience a shift in perspective during a reading, they will project the reason for the breakthrough onto the astrologer. But it is important to remember that the astrologer is only the guide or facilitator—not the actual agent of transformation. The outer planets often hold the key to helping our clients unlock their potential for such transformation.

As we'll see, the outer planets can be further understood in relationship to the inner planets (Mercury, Venus and Mars) as higher octave expressions of those planets. As such, the outer planets represent the transpersonal dimension of the same qualities connected with the inner/personal planetary functions. The outer planets are therefore essential to consider in all deep healing work, whether their archetypal fields are fully conscious within the individual or not.

The Outer Planets as Higher Octaves

To more deeply understand the outer planets, let's first explore their role as *higher octaves* of the three inner planets. Just as we did with Saturn, we'll need to intentionally prepare in advance by becoming intimately familiar with the terrain each outer planet represents so we can hold transformational space for our clients. The spatial transition from the inner to the outer planets reflects the psyche's movement from the linear to nonlinear realms of experience, in which the very nature of our pre-existing identity must be fundamentally transformed or left behind in order to make the leap.

Dane Rudhyar describes the relationship between inner and outer planets with: ". . . the essential fact is that the activities of Uranus, Neptune and Pluto run counter to the normal functions of Mercury, Venus and Mars. The former are not just personal activities of a 'higher' kind; they are activities meant to disturb and transform—indeed, utterly to repolarize and reorient those of Mercury, Venus and Mars." [1] With that in mind, let's look at each of the three outer planets in more detail.

Uranus as the Higher Octave of Mercury

Mercury represents the mental function and its development: language skills, the capacity to conceptualize and label objects and events, and our ability to orientate to the immediate environment in an intelligible fashion. Mercury corresponds to the function of *memory on a conscious level.*

Traditionally, Mercury is said to rule both Gemini and Virgo. Mercury expresses in a yang role as ruler of Gemini, where it corresponds to curiosity. Through *natural inquisitiveness*, the child learns to name and label his environment and mimic those around him in order to become facile and effortless in his relationship to language and social codes. Gemini corresponds to that same spirit in adulthood that wishes to engage in the environment in a curious and open-minded fashion—to read, to stay abreast of the latest news, and to share and disseminate that information.

In its more inward or yin expression, as the ruler of Virgo, Mercury relates to the vital process of *discrimination*. The self asks, "Of all this information I have gathered, what best suits my real needs and evolutionary goals?" Virgo represents a crisis to the extent that some of the information taken in is contradictory and feedback from the environment is problematic or critical. This crisis leads to an internal mental dialogue with the intention of self-improvement and the discovery of what is most useful.

In its shadow expression, the Virgo sorting process can turn into a problematic loop of endlessly recycling the same negative thoughts and associated reactions to those thoughts. Even the most focused and constructive person will discover elements of this Virgoan kind of dialogue inside herself. Many meditators report an increased awareness of this inner dynamic, especially during longer periods of contemplation, such as a silent retreat.

As we shift from linear Mercury to nonlinear Uranus, we see that Uranus corresponds to the *transpersonal* aspect of the *mind*: the unconscious aspect of memory that, through certain illuminating experiences (meditation, hypnosis, dreams, intuition or active imagination), can become conscious. Symbolizing long-term or far memory, Uranus also represents the legacy of past events that have left an imprint on the subtle mind. This includes significant events from prior-life experience, soul memories from the *bardo* (the life in between lives), and from the womb or very early childhood.

In its pure form, Uranus can be experienced as memory or a mental awareness arising from the *soul*: a blueprint of the energy field of the individual's whole life experienced on a subtle mental level. This includes information as to the nature of past lives, to pre-natal states of existence in the womb and perinatal states. Through Uranus, the individual learns systemically via his own experience from these nonlinear realms.

This concept is grounded in Western philosophy dating back to Socrates, noted in the following passage by Ira Progoff:

"The great task, then, as Socrates envisioned the problem of gaining knowledge, is to remember the things that one has known in earlier lifetimes. It seems clear in this connection that Socrates was interested primarily not in recalling the personal events of previous existences, but in recalling the underlying capacities of knowledge which had been accumulated in the course of its past lives by the person (or specifically by his 'soul' as Socrates conceived of the soul)."[2]

Significant events remembered from prior lives, encapsulated within the far memory of the Uranus function, relate not only to positive experiences but also to difficult or traumatic experiences that have been imprinted within the layers of the higher mind.

In exploring this concept, it makes no difference whether we think of reincarnation literally or symbolically, personally or collectively. As we saw earlier, the history of the human endeavor is, for better or worse, founded on our tendency for criminal dominance over others. And this appears to endlessly repeat in a vicious cycle that the Buddhists call *samsara*, or the wheel of suffering. In realizing that we are all born out of the same history, which is not only the history of progress, but also the history of pain and suffering, we recognize that our Uranian *far memory* will naturally have a prominent association with trauma.

In fact, we can observe that *the great majority of humanity is carrying at least some form of post-traumatic stress disorder originating solely from their participation in our collective history.*

It is important that we not think of this description as a clinical diagnosis in the sense defined by the modern psychiatric movement. This would only limit our thinking about Uranus. But it is *clinically observable* that we repeat patterns—inner templates from deep in our unconscious, whether positive or negative. While our formative childhood experiences can be explored as the basis for understanding unconscious patterning, they are usually not adequate to account for all of the patterns we express. Therefore, we must give this particularly Uranian field of experience special attention. A fundamental blind spot in depth psychology is that it ignores the issue of reincarnation in both its constructive (prior-life knowledge/wisdom) and destructive (prior-life adversity/trauma) forms. Much insight into the human psychological experience is lost due to this omission.

In the simple metaphor of the musical octave, we see that a higher octave is just a step up from the lower note—a similar quality, but moving at a faster rate. This metaphor points us in the right direction for understanding the planetary higher octave dynamic, but falls short when it comes to the transition from the linear rational mind of Mercury to the heightened awareness of Uranus, which is better described as a quantum leap.

When Rudhyar observes how the outer planets can "disturb and transform" what the inner planets symbolize, he illuminates the shift from the personal to the transpersonal in both astrological and evolutionary terms. The term "higher" is useful only in allusion to a *different* order of experience. The shift from the personal to the transpersonal dimension involves a shift from the constructed or conditioned realm of the personality to the essential life of the soul, in which our previous understanding of life is completely transformed. This process can be likened to waking from a dream.

The quality of awareness symbolized by Uranus is in a different category than the limited conceptual powers of the waking mind. When Uranian awareness is experienced—say through a revelatory experience during therapy—the results can seem completely opposite to "normal" mental functioning (Mercury), sometimes silencing the mind altogether.

I recently witnessed such a shift occur in a long-term client who holds a senior position at a media company. Arriving at our session right after work, she found herself acknowledging the contrast between her usual work mental state of overwhelm and the feeling of self-confidence that she experienced in the therapy room. She was courageous enough to remain with that contrast without trying to change it. And in visualizing the two different states as two selves on two different chairs sitting in front of us, she was able to approach the overwhelmed self as a direct experience. She described that state as "without history," and as a raw being, alone in a "brown wasteland." She found this experiential exercise completely shocking—her usual mental functioning was suspended.

Only afterwards was she able to reflect, with my assistance, on how this mental state of stress also included memories herself as a young, preverbal child, left alone in the presence of difficulty in the family environment. Her early childhood experience sowed the seeds for an excessive sensitivity to bearing responsibility. Intellectually, she had previously understood this. But in this new (Uranian) experiential state, she had fully seen and felt it as truth.

This level of insight is especially transformative therapeutically. In this particular case, while my client may need to rehash the same emotional ground in search of balance, she also has a new clarity about the issue which will never leave her. This can be likened to the flash of sudden insight which is symbolized by Uranus, in contrast to the systematic learning, mental understanding and verbal communication symbolized by Mercury.

Going further, challenging aspects from Uranus to Mercury or the other personal planets can indicate a core shock or difficulty in adjusting our personality to the soul as experienced on the subtle mental level. The nature of the aspects between Uranus and Mercury refer to our capacity to integrate or communicate (Mercury) about the more essential states of direct knowing that are symbolized by Uranus.

Uranus as a Trauma Indicator

Using data from my clinical practice to build on the pioneering work of Jeffrey Wolf Green in *Uranus: Freedom from The Known,* I have gained insight into the concept of the *trauma signature* in the birth chart. I wrote about this in detail in Chapter 3 of *Healing the Soul: Pluto, Uranus and the Lunar Nodes.* To sum up those findings in brief, a stressful aspect in the natal chart involving the planet Uranus, any planet in the 11th house or in the sign Aquarius reveals a potential *trauma signature.* This can point to an unhealed event from a prior life held as a wound in the higher mind, expressing as a form of post-traumatic stress in the current life. The stressful aspects to consider are the conjunction (0 degrees), square (90 degrees), sesquiquadrate (135 degrees), inconjunct or quincunx (150 degrees) and opposition (180 degrees).

Briefly contemplating the above paragraph will quickly reveal the implications, the most important of which is that there are a great deal of trauma signatures in a vast number of birth charts. If this sounds far-fetched, consider that our collective history is flooded with traumatic events. If we hold the premise that all traumatic experiences require healing, and we contemplate that all our past unhealed traumas seek healing in the present, we see the extent to which our wounded unconscious drives and motivations directly influence us in the present.

Pluto as the Higher Octave of Mars

Mars corresponds to the instinctual and personal will, to the desire nature in its outgoing, expansive form. It symbolizes our individual need for the freedom to perpetually self-discover through the instinctual immediacy of our own experience. Mars symbolizes aggression in service of self: the right to defend our freedom to express our will.

As the natural ruler of Aries, Mars represents birth. An analysis of the Mars placement, the house with Aries on the cusp, any planets in Aries, the first house, Ascendant and ruler of the Ascendant, will reveal information about the nature of our birth process as well as how we react to the perpetual birth of each new moment as we live our lives. By extension, we can see how we react to new situations in which we project ourselves into experience on a completely instinctual level. In this way, those who say the Ascendant relates to the *persona* of the individual, the mask they put on for others, have confused the Descendant with the Ascendant, because here the process is purely instinctual and perpetually new.

Mars represents the nature and function of the personal will: that abiding sense of instinctual power within us. In operating on a primarily instinctual level, Mars can be experienced as a gut feeling (whether attraction or repulsion), as the need to leave a confining space, or even as predilections for certain foods. Mars represents the quality of the outgoing expression of our instinctual desires. At the core of Mars, Aries and the 1st house, is the primal need for a basic level of freedom for the organism to experience itself and the fulfillment of its core desires. Restriction of this freedom becomes the basis for anger or rage, which is in defense of self. If freedom is restricted and anger also suppressed, then there is a potential for depression, or a sense of futility about the lack of permission for the core desires to be realized.

In contrast, Pluto represents the primary emotional and psychological orientation of the *soul* towards evolutionary concerns of the deepest kind. This more transpersonal experience, which is often unconscious (at least in part), represents the source of security at a primary level. This is the level of our core filter or orientation towards the world and life itself. As a reflection of Mars, this deepest level of soul interest can be experienced as desire: the attraction towards certain experiences in order for the soul to know itself and evolve.

Mars and Pluto can be compared and contrasted in terms of will: Mars is the will of the personality, while Pluto is the will of the soul. Both require the freedom to be and to become.

A look at planetary rulership reveals additional insight. Mars is the traditional ruler of both Aries and Scorpio. Pluto is thought by some, myself included, to be the modern ruler of Scorpio. The aspect from Aries to Scorpio is a quincunx (150°), which reveals that tension and potential crisis are implicit between the will of the soul and that of the personality.

Pluto, as the higher octave of Mars, represents the will of the *deeper self* as it then manifests in relationship to Mars as personal will or an attraction of the instinctual will. This relationship implies that what we are instinctively attracted towards (Mars) will reveal deeper needs and motivations of the core psychological self or soul (Pluto). Buber sheds light on this process with his insight: "He must sacrifice his puny unfree will, that is controlled by things and instincts, to his grand will, which quits defined for destined being."[3]

So we can see that what we are led towards via our instinctual attractions to certain people, teachings, experiences, even certain foods, stems from impulses within the deeper self that exist to expose certain emotional realities and psychological truths about ourselves.

As ruler of the Ascendant in the natural zodiac, Mars (Aries) represents a birth into the new, just as Pluto (Scorpio) reveals the truth that every birth into the new also marks the death of a previous state or condition. To be born is to die to our previous state. This was exemplified for me with my client Kay, who was the case study in chapter 2 of *Healing the Soul*. During regression, Kay entered a state of consciousness that seemed to exist *prior* to the difficult experience she was reliving in the womb, and found herself instead in a state she called the *"land of celebration."* She was greeted by an empathic group of beings who totally validated her existence in a way that she had never previously known. And from that state she witnessed herself being born into her current life.

While Mars (Aries) represents the desire for personal freedom, Pluto represents the need for transpersonal freedom—the deep unconscious need to explore certain core emotional and psychological realities that stem from the higher/deeper self. The natural inconjunct between Pluto and Mars represents the crisis that can occur when one's personal will seems at odds with one's higher will.

At times it seems that the higher will has to metabolize the personal will to achieve its evolutionary ends. This dynamic has been explored within the Alcoholics Anonymous program. When dealing with crippling addiction and the subsequent loss of power or control, the personal will is often not strong enough to rescue or transform the situation. When the personality is overwhelmed by a self-destructive pattern of behavior, the first step towards healing is to recognize that loss of control and to admit the possibility of a higher power.

In Pluto terms, only by acknowledging the presence of a higher will can certain states of personal negativity be understood and overcome. This higher will operates on a different level of power. To extend our earlier metaphor of the octaves as quantum leaps, if personal will is 400 Hz then higher will is more like 4,000 Hz than 800 Hz.

For a lengthy description of the way higher will impacts the personal will, see *Transcending the Levels of Consciousness*, by Dr. David Hawkins. I often refer to it in my teaching and writing because it expresses such a profound point about healing, and indeed the nature of being alive:

"Although the suffering of loss is triggered by a specific event, the painful emotions of attachment have actually arisen from multiple sources over time, and there may be more of it below the surface than was first expected. Thus, each loss actually represents all loss, for the experience is of loss itself and not just the specific event that brought it up to awareness. A helpful source of strength during the processing out of painful emotions is to identify with all of humanity and realize that suffering is universal and innate to the phenomenon of being human and the evolution of the ego."[4]

This insight can be likened to an image of an iceberg, in which only a small part of the entire mass of the object is actually visible above the surface. Below the surface of our day-to-day awareness lies a vast mass of additional material, memory and awareness. The difference between the tip of the iceberg and the mass lying under the water can be likened to the difference between the inner (tip) planets and the outer (hidden mass) planets.

Returning to Pluto, the transpersonal aspect of the freedom of expression includes psychological experiences from prior lives. Pluto represents the *core emotional attachments* and sense of purpose from prior lives, just as Uranus represents the aspect of the soul found in the higher mind: a subtle aspect of the mental body that *remembers* significant experiences from prior lives.

We could say that a commitment to revealing and acknowledging our deepest truth in ongoing soul work, regardless of its impact on the personal life, is what enables increasing harmony to emerge between our personal desires (Mars) and the intentions of the soul (Pluto). Significant aspects between Mars and Pluto can indicate that the current life is one in which that soul work will be emphasized. Pluto (the will of the soul) is impacting (aspecting) the personal will (Mars) in order to bring about transformation. The nature of the aspect and the position of Mars and Pluto by house and sign will more specifically describe the nature of that work.

Neptune as the Higher Octave of Venus

Venus corresponds to our innermost *relationship* with ourselves: how we understand and meet our own core needs, and how we then project those needs as expectations onto others. Our relationship with the other is a mirror to our relationship with our self.

Venus symbolizes our potential for self-love and love for another. These are actually two sides of the same coin, represented astrologically by the dual rulership of Venus in Taurus and Libra. In Venus we find the love for self and other and any challenges or blocks to that love.

Through the Taurus aspect of Venus, we see a correlation with the survival instinct: how to establish and maintain biological survival and to secure one's core emotional needs. The Libra aspect of Venus relates to the way these needs are then projected outwards via our relationships.

Venus is linked with the integrity of the biological and emotional being. This is evident in that sometimes failure in relationship threatens (or *seems* to threaten) our survival or will to live. Psychoanalytically, we call this *"object constancy,"* where the interiorization of a stable parental image in childhood enables the individual to feel secure even when apart from the primary caregivers. The primary need for meaningful attachments in infancy is a survival issue. Disruptions or anxiety at this critical stage of our development can manifest in later life as core insecurity or anxiety when separated from loved ones.

We can observe that most healthy relationships (Libra) emerge from a basic maturity in the way we meet our own needs (Taurus), so that we don't overburden others with core unresolved feelings about ourselves. Conversely, we can observe that most relationship problems stem from unresolved personal feelings that interfere with our capacity to meet our inner needs (Taurus). These unresolved feelings can color our relationships (Libra), tainting them with the disappointments we carry from our inability to meet our own needs, or with unrealistic projections of how the other (Libra) might save us.

The core influence on the way we relate to ourselves (Taurus) is the nature of relationships (Libra) in our early home environment (Cancer-Capricorn). Understand this process and you will see how people recreate unresolved issues from their early home life in their marriages and long-term relationships. [5]

As the higher octave of Venus, Neptune symbolizes *universal or transpersonal* love for all of life. Neptune is *Agape*, while Venus is *Eros*. The Neptunian expression of love inspires the sacrifice of self to a higher calling. In a very real sense, every small personal sacrifice that we make in service of another, or of life itself, is a preparation, a step closer toward, a higher expression of Neptune. Neptune relates to the ultimate sacrifice of the ego in the service of soul: the enlightened state of identity in which the inherent divinity of consciousness is the primary focus of awareness.

This kind of sacrifice can be spiritually transcendent in a positive way, but it also has a shadow expression. Trauma signatures involving Neptune in the natal chart could point towards an experience of an overwhelming force drowning the ego identity, a negative experience of self-sacrifice, or a core disillusionment or despair at life as we are overwhelmed by its sheer scale.

Spiritually, Neptune symbolizes the infinite field of reality, from the most material to the most subtle levels, all of which are inherently aspects of the sacred nature of life—the inner divinity of consciousness in all its myriad forms. The nature of Neptune is that of transpersonal love—the nature of spirit itself. This is an unconditional love that manifests as a total experience of immersion and that leads to an understanding that creation and love are intertwined. As David Hawkins explains, "To understand the nature of God, it is necessary only to know the nature of love itself. To truly know love is to know and understand God; and to know God is to understand love."[6]

Neptunian transpersonal love or sacrifice can be experienced positively, but trauma signatures in the birth chart can point to a more negative experience of love as an overwhelming force that drowns the ego identity, or is experienced as core disillusionment or despair as we are overcome by its sheer scale.

Our self-love, evidenced in meeting our own needs (Taurus), and our love for others (Libra), both arise from the greater field of love that interpenetrates the Cosmos. When we are lost in personal vanity (Taurus) or projecting our displaced childhood emotions (Cancer) onto others (Libra), it may seem that we have shut ourselves off from this higher love (Pisces). Yet, when one experiences the all-inclusive nature of the love, one recognizes that this field encompasses all states of being, no matter how selfish or narrow.

In this sense, personal regard and the belief that others should fulfill our unmet needs occupy a fundamentally different category than the love that arises in response to the totality of another's being. Nevertheless, real love can embrace more self-involved states of being effortlessly. In the radical opening created by an experience of real love, we can see that our regard for the self, the personality and the ego all arise as a defense against the overwhelming inclusivity of the all.

With this in mind, we can see the Biblical myth of the Fall as relating to the part of our own nature that cannot bear the field of unconditional love. Through ignorance, fear and hurt, we turn against it and form a personality. And yet, when one experiences the Neptune level of surrender to the all—the core nature of which is love—the "isolated" personality is found not to exist independently.

Our true nature, exposed by the brilliance of real love, is found to comprise numerous core elements, of which joy, dedication to truth, wisdom, infinite love and gratitude are key. We realize then as these essential Soul states begin to unfold within us that the apparent loss that the ego projects onto the reality of the *deep self* is no real loss at all. In fact, what arises in place of what we believed was our self is an all-embracing inclusive presence; we feel cared for so completely that all previous notions of what constituted contentment or satisfaction are found to be mere shadows in comparison.

Neptune relates to the *collective unconscious* as described by post-Jungian depth psychology. It is the "virtually immortal" (to recontextualize Freud) collective repository of the archetypes—of all the possible templates for the human story, action and myth.

In one sense, history is the collapse of the wave function of the collective unconscious into form. The nonlinear potential of humanity as a whole, represented by the collective unconscious, manifests in form as the events of history when the conditions are right.

This initially complex idea becomes increasingly comfortable the more one surrenders a linear or causal view of history as a sequence of interlocking events. When we hold the concept of the relativity of the space-time continuum, and the acausal connecting principle (which Jung christened *synchronicity*) manifesting throughout space and time, we enter markedly Neptunian territory.

Neptune symbolizes the inter-connective unifying or "knowing field" in which all things are held. This *knowing field* contains a level of collective memory, the repository of all archetypes (the essences that precede form), but it is also an *impersonal* field of love. In Christian language, we could refer to this as the Holy Spirit. At this level of experience, everything is literally made from love. Creation/love renews itself in every moment, and what is seemingly a sequential experience of time is really a manifestation of the totality of everything, forever, all moments, eternal and inviolate. If only for a moment, when we see everything as one, the whole world is forever transformed.

To summarize the outer planets, Neptune represents a shift from personal love and love of others for how they relate to us and fulfill our needs (Venus ruling Taurus and Libra) towards a universal love that spontaneously arises when the true nature of experience is seen. Pluto represents the shift from the personal will instinctively acting on behalf of the self (Mars) to a higher will that represents the desire of the soul to fulfill its evolutionary potential in ways that may run counter to the ideas of the personality. Uranus represents the shift from the mental labeling of experience (Mercury) towards a direct encounter, beyond concepts or positions.

When we combine the archetypes of Uranus, Pluto and Neptune, we realize that the transpersonal dimension of experience completely alters the more conventional experience of the personality. From the transpersonal perspective, all that exists is an expression of its own true nature, and is, therefore, just how it is meant to be. As Hawkins eloquently teaches us:

> *"In reality, everything occurs of its own, with no exterior cause. Every thing and every event is a manifestation of the totality of All That Is. Once seen in its totality, everything is perfect at all times and nothing needs an external cause to change it in any way. From the viewpoint of the ego's positionality and limited scope, the world seems to need endless fixing and correction. This illusion collapses as a vanity. In reality, everything is automatically manifesting the inherent destiny of its existence; it doesn't*

need external help to do this. With humility, one can relinquish the ego's self-appointed role as savior of the world and surrender it straight to God. The world that the ego pictures is a projection of its own illusions and arbitrary positionalities. No such world exists." [7]

6

---❧---

The Developing Self:
The Saturn and Uranus Cycles

"Astrology can be defined as a technique for the study of life-cycles. Its main purpose (is to establish) the existence of regular patterns in the sequence of events constituting man's inner and outer experience; then, to use the knowledge of these patterns in order to control or give meaning to these experiences . . . Indeed, the study of cycles—that is, of periodical activities in nature, human and otherwise—is the root of all significant knowledge, be it scientific or philosophical. And the study of cycles is a study of time." –Dane Rudhyar [1]

The dynamic of change is a constant in a counseling practice. After all, no one undertakes therapy to remain the same. With this in mind, the background context of the individual is of major importance in a consultation. Psychology and psychotherapy have traditionally placed strong emphasis on how past development, particularly from childhood through adolescence, has crucially shaped the individual in the present. The goal in psychotherapy is to understand how this evolution took place and apply that understanding to overcoming present limitations.

In an astrology reading, we may not have the luxury of working with a client over time to address the nuances of her past, especially if we only see her once. However, we have many timing techniques at our disposal that can give us a snapshot of the context in which our client comes to the reading. We will not know the exact particulars, but we can identify overarching themes by looking at previous transits or progressions up to the moment of the reading. Taking a look at the context in which a client arrives can help you prepare space to energetically meet her where she is.

Although we won't have time to look at every possible transit that a client may have had before showing up on our doorstep, we will spend some time looking at some of the transit cycles of Saturn and Uranus as they relate to the essential unfolding structures of self-identity. Saturn is the crucial boundary of the personality, the symbol of the fastening of the structure of the self into a consistent form. Uranus is the challenging, liberating force that is always testing the limits of that safe structure in order to facilitate growth. If you become proficient at understanding these important cycles, which will impact every client you see, you will have another substantial tool to support the growth process.

This chapter will focus on the *developing* self, paying close attention to the ways Saturn and Uranus influence that growth. We will limit our analysis to the first Saturn return and Uranus opposition. Many will reach their second Saturn return in their early 60s, and a lucky few will reach a second Uranian opposition at age 84. However, those cycles represent culmination and dissemination, so we'll save those for another time.

The First Saturn Square

At about age 7, we come to our first Saturn square, as transiting Saturn has moved to square (90° angle) its natal placement. The exact aspect takes place a little earlier or later for some people due to the retrograde motion of Saturn. [2] *The first Saturn square symbolizes the formation of the ego identity of the individual.*

In terms of identity, Saturn relates to personal limitations and the boundary of the self. The first quarter square is resonant with the sign Cancer. This is because Cancer forms a 90-degree aspect from the Ascendant of the *Natural Zodiac* or *Archetypal Zodiac* in which Aries is the first sign, on the Ascendant.

Cancer symbolizes the emergence of the conditioned ego self, or "I" (the Moon). This self-development process is expressed clearly by Ken Wilber in his book *Integral Psychology*:

> *"The self starts out relatively undifferentiated from its environment. That is, it cannot easily tell where its body stops and the physical environment begins ... Somewhere during the first year, the infant learns that if it bites a blanket, it does not hurt, but if it bites its thumb, it hurts; there is a difference between body and matter. The infant differentiates its body from the environment, and thus its identity switches from fusion with the material world to an identity with the emotional-feeling body ... As the conceptual mind begins to emerge and develop (especially around 3 to 6 years), the child eventually differentiates the conceptual mind and the emotional body ... "*[3]

Here Wilber denotes the three earliest stages of human development, which we can relate to the first three astrological archetypes: Aries (instinctual body/environment), Taurus (feeling body, internal needs) and Gemini (development of conceptual mind and language). These three stages (physical, emotional and mental) in their earliest formation coalesce into an overall personality that relates to the Moon, Cancer and the 4th house.

Cancer (4th house and the Moon) relates to the time when the conscious self begins to form from the early fusion of the instinctual-physical sense of self with the feeling body and the development of language and conceptual faculties. This formation tends to clarify around the time of the first Saturn square, during which the individual often has experiences that provoke a sense of limitation—realizations about the boundary of the self.

In *A Criminal History of Mankind*, Colin Wilson demonstrates how we begin to separate from a living sense of participation in the world around us through developing increasing complexity in our conceptual ability and use of language. Studies show that at age 7, the two halves of the brain begin to specialize; the left brain develops language capacities, while the right brain develops on another path. [4] Up to age 7, children with left brain damage can compensate, learning language with their right brain. But beyond that age, they cannot continue, as the two parts of the brain become so distinct.

This is an example of the crucial formative impact of the first Saturn square in creating the conditioned self. The two hemispheres of the brain physically conform to separate functioning, establishing boundary. This is a crucial feature of the conditioned self, or the human ego—that it is able to separate from experience and compartmentalize a response to different parts of that experience. This step along the way to mature development is one in which we see a potential loss of immediacy from the earlier stages marked by spontaneous participation during infancy. Saturnian structure develops within us, but each stage of development also involves loss. It is worth noting that Rudolf Steiner's Waldorf educational approach delays learning to read until the time of the Saturn square to preserve as much of the earlier-stage experience as possible.

At the time of the first Saturn square, children begin to have a clearer sense of their emerging beings as separate entities in their own right, increasingly free from the parental reality and the reality of others. Often this includes a new awareness of death, or of the fragility of the human form, for that is the ultimate boundary of human life.

At the end of my first Saturn square, my father took my sister and me to see *Star Wars*. During the scene where Darth Vader destroys Princess Leia's home planet, I was deeply shocked by the idea that a whole world could be destroyed. The scale of such an act of violence left me with a sense of separation and helplessness that I still remember well.

In his autobiography *And There Was Light*, Jacques Lusseyran records his experience of blindness occurring during his first Saturn square (see chart graphic). Lusseyran's natal Saturn is in Scorpio in the 11th house, and transiting Saturn was squaring from Aquarius. The accident took place in a classroom. His natal Saturn forms a *trauma signature*, being in a wide square to Venus in Leo in the 9th house. Transiting Saturn forming the square to itself activated this *trauma signature*. (For a detailed discussion of *trauma signatures* see Chapter 3 in *Healing the Soul*).

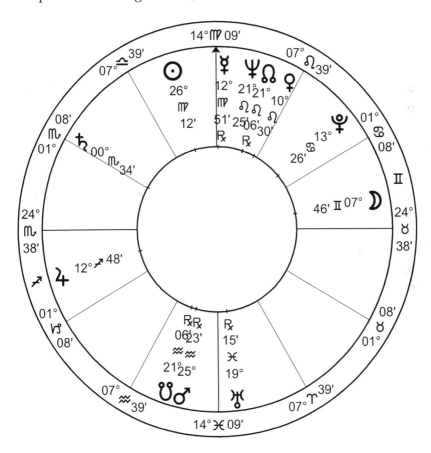

Jacques Lusseyran
September 19, 1924 at 12:00 p.m. in Paris, France
Rodden Rating: B

Rushing to the playground from a village classroom in rural France, Jacques was caught unawares by the movement of an older boy. He went crashing into the sharp corner of the teacher's desk. The extra strength of his shatterproof glasses kept them intact, but one of the temples scooped out his right eye. Afterward, as sympathetic opthalmia swelled and inflamed Jacques' other eye, blindness descended. In his autobiography he writes, "Every day since then I have thanked heaven for making me blind while I was still a child."[5]

Why such thanks for what, to all appearances, was a truly terrible childhood injury? During his Saturn square, Lusseyran also experienced transiting Neptune square his Moon, which we can read as loss (one meaning of Neptune) of an eye (the Moon, a luminary).

Transiting Jupiter was applying to the conjunction of his natal Neptune-North Node conjunction. As I have explained elsewhere (*Healing the Soul* and the introductory Pluto School Training Course), a planet conjuncting the North Node represents a quality developed recently (in the last or very recent prior life, or in childhood). It is the evolutionary intention of the current life situation (North Node) to bring the North Node archetype, carried as a potential in the unconscious, into conscious experience. Lusseyran's natal Neptune conjunct North Node in Leo indicates the potential for creative breakthrough in terms of the life of spirit which Lusseyran had developed in a recent prior life. This potential—a latent gift—sought development in the current life. Ironically, this gift began to manifest only once he had lost his eyesight. He recounts his experience:

"Immediately, the substance of the universe drew together, redefined and peopled itself anew. I was aware of a radiance emanating from a place I knew nothing about, a place which might as well have been outside me as within. But radiance was there, or, to put it more precisely, light. It was a fact, for light was there.

"I felt indescribable relief, and happiness so great it almost made me laugh. Confidence and gratitude came as if a prayer had been answered. I found light and joy at the same moment, and I can say without hesitation that from that time on light and joy have never been separated in my experience. I have had them or lost them together." [6]

The life and work of Jacques Lusseyran has, I believe, many profound implications for our understanding about identity, the life of the spirit, and the nature of courage. Lusseyran used his ability to read people to become a leader in the French resistance under the Nazi occupation and survived Buchenwald. His experience of light at the time of the accident was part of an inner truth which brightened the more he trusted life and dimmed if he held onto fear. This speaks of the relationship of the Saturn cycle to our foundation of trust in the world, which is the key to genuine emotional and psychological stability.

The First Saturn Opposition

To gain insight into the first Saturn opposition, we can return to Lusseyran, whose insights reveal a lifelong sensitivity to the Saturn cycle. He writes, "Until I was nearly fourteen I remember calling the experience, which kept renewing itself inside me, 'my secret', and speaking of it only to intimate friends." [7]

At his Saturn opposition, around age 14, young Lusseyran finally felt safe enough to share his inner experience with others. This corresponds to the social understanding that begins to enter awareness at the Saturn opposition. The Saturn opposition can be understood via the Natural Zodiac as a Libran aspect: starting with Aries at the Ascendant (conjunction), Libra is the opposing sign. With Saturn opposing its natal position, the awareness of the socio-sexual world grows during adolescence, when suddenly the "others" to whom we are attracted become objects of fascination and mystery.

This natural evolution of the ego self is shaped by the movements of the Saturn cycle. Saturn is the great bridge between the inner planets (personal identity) and the outer planets (transpersonal forces). Saturn forms the boundary between these two poles.

Many hunter-gatherers and indigenous cultures mark the Saturn opposition time with initiation rites. Many of these involve closeting the individual away from other people and then reintroducing him to the tribe only after he has accomplished some feat or test of his courage and capacity. In this way, the entrance of the youth into the social world is given a form that he can celebrate. The rite is often memorialized with permanent body markings to commemorate its power.

Some tribal social inductions involve ceremonial dancing or ritual contact where the young men symbolically display their attributes to the young women and vice versa. Many such rituals involve a sexual initiation intended to introduce them to the power of their bodies. Others involve painful mutilations. Each of these tribal cultures ritually embodies the energy of the first Saturn opposition, while most modern societies fail to provide their teenagers with anything equivalent. School dances, with boys painfully lined up on one side of the room, girls on the other, are a poor substitute. The lack of initiation rituals has been observed by many modern thinkers. In *Iron John*, Robert Bly notes the explicit sense of loss for young men due to a lack of form through which to channel their libidinous potential.

The Second Saturn Square & The First Uranus Square

The second square of transiting Saturn to natal Saturn interfaces chronologically with the first square that transiting Uranus makes to its natal position, around the age of 21. The significance that many Western cultures place on this age is borne of this powerful astrological meeting point.

The second Saturn square coincides with the realization that after the hard work of education—school and college programs, apprenticeships, travel—the quickly maturing individual needs to find work to support herself. There is a pressure to find a meaningful role within the given culture. The crisis of consciousness at the second square concerns finding a way to feel meaningful while expressing self-identity *within* the collective.

The first Uranus square affords a second crucial challenge alongside the Saturnian pressure to fit *into* society: that of how to *act* while aligning with one's *true nature* and inspiration (Uranus). This is a massive combined pressure—to both individuate and fit in. And many struggle with these coexisting archetypal impulses. Facing the world after college or a first job or apprenticeship, or contemplating adult life outside the parental home, many are overwhelmed.

Arrested Development is Possible at Any Stage

This raises the crucial issue of developmental failure in the face of multiple challenges. Many people never discover how to fit into society in a meaningful fashion. This is essentially a Saturn failure. Still others struggle to find a meaningful role while preserving some sense of their own individuality or inspiration—essentially a Uranus failure.

Others struggle to integrate the earlier Saturn stresses. Some never get over the anxiety that arises during the first encounter with limitation and death from the first Saturn square. In fact, one could argue that our entire society denies mortality and inherent limitations. [8] This leads to many collective shadows arising from insecurity about our individual and collective significance.

Still others never make the leap into the social world during the first Saturn opposition. Personal insecurities make entering the greater social milieu seem too frightening. Realization of our fundamental incapacity to control other people leads to feelings of helplessness and inadequacy. Some choose (consciously or unconsciously) to live alone so as to minimize the anxiety experienced in the presence of other people. Many create their own purgatory of isolation rather than risk rejection or betrayal.

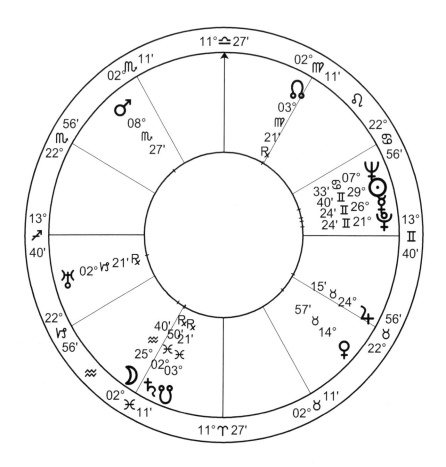

Jean-Paul Sartre
June 21, 1905, 6:45 p.m., Paris, France
Rodden Rating: AA

Embodying a strong Saturn archetype, Jean-Paul Sartre was born with Saturn at 2° Pisces in the 3rd house conjunct the south node of the Moon, and also widely conjunct the Moon at 25° Aquarius. With Pluto conjunct Mercury in his 7th house in Gemini, we see an inquiring and restless mind that, in the past (south node of the Moon), has come up against a limitation of meaning (Saturn in Pisces in the 3rd house; Jupiter in a wide square to the Nodal Axis of the Moon), and has struggled to overcome a core futility and despair (Saturn-south node of Moon-Moon). He explored this karmic dynamic consistently through his writing (Pluto in Gemini, Saturn conjunct south node of the Moon in the 3rd house), which we can observe as linked to the expression of the unrealized Saturn archetype.

At the personal level, developmental issues in one's early home life can leave some people prone to an emphasized sense of struggle against the challenges presented during the Saturn (and Uranus) cycle. If the individual's mother is intensely anxious or depressed during the early phase of infancy, then the anxiety of death or danger at the first Saturn square may be experienced as extra scary. If the individual responds with withdrawal and denial, the Saturn opposition is an initiation experienced as anxiety-provoking, as there is no model for pressurized interpersonal dialogue. And most teenage dialogue already has a certain underlying tension.

In a family in which duty has been emphasized over and above love or creativity, the second Saturn square may be easier to navigate than the concurrent first Uranus square. The individual may settle into a job and a seemingly placid and successful life—only for the unlived life potential to erupt down the line.

Conversely, in the family in which individual creativity and "doing your own thing" has been the prevailing message, a person may feel quite inspired. She might travel the world or form a band. And yet the social pressure to conform or to make a living may prove to be stressful in a whole other way. This can lead to the perpetual teenager feeling common among those who seek recognition of their creativity while failing to exercise the discipline necessary to produce the economic and social rewards of their gifts.

The Importance of the First Saturn Return

Astrology offers the profound gift of insight into the full potential of key time periods in the individual life cycle. In a culture in which rituals of initiation are few and far between, astrology can reinstate awareness of the initiatory power inherent in timing. The Saturn Return is often the most significant universal life cycle transit that will have occurred up until that point. This transit marks a turning point—closing the chapter on one phase of life and beginning a new one.

In his book *The Seasons of a Man's Life*, Daniel J. Levinson presents the findings from his research team, which developed a detailed survey of adult development. Levinson applies this research specifically to the study of male development. Levinson's findings reveal a remarkable structural similarity with the Saturn and Uranus cycles of adult development.

Levinson and his group found significance in what we know as the first Saturn Return, which they refer to as "*The Age Thirty Transition.*" During that time, their study participant Paulsen went through changes that "represented a substantial advance in his development. Paulsen came to act less like a carefree boy and more like a man who wants to make his place in the world and is ready to take responsibility for doing this." [9] They proved what astrologers have long known, that this stage of life carries a near universal significance.

The first Saturn Return contains a great rebirth potential. The planet that symbolizes how we structure our consciousness and our psychological maturation returns to its natal position holding all of the information gathered during its first cycle.

Although certain key ages are celebrated ritually, such as 18 or 21, and although the Jupiter Return at age 24 can bring a period marked by expansive vision, at the first Saturn Return around the ages of 28 to 30 is when the individual is presented an opportunity for true maturation into adulthood. Many people who fail to fulfill their potential at this time, especially those who deny or struggle to accept that failure, will continue to face difficulty throughout their 30s. The significance of this transit as a psychological foundation for adult life can hardly be overemphasized.

The Nodal Opposition Prior to the Saturn Return

At 27, we experience a significant precursor to the Saturn Return when the transiting lunar nodes oppose their natal placement. The Nodal transit cycle takes 18 years, so at 27, the transiting north node of the Moon conjuncts the natal south node of the Moon. At this time, the current evolutionary intention (transit of the north node) is to explore the past (conjunct the natal south node). We are encouraged to go back into the past (of the current life) and identify what is best from it, and carry that with us into the future.

Although karmic or past-life material may come into consciousness at this time, our focus is on the psychological development marked by the fourth harmonic Saturn aspects (first square, opposition, second square) and the way that the recent past of the current life carries subconscious traces of prior karma from recent prior lives (deeper meaning of the south node of the Moon). So when we go back into the past at the nodal opposition, we are going back to a rich seam of all the conscious memories of the current life and all the unconscious memories of early infancy, which carry traces of prior-life memories.

Done consciously, this process prepares us for the forthcoming maturation struggle of our first Saturn Return, when we identify and collect the best of ourselves for the next phase of life and align with our deepest potential.

First Steps Toward Karmic Freedom

Our early lives are shaped by our past karma. In *Healing the Soul*, I explain in detail how Pluto, Uranus and the Lunar Nodes can be analyzed to reveal the patterns from our karmic past and the way those patterns inform the current life. Our family of origin and our earliest experiences with caregivers echo prior-life events, which then shape our responses to these situations in order to provide the perfect environment for our evolutionary growth. Karma is not an arbitrary judgment determined by an impersonal higher power or cosmic principle of justice. Karma is the deeply personal recognition of who we really are and how the inner truth of our nature manifests reality in order to reveal our true nature to ourselves, the world and the Divine.

The rebirth potential of the Saturn Return represents the opportunity for the creative will to structure the consciousness in the current life from a position of having cleared the momentum of the wave of prior karma. The only exception to this is when Pluto is conjunct the south node of the Moon. This configuration indicates a strong intention to repeat prior karma, in which case this clarity to act free from that prominent past influence in the current life tends to manifest later on instead, sometimes as late as the second Saturn Return. [10]

The first Saturn Return, after childhood and the encounter with our karmic past at the nodal opposition, presents the first clear opportunity we have to shape our current life with our creative will—maturing, fully conscious, and present.

Prince Siddhartha

When the Buddha was born, a seer at court predicted that he would either become a great ruler over many lands or a great teacher of men. His father, the King, was very much into the idea of him becoming an all-powerful ruler and was afraid of him becoming an ascetic. So he created a perfect environment for the young prince in his palace so that he would not want for anything. It wasn't until Prince Siddhartha reached his first Saturn Return that left the palace.

During his first three trips outside the palace, the young Siddhartha came face to face with the reality of old age, sickness and death. The contrast with his own life made a profound impact on him, such that he resolved to leave the palace, his wife and children, and seek the origin of suffering and the path of liberation from it.

That he did so is one of the great events of world history. Siddhartha remains the shining example of the perfected human, enlightened and free from the cycle of rebirth and the world of *samsara* (literally "continuous flow" of life). His life provides a blueprint of the potential within every human and the primary goal of the Buddhist path.

We can learn something essential about the first Saturn Return with the revelation that it was only during that phase of life that the Buddha's intention arose to penetrate the heart of suffering. At the first Saturn Return, we gain recognition of our mortality and a resulting sense of seriousness about achieving our life's purpose or goals.

Puer and Senex

When we are young, we have a naïve sense of endless time and possibility. We can imagine ourselves doing many things and nothing seems fixed. At the first Saturn Return, our choices begin to be limited and opportunities solidify. We become aware that there are only so many things we can actually achieve in one lifetime. This recognition, often only partially conscious, begins to alter the youthful self and brings a growing internal pressure to commit to that which will form the structure of one's adult life.

The words *puer aeternus*, Latin for "eternal boy," first appear in Ovid's *Metamorphoses*. Carl Jung spent considerable time exploring the archetype in his paper "The Psychology of the Child Archetype." But *Peter Pan*, the creation of J.M. Barrie, is perhaps the most memorable expression of the archetype in the modern imagination. This beloved story about a young boy who never grows up and lives in the world of Neverland speaks to a common fantasy to avoid adulthood altogether. But the *puer aeternus* can be best understood in relationship to its antithetical or polarity archetype—the *senex*.

The *senex* is an archetype described by Jung in Saturnian terms as an old man, in contrast to the youthful Peter Pan figure of the *puer*. The *senex* represents the power of time, of hard work and the understanding that is born from loss. Loss is always associated with time, in part because loss occurs and heals in time—but most practically because the longer we stick around, the more we lose people whom we know and love.

The first Saturn Return includes a primordial encounter between the *puer* and *senex* as the wave of youth crashes into the cliff-face of time. Without dedication, the default setting of life ensures that very little will happen. Many people do not grow or evolve significantly their entire lives. Without commitment and the development of the will to serve the highest potential of the self and of others, evolution is difficult. We can observe that an individual's psychological and biological ages may be very different. Many people get stuck at a particular developmental stage and do not significantly advance beyond that.

An attachment to the youthful state of possibility represents a particular sticking point in the *puer* archetype. On the positive side of the *puer* archetype, we find the power of the imagination to dream beyond the limitations of our day-to-day concerns. We also find the joy of life, the appreciation of beauty in the arts, nature and the erotic realm. Yet, excessive attachment to the *puer* consciousness is linked with failure to mature and grow. What is attractive in a children's story about the magic of fairies changes with age. Excessive *puer* behavior is tiresome in someone in their 30s or 40s who cannot commit, lets his children down, and chases every passing new attraction as if it were as alluring as the first.

Michael Jackson famously named his estate Neverland, perhaps dreaming of it as an antidote to the brutality of his own childhood. But whatever our compassion for his brutal parenting, early training and hectic tour schedule, a man in his 40s having "sleepovers" with children is problematic.

Many drink and drug addicts, sex addicts and compulsives of all kinds have an identification with the *puer* in which they want to feel the freedom of flight (or escape), but end up thwarted in the face of Saturn (*senex*) and ruining their lives.

Icarus and Daedalus

The *puer* and *senex* dilemma unfolded in Greek mythology through the story of Daedalus and his son, Icarus. The story goes that Daedalus (literally "clever worker") was the great craftsman of his time. He was a master of his art through his intense labor of many years. His skill had made him famous, and he was asked to create the labyrinth in which the Minotaur would be housed. After finishing the labyrinth, even though the King was pleased with his work, Daedalus and his son were imprisoned in a tower on the island of Crete to guarantee that he would never speak of the secrets of the labyrinth to anyone. Daedalus then used his skills to create two sets of wings using wax and the feathers of seabirds so that he and his son could escape their captivity.

As they escaped, he and Icarus sailed off into the sky above Crete. Problems quickly ensued because Icarus enjoyed the feeling of flying so much that he began to soar ever higher, intoxicated by the feeling of being on top of the world. Daedalus shouted warnings to his son, explaining that the wings were only temporary constructions and that the wax holding the feathers together would not withstand the heat of the sun. But Icarus flew on, closer and closer to the sun. Eventually the inevitable happened and the wax melted. Icarus fell to his death, Daedalus lost his only son while trying to free him.

There is a wonderful painting by Pieter Bruegel called *Landscape with the Fall of Icarus* in which Icarus is shown falling into the sea—just a tiny splash in the vast water. When first viewing the painting, it is hard to even find the figure of Icarus. He is such a small event in this painting that lovingly depicts a farmer plowing a field next to a cliff with bright ships in the water below him. Icarus is a footnote in the scene. The *senex* reality of this scene is that life goes on despite the loss.

In keeping with much of Greek thought, the story of Icarus is a critique of hubris. Ancient Greek philosophy saw this form of pride as the central problem of the human condition. The positive quality of the *puer* is also its undoing. The joy of flight becomes intoxicating, which leads to the loss of judgment that brings one crashing back to earth.

The Wake-Up Call

The first Saturn Return marks the moment we need to return, safely, to solid ground, releasing the unrealistic fantasies of childhood. At this juncture, it pays to contemplate a grounded vision of one's true capacities and how one might make one's way in the world. Realism is essential, because self-delusion at this point is dangerous. When "getting real," it is important not to take things too far or become completely disenchanted. Depression can quickly replace realism, and negative self-esteem can become as much of a problem as a grandiose self-image.

In the ideal alchemy of this wake-up call, the qualities of the *puer* and *senex* combine to produce an inspirational but grounded vision of how to go forth into the world based on a genuine and sober assessment of one's assets. This requires a relatively stable self-image and adequate self-worth. If these qualities are lacking—or if the individual is carrying residual damage from the family of origin—it can be hard to find a stable enough sense of identity to undertake the process in a balanced manner.

Success and Failure at Work

Saturn rules Capricorn and the 10th house, the cusp of which is the Midheaven: an angle critical in representing our self-expression in the world. Saturn teaches us how to deal with failure. One key arena in which success or failure plays out during the first Saturn Return is the workplace. Keep in mind that fantasies of success and failure are as just powerful in their impact as the real thing.

We can make a simple but effective threefold distinction here between having a job, a career and a vocation. Now, just to have a job is a major accomplishment in the material world. Western economies are currently reeling from the failures of the secretive investment banking industry and the subsequent withdrawal of capital for small businesses and homeowners as an overreaction to the *laissez faire* attitude they previously held. So, for some, simply getting a job is the primary achievement of the first Saturn Return. For the not-so-fortunate, failure to find employment is part of the Saturnian theme of dealing with limitation that this transit can bring. In Spain—which is the fifth largest economy in Europe (the thirteenth largest in the world)—at the time of writing, unemployment nationwide had passed 25% and youth unemployment had passed 50%. In such a world, many people will fail to find work, Saturn Return lessons learned or not.

For some who have worked throughout their 20s, the first Saturn Return represents the evolution from having a job to embarking on a career. The first Saturn Return is a good time to make this self-investment, whether that involves funds or time for training or promotion. The reality of most peoples' lives is that they will spend an inordinate number of their waking hours working. With this core Saturn realization firmly in place, it behooves any sane person who cares about her well-being to find a job or career that is at the least a bearable way of making a living. Ideally, it is one she will also find enjoyable and personally fulfilling.

Many adults will find their job or career to be the arena in which their greatest creative expression and personal effort manifests. Positive recognition of the importance of work/career at the first Saturn Return leads to sensible choices and self-investment which lay the foundations for a successful working life. Failure to do so, or a sense of futility at the prospect, can lead to settling for jobs that are a poor fit. This can later lead to feelings of ambivalence at best, or at worst, feelings of aversion and anger at one's lot.

I have assisted many people with life transitions in which a key part of their personal transformation revolved around changing job or career to a more appropriate choice. It cannot be overstated how damaging it is to spend forty or so hours a week (sometimes more like fifty or sixty with travel) doing daily work that is harming the self. Many will seek help out of despair that becomes unbearable during a Saturn time. To help a person with this kind of issue, we simply need to provide space for the individual to realize that he does not have to continue in work that is painful or harmful to the self. Insight usually occurs when the client has connected to a greater sense of self-value or potential, initially mirrored by the therapist. When the sense of potential is adequately internalized, it is easy for the client to begin thinking of creative ways to actualize it.

A career is a job structure that progresses over time and produces rewards that can be financially and creatively empowering. A vocation (from the Latin meaning call or summons) is more of a calling: a sense of being inspired by some higher power or principle (which may not be consciously realized) in order to express one's gifts or fulfill a given role within the collective. Such an inner prompting can occur at any stage in life but is often felt early on as a compelling drive. Sometimes this drive is repressed or locked away until later events or a change of heart bring the issue back into consciousness. For those who feel a calling to a vocation, the Saturn Return marks a critical juncture in terms of making a commitment to that calling. This usually involves taking on more responsibility in the given field, a more prominent role, or at least working towards that prominence. Sometimes the calling takes the form of a seemingly random invitation or opportunity which places the individual in a public role in which she begins to embody the nature of her vocation.

It's not uncommon for people to have a lot of stress about vocation, calling and career. It's helpful to remember here that *life is a meaningful journey to which we are all called to fully participate if we are open.* This is the spiritual truth about vocation that we might call the "open secret," or as a friend of mine used to say, "An elite club to which everyone is invited." Life presents all of us an open invitation to enter willingly into the adventure. Unfortunately, many people choose not to hear or believe the invitation. For a wonderful consideration of the subject, see Gregg Levoy's *Callings: Finding and Following an Authentic Life.*

A young person confronting his Saturn Return may face losses that already threaten his sense of meaning and his capacity to engage with the tasks of adult life with optimism about his own abilities. As astrologers, we are charged with helping such clients reengage with this necessary primary sense of possibility so that the demands of the Saturn Return are met by a robust self. We can explore this process with an example.

Saturn Return Case Study

Recently I did a reading for a young man who traveled several hours to seek my advice. Looking at his chart, which follows, we can see with his 1st house Pluto in Scorpio that Tom has a central need for the space to explore his instinctual process and freedom to self-discover. This will be experienced as an intense urge from within (Pluto) that can lead to inner crisis if not acknowledged. In combining the two archetypes, the quincunx from Aries/1st house to Pluto/8th house reflects a tremendous source of crisis. The concept of the quincunx as a crisis comes from an understanding of the natural zodiac, with Aries on the Ascendant, and its relationship with Virgo/6th house as the blueprint for the aspect. Tom expressed how important it was that he see me in person (1st house Pluto). He needed the emotional and physical immediacy of a face-to-face encounter.

With Venus in Libra conjunct Pluto in Scorpio, we see an intensification of relationship concerns central to his need for focused exploration of personal freedom. We further observe that a number of paradoxes could originate from these two needs operating together. To the extent that personal freedom is the bottom line of Tom's personal identity, he will be content to be alone. As being alone becomes restrictive, boring even, there emerges an attraction to the shared reality of the other. The other then represents a new journey—a shared adventure. As the needs of the other become more central in his experience (and with Venus in Libra he is very sensitive to the feelings of others), and as the potential for deepening commitment emerges, his original need for personal freedom may become threatened.

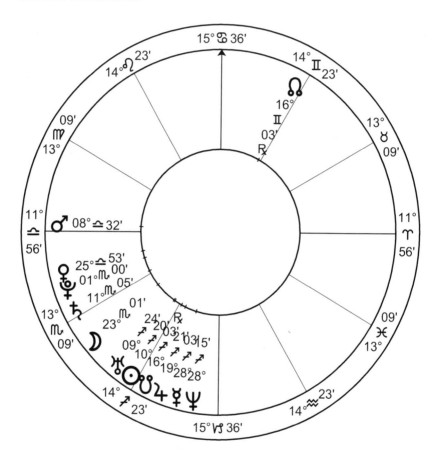

Tom
December 3, 1983, 2:23 a.m., London, UK

The Libran sensitivity to others may create a feeling of being torn between his deep personal orientation (Pluto in the 1st house in its own sign) and that of the other (Venus). As such, Tom may struggle to articulate the strength (Pluto) of his own need honestly. If this continues, his need for personal freedom is likely to lead to an eruption of conflict that could be destructive to a relationship—especially if he has pandered to the other's expectations (Venus in Libra) and he/she is unaware of the full extent of Tom's personal drive.

The 1st house Pluto person can struggle with relationship commitment to the extent that such a commitment might compromise the primacy of the individual need for unimpeded self exploration. This inherent 1st house Pluto conflict is exacerbated in Tom's chart through his Venus placement. Tom's Venus in Libra is in *balsamic conjunction* to Pluto. As the final phase, the balsamic conjunction has a Pisces-like imprint that, in Tom's case, reflects that these issues are *culminating* and that an intense inner conflict on a private or secret level is possible. He is at risk of carrying the pressure of this conflict privately and, without expressing it, imploding.

That Saturn is in Scorpio in the 1st house, widely conjunct Pluto, shows that the issues of his Saturn Return are pressing and that the issue of commitment (Saturn in Scorpio) is central. That Pluto aspects Saturn reveals that a core component of Tom's life has to do with the transformation of his personal authority. Saturn in Scorpio in the 1st house only emphasizes the issue of self-commitment which, if not understood, could lead to a struggle to commit to another.

Further information about the need for relationship is shown by the Mars-Venus phase, which is *new phase*. This means that Venus is separating from the slower moving Mars, and the phase is akin to an Aries/1st house dynamic. This is in contrast with the balsamic or Pisces-like conjunction of Venus and Pluto. People with a new phase Mars-Venus placement often need to experience a few relationships before recognizing what it is they really need from intimacy. A number of factors in this chart would point to some risk in prematurely settling with a partner, or the danger of compromising the needs of the self. This chart necessitates having freedom to grow. The 1st house Pluto and the new Mars-Venus phase reveal a greater than average need for personal exploration of relationships before the individual may be able to resolve the powerful personal impulse for freedom with another.

Tom's stellium in Sagittarius on the south node speaks to why I personally nicknamed this client "The Seeker." A large part of our reading was taken up in his sharing of his spiritual journey and his exploring a number of altered states of consciousness in order to clarify his understanding. He shared a story that began while preparing to board a train after an aikido retreat. As he waited for the train, he wrote a letter to thank the master for a wonderful time, underlining the word "wonderful." Just before boarding the train, he looked up at an advertising board in which a slogan appeared with the word "wonderful" also underlined. As he rode the train, a profound state of peace enveloped him. Just then, his breath stopped and he sensed that he might die—and that he would not mind if he did. At this point, he started breathing again.

A lack of concern about physical death often accompanies powerful altered states or incursions of the transpersonal dimensions. This is because, as the word 'transpersonal' suggests, the experience leads to an understanding that the inner life exists beyond the personal, including the biology of the physical form. However, that such an awareness of death seemed to arise so quickly with the expansion of Tom's mental awareness is evocative. His planets near the south node show the considerable energy from the past that he is bringing in. With the north node ruler, Jupiter, conjunct the south node, we see the intention to repeat those experiences (south node) in order to mentally integrate them into a more coherent overall philosophy or understanding (north node in Gemini in the 9th house). The combination of the planets conjunct the south node, the Pluto-Venus signature with Pluto also ruling the 2nd house cusp, the archetype of Venus/Taurus corresponding in part to our biological survival, combine to suggest that some of the past experience he intends to repeat involves memories of his own death. The experience he had on the train suggests lifetimes in which consciousness expansion or some form of higher values are aligned in his subconscious with death. We could envision a warrior dying for a cause, a holy war, or perhaps ascetic lifetimes in which his body was manipulated or ignored in the service of expanding consciousness.

Our reading focused on the first real love of his life, whom he had met traveling. After a period of living with her family, they planned to marry. Fueling this serious commitment was the fact that she was pregnant with his child. When they had first met, Tom had explained he felt a powerful intuition that he would need to be alone for three months at some point in the development of their relationship. At the time he interpreted this as a premonition, and we could also observe that it was a kind of warning arising from his inner self. Already we see the key stress of relationship commitment conflicting with his intense personal motivation for freedom. Tom's partner listened to this message and said that although it would be very hard, she would do her best to understand and accept his absence if need be. Mere weeks before the wedding, with Tom's partner heavily pregnant, huge internal pressures finally prompted Tom to follow through and take his leave. We can only imagine how his partner would have struggled to accept his extreme personal need and resulting action. He was sensitive to that struggle in her and therefore felt unable to tell her when the time came.

Tom's internal pressures involved increasingly intense bursts of paranoia about the hierarchical nature of Western civilization. He grew concerned about world conflict and became attached to certain conspiracy theories. Just prior to his departure for New Zealand, his chosen retreat location, he was desperately convinced that a huge terrorist attack was imminent and that the world he knew was fundamentally unsafe. Although members of his girlfriend's family had begun to notice his increasingly intense and erratic state, none recognized its depth or severity. Tom felt he *had* to go—it was that or psychiatric internment. Although leaving was an abandonment that cost the family a great deal of money and stress, he did not intend to abandon his partner. After spending time in a healing center in New

Zealand, which stabilized his psyche, he returned to work things out. Unfortunately, this was too late for his girlfriend and family.

To further understand the situation with Tom's partner, we need to go back to the time of the proposal. They had been visiting New Zealand, where they were planning to emigrate, and she was increasingly pressuring him to marry her. She was older and had experienced a string of failed relationships with boyfriends whose personal problems had derailed the partnerships. Tom, in his first proper relationship, his first love, was naïve about the importance of her need for public commitment. This prompted his partner to summon her family's support and pressure Tom for marriage.

Initially, his stated resistance was not consciously against marriage, but instead fixated on the formal social contract (Saturn). His strong Sagittarius nature struggled with the question, "Why do we need a piece of paper to confirm our love?" Her family was not impressed. They said they would not pay for a wedding that was simply a "big party." They spoke with his mother, who then called him. There were a lot of tears, and a lot of pressure, to which he eventually gave in. When the arguments were over and the marriage plans agreed on, the child was conceived that very night. Fateful stuff! We can see that his compromise concealed the depth of his own needs and these would only emerge later.

With the marriage just round the corner, Tom was drawn to return to the place they had the original fight over marriage plans and conceived their child. He met someone on the plane who offered him a place to stay his first night and then went to live in a spiritual community. He did return home three months later. But his choice to leave was enough to end his relationship and to strain his bond with his daughter. His ex-fiancée is still cold, and her father will not speak to Tom at all.

Interestingly, Tom did not consciously experience pressure building up prior to the wedding. Very much the 1st house Pluto, he felt the powerful feelings *in his body* and on an *instinctual level* but he was not able to articulate why they were there. But just before his departure, those stressful feelings mounted until he felt strongly compelled to leave or face imminent breakdown.

We can see from our astrological analysis and our understanding of the timing of the Saturn return that Tom was unconsciously expressing his unresolved struggle with Saturn. When the Saturn function remains unresolved or in an immature state, it is easy for a person to project Saturn outwardly. In Tom's case, he saw the world's authorities as hostile and lacking integrity. This is, in part, an expression of his felt sense of a lack of power and personal authority.

During the reading, Tom gained insight from our discussion of the dynamics of his Saturn Return. He began to see the connection between his conspiracy theory fears and the pressure of others lining up against him: his lover, her family, and his mother. Although his partner was his first love, the two had spent much of their time together traveling the world or living with her parents. There was no sense of how they would actually be together while working and raising a child. It was his girlfriend's need that they marry, and leaning to the Venus in Libra side of the core conflict at the heart of his chart, he had compromised on his own 1st house Pluto drives and instincts. Ultimately, his psyche could not bear the compromise.

Saturn and the Family Trance

Tom's fiancée's family represented a Saturnian collective response against him—an example of the "family myth" or the "family trance" as an obstacle to personal growth and freedom. After his departure, they cut him off altogether, including any acknowledgment that he was the father of his daughter.

Let's pause our Saturn Return case study to contemplate the profound role Saturn plays within the family myth or trance. The family trance is subconscious—a series of messages or codes that the family lives by. For example, some families carry the belief that "whatever happens, the family deals with it." This popular family myth plays out in Tom's ex-partner's family. In some families, the key component to this particular myth is that outsiders are kept from seeing the family problems, which are to be dealt with (or ignored) privately. There is a fear of the neighbors knowing. We can see that this trance has its roots in the perception of social hierarchies with the fear that other people will look down on them. This is the family's attempt to manage the Saturn shadow. Shame fuels this trance state. Often with the family trance, a seemingly positive message or myth has at its core a negative emotion, the fear of which is the true motivational energy driving the trance.

Though the family trance or myth of "we take care of our own" or "we deal with our problems without anyone else needing to intrude" is very common, it can take myriad forms through the variety of emotional states that may drive its expression. Some people are dominated by the shame of having others see their personal or family problems, and they are defending themselves from hostile perceptions.

In another expression of this "we take care of our own" family myth, an internal fear of chaos is the motivator. This unconscious fear dictates a prompt resolution of problems to stave off internal forces that threaten to override the parent(s) and therefore the family. So, some families are preoccupied by an externalization of the fear of the Saturn shadow (external judgment, condemnation and internal shame). Others are preoccupied by the internalization of the fear of the Saturn shadow (as in, "If we don't keep it together we will fail, and our family will lose our home and be out on the streets").

Other families will express the same myth in seemingly diametrically opposed ways. Note the difference in emphasis between the ideas, "we take care of our own" and "we can deal with our problems on our own." Both have an underlying archetypal similarity. The first emphasizes the internal bond of the family out of fear of it will somehow dissolve. The second case involves the fear of others looking down from a place of superiority. In this manner, families can differ based on whether they are essentially an open or closed system.

In open-family systems, people literally do not like to close the doors—bedrooms and bathrooms may even be left open. In such a family, the caretaking is held within an emotional living thread between the participants. In a closed-family system, people tend to want to shut themselves off from the others, who are experienced as overwhelming. In the open system, the danger is enmeshment, and the unresolved Saturn function is fear and anxiety. The family care-taking myth is a mantra to channel the anxiety. In the closed system, the unresolved Saturn issues tend to fixate around guilt and grief. The thinking is that people are intrusive because they judge (guilt) and this creates core emotional isolation (grief). In such systems, the family trance actually represents a defense against contact.

In extreme cases, this myth only exists to push other prying eyes away so that the family can maintain the strongest defense—denial. In these cases, the family trance is a conscious lie. We have explored how even well-meaning family myths are actually fueled primarily through negative emotional states. But when denial is the prime op-erating factor, there is not even the pretense of good intention. The family trance is then a hypnotic suggestion for its members to shut down. This is a hallmark of dysfunctional families and its destructive impact can hardly be overstated. Though it is more often apparent in the closed-style system, both open and closed systems can fall prey to denial.

We can see that these Saturnian defensive structures, while in-dividual, have their roots in our conditioning and particularly our upbringing. This means that they will have collective elements to them. This is a potential in all natal charts because defense is a fun-damental characteristic of the ego itself. But especially vulnerable are those who have Saturn in Cancer or Capricorn, the 4th or 10th houses, or Saturn in major aspect to Pluto and/or the nodes of the Moon.

Tom's Saturn Return

When much of his paranoia about international conspiracy theories was rife, transiting Saturn was in Libra in Tom's 12th house, where it formed a conjunction with his natal Mars. He was expressing an un-developed Saturn function that indirectly arose out of the "conspir-acy" that everyone close to him was pushing him towards marriage. As Saturn later moved into his 1st house, it would conjunct Venus and then enter Scorpio, where it would conjunct his natal Pluto at 1° Scorpio and then Saturn at 11° Scorpio. It was at his Saturn Return that Tom began to realize the consequences of his actions, coming to terms with these events relative to his inner commitment to himself (Scorpio in the 1st house). His own abandonment of the situation for which he had, under pressure, signed up, directly reflected the self-abandonment that the capitulation actually represented to the core value of his deeper self: Pluto in the 1st house.

When Tom arrived for his reading, a strong part of him was still in the doghouse and holding onto personal guilt about every-thing that had transpired. As we were able to contextualize his ac-tions, namely his leaving—that was and is viewed so punitively by others—we understood that in his own primitive fashion, he was serving his deepest needs. We unpacked the events surrounding the decision to marry. Instead of the joy of mutual love, we found only anxiety, profound ambivalence and a degree of coercion. This was not the recipe for a marriage made in heaven. In fact, at one point, Tom recognized that he really would have preferred not to marry this person at all—or at least, certainly not under those circumstances. The very feelings he'd been unable to express verbally at the time were enacted instead by his instinctual body, which went into fight-or-flight mode.

With his Mars in the 12th house, conjunct the Ascendant in Libra, and his prominent Venus in Libra conjunct Pluto in Scor-pio (within 6°), he was unable to honor his own self commitment (Pluto-Saturn Scorpio in the 1st house). With hindsight, his Saturn

Return could be seen as the attempt to consciously live what his body had already enacted.

As is so often the case with coercion that is resisted or unconsciously escaped, it bit back. Tom had every intention of recommitting to the relationship upon his return. But the domestic tragedy he now faces is that the mother of his child is still very angry with him and has moved to a place where it is hard for him to visit. She lives with another man to whom she is engaged, and her family will not acknowledge Tom (or even speak to him), which makes being involved in his daughter's life difficult. Tom never wanted to be an absent father but is in a situation in which that is inevitable. In fact, Tom is faced with an awareness of a common dynamic at the Saturn Return—that of failure. During the Saturn return, it can actually be constructive to accept loss, to retreat and regroup. When asked for his opinion on the best test of greatness, the Duke of Wellington replied, "To know when to retreat; and to dare to do it."[11]

Saturn can relate to the father, and another issue that arose for Tom during his Saturn Return was the need to come to terms with his father issues—namely the lack of an active relationship with his father during childhood. When a young (heterosexual) man's only steady parent is his mother, he often struggles later to articulate his conflicts with women. This happens because there was no modeling for expressing individual needs that might be contrary to the relationship needs, since the parents' bond was entirely broken. Often, when you see Saturn in the 4th house, or ruling the 4th house (and sometimes when square or opposite a planet in the 4th house) as it does in Tom's chart, you encounter a situation where the mother was the primary authority in the family. This is not always because of a physically absent father. Often it can just mean that the mother is the more dominant figure in the marriage and her strength overturns a more preoccupied father, or her anxiety and control issues dominate the father.

Since Tom had an absent father (and a compensatory bond with his mother), we can understand why this relatively independent young man, capable of traveling the world on his own, might have found it exceptionally difficult to voice disagreement with a significant other. Love is a moral imperative—but one that cannot be commanded—because it requires freedom. And in the expression of love, it bestows freedom. We might wonder, given Tom's marked agitation with a child on the way, how things could have played out if the plan to marry had been granted a gentler timescale—one that allowed the couple to live together first to see how they coped with new parenthood.

We can see how the Saturn Return operates here as an opportunity to consciously understand the events of one's earlier life and to make decisions based upon that understanding as a foundation for the future. We can also observe that this is often a difficult period. Tom has felt the benefit of understanding how his actions were a flawed attempt to serve a genuine need in his psyche. This has helped him remove much of the guilt that was weighing upon him. Relieved of that burden, he must now undertake the task of maturation itself, which requires that he accept the consequences of his prior actions.

We can observe here the transition from what we might term a neurotic burden: that of guilt for failing other people's expectations of him— expectations which in some cases were coercive or opposed to Tom's true nature and needs— towards the shouldering of genuine *gravitas*. By that, I mean the mature ability to acknowledge the events that have occurred and take responsibility, to whatever extent that one is able, for one's part in them. For Tom, the conscious dilemma of how to play a part in his daughter's life is a real struggle in which acceptance of loss will play a part, because it is a real compromise. The guilt carried for his own actions hurting others is psychologically more of a neurotic pain; I say this because it is a remnant of the experience of pressure from others that led to some of the problem in the first place. It does not help in this instance to make amends, to try to make what already happened all right. Though Tom wanted to do this at first, he later understood his actions in the context of the unresolved struggle between self and other at the heart of his chart and his life. In Tom's case, the past cannot be un-made but must be accepted, lived through and with.

The First Saturn Square After the Return

In the first Saturn square following the first Saturn Return (about 7 ½ years later), the individual experiences the challenge and/or reward of the conscious potential unearthed at the Saturn Return. Some people fail to activate the conscious rebirth potential of the Saturn Return, in which case the Saturn function remains dormant and expresses itself in an unconscious and unresolved fashion. In such cases, the Saturn square can be a jolt that provides a new chance to engage with the repressed parts of themselves.

If a person rejected outright the potential of the Saturn Return, the Uranus opposition at midlife often provides the most significant opportunity for him to overcome his resistance to himself, or to life. (This assumes a lack of any personal significant transit activity, or the Pluto square Pluto transit depending on its elusive orb.) Many people, however, never learn the core lessons of Saturn: maturation; healthy boundaries; discipline; commitment. They may remain inwardly infantile, blaming others for perceived lack or the failures of their lives. Behavior that is frustrating but understandable in a child becomes incredibly destructive in an immature adult. Such a person may saturate relationships with decades-old resentment, finding fault with everything and everyone but herself.

For those who do consciously embrace the Saturn Return process—with its difficult rewards—the square is a chance to take stock of the potential sensed at the Return. When we look at life with the long-term view provided by Saturn and the outer planets, the seven years following the Saturn Return is just about the shortest time that it takes to build anything of consequence in life. At my Saturn Return, my central career focus was to build my own private practice as a therapist and to find an outlet to teach astrology to sincere students. At the time of the first square, I was paying the mortgage on my first home with income from my client practice, I had taught three astrology workshops in the UK and had begun regular teaching work in the United States. I was teaching myself how to run a business and getting used to the physical and psychic strain of working with people's most significant and problematic issues. As one is in a building phase, it is only over time that one appreciates the significance of that period of building and growth.

Saturn rules the linear progression of time. One must steadily adhere to the commitments one makes at the Saturn Return to see results. In my case, gaining a clear perspective on my progress required conversations with my supervisor. The repetitive focus and sheer accumulation of hours provided the forge on which I shaped my increasing ability to be skillful at my work. It took perseverance at various roles in order to transcend those roles. It took total concentration on being the best possible therapist I could be to come to the place where I just surrendered. I no longer even experience work in those terms. I do not even think of it as work when I am in the work; it is just the expression of who I am. But that awareness only came with time.

Midlife Transits: Saturn and Uranus

In our early 40s we come to the most significant interconnection of the Saturn and Uranus cycles: transiting Uranus opposite natal Uranus and transiting Saturn opposite natal Saturn. In fact, midlife marks the most significant transit activity in the human life span in general (individuals will have more or less intense periods depending on the arrangement of the planets in their natal charts). The transits of midlife also include Neptune square Neptune and for some, Pluto square Pluto (some generations experience this transit at midlife while others get it near the end of life). Here, we'll just focus on the midlife transits of Saturn and Uranus. The first Saturn opposition after the Saturn Return (14 years later) marks another moment of key dialogue with the meaning established during the

Saturn Return. The second Saturn opposition sometimes occurs concurrently with the Uranus opposition and sometimes just after; it varies depending on the chart.

The Uranus Opposition and its Meaning

"Though we would like to live without regrets, and sometimes proudly insist that we have none, this is not really possible, if only because we are mortal. When more time stretches behind than stretches before one, some assessments, however reluctantly and incompletely, begin to be made. Between what one wishes to become and what one has become there is a momentous gap, which will now never be closed. And this gap seems to operate as one's final margin, one's last opportunity for creation. And between the self as it is and the self as one sees it, there is also a distance, even harder to gauge. Some of us are compelled, around the middle of our lives, to make a study of this baffling geography, less in the hope of conquering these distances than in the determination that the distance shall not become any greater."
-James Baldwin, from his review of Elia Kazan's *The Arrangement* [12]

In his book *The Seasons of a Man's Life*, from which the above quote is taken, Daniel J. Levinson found that the ages 31-38 corresponded to what he called *Becoming One's Own Man*, in which the core aspiration or dream is expressed—or at least chased. Then, he writes, "at around 40, a new period gets under way." [13] This midlife transition period is of such significance that Levinson devotes nearly a third of his book to it. To expand on the phrase "around 40" Levinson goes on to add, "We doubt that a true Midlife transition can begin before age 38 or after 43."

Levinson refers to an independent study of adult development conducted at Yale between the years 1966-1973 that concluded that 38-43 years is the age for the midlife transition—corresponding to

the time period that includes the universal transit of Uranus opposite natal Uranus. [14]

Referring to the period of ages 31-38 as *"Becoming One's Own
Man,"* Levinson found that men tended to envisage their life as a
heroic enterprise, or "myth-drama." Holding this image, part of the
power at the *Midlife Transition* is attained through the reevalua-
tion of one's single-minded pursuit of the dream or life mission. He
writes:

"The illusions, the sense of omnipotence and the excitement of
heroic drama give the Dream its intensity and inspirational qualities. But they also contribute to the *tyranny* of the Dream. Reducing
this tyranny is a major task of the Midlife Transition, whenever the
Dream has had an important place in a man's life and he is in the
grip of its myth. The task is not to get rid of the Dream altogether
but to reduce its excessive power: to make its demands less absolute;
to make success less essential and failure less disastrous; to diminish
the magical-illusory qualities." [15]

So at the Uranus opposition (Midlife Transition), to the extent that the hero "can have no flaws," the imagined perfection of
the dream/mission will be challenged, nay, annihilated. Levinson's
"Dream" could actually evolve into a conscious attitude, a directed
idealism for the ego to aspire towards, rather than a punitive perfection for which it always falls short.

Carl Jung

Carl Jung's stage of *Becoming One's Own Man* began with meeting
Sigmund Freud when he was 31, just after his Saturn Return. Their
meeting took place in Vienna at Freud's house on March 3, 1907.
They met at 1:00 p.m. for lunch and did not part until 2:00 a.m. The
two men had been talking without significant interruption for thir-
teen hours! Their relationship was extremely productive during this
period; Freud felt Jung was the crown prince of psychoanalysis, and
Jung enjoyed the attention of his then-mentor, Freud.

During this phase (31-38 years) of becoming, Jung was content to develop his link with Freud and to sideline concerns he had about Freud's metaphysical bias. Nevertheless, at age 38, at the build-up to his Uranus opposition, Jung separated from Freud and started a process of breaking down to break through. Luckily, he left us a map of what he experienced in his psyche at the time in his enormous artistic-magical tome, the *Red Book*.

Within the breakdown phase, Jung felt completely at a loss within himself, for he had valued the connection with Freud enormously. But he felt he could not stay with it because it was not wholly true. Jung had reached the point where his own individuation began to clash too harshly with the vision Freud had of him. He had to break with his mentor to express his greatest gifts—which included his theories on the collective unconscious. This is an aspect of the quickening potential of the Uranus opposition transit. Life seems to ask us what is most important to us, and to define what we really think and feel about things. The issues that arise may have been present for a long time when their importance suddenly starts to manifest, often via surprising events or flashes of insight.

The main issue we wrestle with during this transition is how to live with the unfolding change that comes about when we commit to a more deeply authentic path. The film *American Beauty* explores this theme of the *Midlife Transition* and how to respond to the realization that the details of one's life, even those that may appear outwardly successful, may actually leave one feeling empty and alone if they lack authenticity. This juncture proves too challenging for some, who can never fully embody their authenticity. Others can admit what is unsatisfactory or out of balance but then struggle to know what to do about it. When managed well, the process is fruitful and, after a period of adjustment, leads to a time of feeling "more oneself."

Jung, who had the courage to go with very deep changes within, managed to allow himself to break down, having faith that his unraveling would lead somewhere fruitful. He trusted in the process, unaware at the time of how his actions would lead to later innovations in counseling. For instance, he found himself playing in the sand by the lake, building mandala patterns to soothe his psyche, which eventually led to the *Sandplay* movement. His dialogue with certain inner figures and guides became an aspect of the art of *active imagination*, which is still used in therapy today. Jung was able to explore the other side of the conscious ego ideal that Levinson calls the *Tyranny of the Dream* and find the unconscious counterpoint to balance it.

Uranus Opposition: Lightning Strikes

Seeing past the *Tyranny of the Dream* opens one to a part of the unconscious that lies beyond the conscious ideals held by the personality. Sometimes this transition can be very intense, even shocking—hence, the image of the lightning strike. Sometimes this is not just a symbolic image.

In 1994, orthopedic surgeon Tony Cicoria had just used a public telephone in Albany, New York, when he was struck by lightning. He then experienced his consciousness hovering above his own body, which he saw surrounded by a white light with a distinct blue tinge, while the woman who had been waiting behind him to use the phone approached his supine comatose form. As it happened, she was an intensive care nurse. She recognized that his heart had stopped beating and promptly resuscitated him. It was this act that surely saved his life. [16]

When Cicoria returned to his body, he experienced pain. He remembers thinking, 'only bodies have pain.' He wanted to return to the unembodied state, to ask the woman to stop saving him! Even when the ambulance arrived, he insisted they take him home rather than to the hospital. He was 42 years old, in the aftermath of his Uranus opposition. [17]

Months later, after a marvelous physical recovery that left only traces of the burn marks on his face and his foot where the lightning had entered and exited his body, Cicoria began to experience difficulties with his short-term memory and felt sluggish. He received a thorough neurological examination, including an MRI scan and an EEG test. Nothing out of the ordinary showed up, and a week or two later, he was no longer experiencing any problems. Yet, Cicoria began to develop an unusually intense interest in piano music.

Up until then, his experience with piano had consisted of taking a handful of lessons as a boy. He had not played since. Along with Cicoria's new desire came the ability to hear music in his head, initially through a dream. He awoke so inspired that he leapt out of bed to write down the music he was hearing. He had never tried to notate or write music before! As he sat at the piano to play Chopin's compositions, his own music "would come and take me over. It had a very powerful presence." [18] Furthermore, the experience of having the music inside was becoming more and more intense: "It's like a frequency, a radio band. If I open myself up, it comes. I want to say, 'It comes from heaven,' as Mozart said. It never runs dry . . . If anything I have to turn it off."

This was all within three months of being struck by lightning. I do not have chart data for Tony Cicoria, aside from his birth year of 1952. Yet, simply from his age we know that he was undergoing his Uranus opposition and that it was his karma, fate or destiny to experience the significance of this transit in a very radical fashion. The radical nature of this example illustrates the principles contained in the Midlife Transition.

This change in Cicoria was accompanied by *a radical shift in perspective* across the board. For example, following the lighting strike, he began to believe in reincarnation. He did not study to achieve this shift. He did not become a Hindu, Buddhist or Theosophist. He just felt, after his experience, that he knew that we were here before and would come back again. Perhaps implicitly, he realized that the electrical system shock that he experienced triggered prior-life memories and talents. Just as he quoted Mozart saying the music "comes from heaven," he recognized a similar process within himself.

Wolfgang Amadeus Mozart

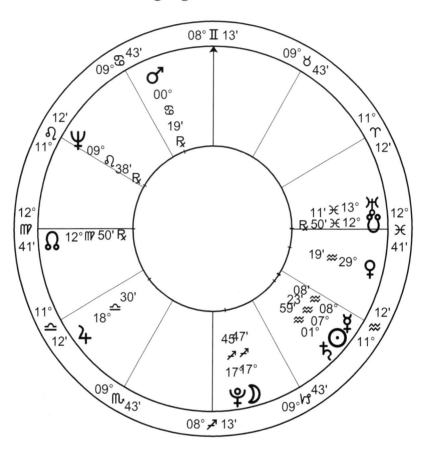

Wolfgang Amadeus Mozart
January 27, 1756, 8:00 p.m., Salzburg, Austria
Rodden Rating: AA

We can see the potential for prior-life recall, as well as innate talent, indicated in Mozart's chart. Mozart's Uranus in Pisces is closely
conjunct the south node of the Moon in Pisces, speaking of bringing
in a deep memory (Uranus) from the past (south node of the Moon).
That this then squares the Moon reveals the precocity of the young
Mozart (Moon-Uranus), who was famously able to channel his gifts

into marvelous playing and even detailed composition from a young age. Pluto conjunct the Moon reveals the emotional and psychological intensity of the precocity: literally the deep self (Pluto) is almost exactly conjunct the ego or conditioned self (Moon), and we see that a resulting power from the Soul infuses the creative expression of the self.

Mozart's Moon is separating from Pluto. This is a new phase conjunction that is analogous to an Aries type conjunction. The expression of his talent, the power of his connection, is completely instinctual and effortless. This is encapsulated beautifully—whether it actually happened or not—in the film *Amadeus* when Salieri, the court composer, brings in a new piece of music to the Duke. After hearing it only once, Mozart starts spontaneously improvising around it. His talent was effortless. Mozart was able to jam on the bedrock of the classical foundation like the best jazz musician.

Tony Cicoria's experience was akin to a spiritual conversion. That such a conversion was accompanied by a tangible expression of a new perspective and talent is extra useful in a culture such as ours, which tends to only focus on the form. Cicoria could suddenly play music in a way he could not before. He went on to write and perform his own compositions. Yet even if he had not, his inner conversion experience would have still been valid. He had what could be likened to a peak experience that utterly changed his orientation to reality and the meaning of life. The lightning bolt that hit him, and crucially, the near-death experience he had following this, changed his entire orientation to reality. I would say, based on personal and clinical experience, that any genuine experience of full consciousness not attached to the body is completely revelatory as to the nature of reality, and in this case, to the experience in consciousness of the archetype of Uranus.

The Consciousness of Uranus

If we hold that all of us have access to far memory, that we can remember everything and anything, and that Uranus points to that process, we can radically reframe Tony Cicoria's experience. Rather than seeing his out-of-body experience as unusual, or even a seemingly nonlocal accessing of some hitherto unforeseen musical gifts, we can deduce instead that it is actually unusual that we *only* see the limited amount of information that we do in our day-to-day lives. That we manage to reduce the vast ocean of data within which our consciousness swims to various simple parameters for daily living is a sign of the success of the Saturn function (block, limitation) as it then operates throughout the inner planets, and in particular through the Moon. The Moon is the lens through which we identify space/time reality in all its specificity. Yet, when we are shocked or somehow transported into Uranian consciousness, we can escape that filter and return to a more widescreen experience of reality.

Normal waking consciousness filters reality into habit-formed patterns of what is perceived to be useful or functional. We see a door handle as something to turn to open the door. Once we have opened that door several times a day over multiple days and weeks, we barely even see the door handle anymore. Notwithstanding, were we to stop and notice the dull gleam of the porcelain refract the tilted image of the room back at us, we might experience its shape with its strange similarity to a light bulb's as something of aesthetic interest all on its own. People on psychedelics stop and stare at a door handle, a carpet pattern or set of curtains as if they were great works of art. When the filters are removed or reset to fundamentally different parameters, an object as ordinary as a door handle can shine forth with inherent luminosity. As William Blake wrote, "Heaven in a wild flower; Eternity in an hour."

But even within the psychedelic experience there is a limitation: witness the paltry results of people on psychedelic drugs who attempt to record their insights while still high. Yet, insight arises when you realize that it is the vivid flooding of consciousness, filters removed, that provides the absorption of the psychedelic experience.

In a more stable sense, even though it is quite alien to our way of life, the isolated Tibetan hermit alone in a cave in retreat for three years may indeed be considerably more absorbed than we are in our modern lives—with all our multimedia momentum, surfing the web on our smart phones as we commute.

It is this fullness of reality that may paradoxically find us more absorbed, with less going on, than we were with all the stimulation of our more ordinary waking conscious. We can name this distinction as being between the linear and nonlinear parts of the mind. Mercury represents the linear aspect of the mind, and Uranus, its nonlinear aspect. The Uranus opposition then could be likened to a challenge: *to have more in Mind*.

The Butterfly Effect

The Greek word "*psyche*," the root of the word "psychology," comes from a word meaning butterfly. From our caterpillar nature we are surprised at times by a winged vast potential that seems to burst through us. Psychology is the merging of two words: *psyche* (soul, butterfly) and *logos* (word, thought). Psychology can be taken literally to mean "butterfly words." The transformational power of speech, of finding and saying the unsayable, the unspeakable being spoken is the key to talk therapy. Someone silenced for years in her family, or within the confines of an abusive relationship, can find powerful liberation by confiding in a kind, trusted other the shameful secrets whose toxic burden has drained her for so long.

When the caterpillar goes into the structure (Saturn) of the chrysalis to transform, it actually enters a completely liquid state. During this state, certain cells seem to arise from nowhere and as such have been termed *imaginal cells*. These previously nonexistent cells begin to seed DNA and RNA coding into the primordial soup that the caterpillar has regressed into within the safety of its chrysalis. From these new codes, the butterfly is able to grow.

The symbolism is clear—something completely new arises from a state of having not been there (or held in some kind of potential that has not been observed or previously understood) and recreates the new order of being. Carl Jung echoed this potential in his Uranus opposition, finding new creative forms from within a state of breakdown, with his safe haven Bollingen acting as the chrysalis. Tony Cicoria, too, had *imaginal cells* trigger a completely new level of experience with the hearing, playing and composing of music. The Uranus opposition presents one with the opportunity to experience a transformation for which there was no previous knowledge or preparation. It is as if life itself seeks out a wholly new aspect of the person's being and sets the stage for its possible emergence.

Entelechy

Don't you know yet? Fling the emptiness out of your arms into the spaces we breathe; perhaps the birds will feel the expanded air with more passionate flying.

Yes—the springtime's needed you. Often a star was waiting for you to notice it. A wave rolled toward you out of the distant past, or as you walked under an open window, a violin yielded itself to your hearing. All this was mission. But could you accomplish it?

-Rilke's first *Duino Elegy*, Stephen Mitchell translation

Rilke reminds us here that life wants to be lived by us—it actually desires our participation. This is a reference to a profound encounter in the depths of one's being with the very evolutionary nature of the life force that wants to be seen, to be felt. Aristotle coined the term *entelechy* for this movement. He defines motion as the actuality (*entelecheia*) of "potentiality as such." So the motion of life is towards actualizing inherent potential wherever conditions are favorable, wherever the ground is ripe.

This idea is akin in scientific terms to David Bohm's revolutionary concept of an *implicate order* which is enfolded within the *explicate order*, or the form of the universe; when conditions are right, what is enfolded within the physical as potential unfolds as the actual.

In poetry, this is like Rumi's idea expressed in *Desire and the Importance of Failing*:

In fact, all the particles of the world
Are in love and looking for lovers ...

We tremble like iron filings
Welcoming the magnet."

From these perspectives, there is a creative movement within life itself to seek a response. Earlier in Rumi's poem, just as the man cries out for water, the water cries out to be drunk. Life wishes for us to live it. The Uranus opposition is the archetypal, universal transit, the importance of which lies in the growing impulse within the individual—and in life responding to the individual—for more life to be lived. The energy fields of people at this time are being naturally stepped up. Luckily, most of us won't endure an actual lightning bolt, but there will be a quickening.

Your Uranus opposition *mission*—should you chose to accept it—is to feel the expanded air with more passionate flying, to open to more of the source of being and encounter that which enlivens and revivifies as a result.

The Informed Universe

Ervin Laszlo, in his book *Science and the Akashic Field*, presents a remarkable synthesis of modern physics from over forty years of research in the field. He draws awareness to the quantum vacuum, a pleroma, from which all forms arise and receive coherence. This non-material field that underlies all of the metaverse (this universe and all other universes) communicates through torsion waves that operate at billions of times the speed of light. Lest this field, the Zero Point Field, be thought of as too subtle, Laszlo points out its relevance for maintaining planetary motion in our solar system:

"Even the stability of our planet in its orbit around the Sun derives from vacuum-energy inputs. As Earth pursues its orbital path, it loses momentum; given a constant loss of momentum, the gravitational field of the Sun – in the absence of energy from the Zero Point Field – would overcome the centrifugal force that pushes Earth around its orbit and Earth would spiral into the Sun. This means that in addition to inertia, gravity, and mass, the very stability of both atoms and solar systems is due to interaction with the zero-point field of the vacuum." [19]

The crucial point for our analysis is the way that this field carries information of "mind-boggling coherence." Laslo writes: "All that happens in one place happens also in other places; all that happened at one time happens at all times after that. Nothing is 'local', limited to where and when it is happening. All things are global, indeed cosmic, *for the memory of all things extends to all places and all times.* This is the concept of the informed universe ..." [20]

The correspondence to the principle we are exploring is that of the nonlocal aspects of memory. The universe itself experiences a deep memory to which all things are copresent, just as we experience an aspect of our consciousness (Uranus) that can access memory from others times and places. This is the macro- and microcosmic worlds in alignment: As Above, So Below. The Uranus function is to remember *more* of life than the personal planets, surrounded by the ring-pass-not of Saturn, conventionally allow. The zero-point field that carries critical information for the right functioning of the solar system also carries information that can help heal individuals. This field is nonmaterial but underpins all material expression.

In physics, this correlates with the *knowing field*: a transpersonal field of resonance which carries information as to the nature of the human interactions within it. In the therapeutic encounter, one can consciously interact with the field for greater access to this information. Further, the field can increase the power of the *holding environment*, which supports people as they risk change and growth.

This field has a relationship to the archetype of Aquarius, Uranus and the 11th house through the archetype's capacity to access far or deep memory. Such memories may include visions from early childhood, intrauterine states and prior lives. These memories may also include certain past gifts or hitherto unacknowledged capacities within the self. They may touch the ordinary individual and produce something extraordinary. The Uranus opposition is the archetypal transit of the potential of our individual consciousness to *take on a greater memory of its capacity* and even, therefore, to fulfill a role of larger significance within the collective.

The Transformation of the Every Day

On December 1, 1955, in Montgomery, Alabama, having spent a long day bent over an ironing board in a basement tailor shop, a quiet dignified woman is too tired to remember getting on the bus. This is a day like any other: long hours of work, the tired journey back to a modest home. Yet, when moments later, the 42-year-old is asked to leave her seat to make room for a white person who joined at a following stop she says, "No." When the driver threatens to have her arrested she will only say, "You may do that." When a police officer arrives she inquires, "Why do you all push us around?" And he replies that he does not know but that she will have to leave the bus stating, "The law is the law."

Even though "the law is the law," there are times when that law is not worth following. This normally reserved woman had had enough. She did not realize until too late that the bus she had stepped on was driven by the same driver who, 12 years before (at her Saturn Return), had asked her to leave the bus because there were no "colored" seats left. At that time, her response of quiet rebellion was to sit on a white person's seat to tie her shoelaces before leaving the bus, vowing that she would never travel on that man's bus again. But she was too tired that fateful December day years later to remember to look out for him when she boarded.

Rosa Parks

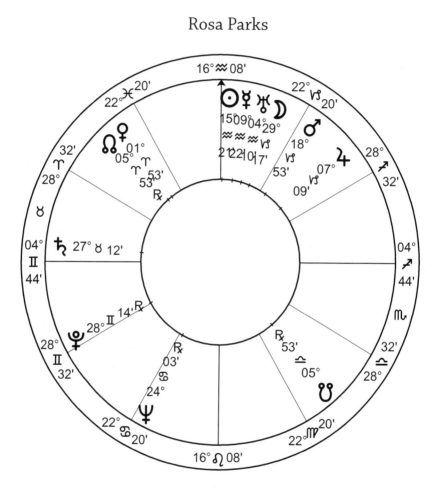

Rosa Parks
February 4, 1913, 12:00 p.m. (no birth time), Tuskegee, AL, USA
Rodden Rating: C

Rosa Parks' brother served his country with honors in the Second World War, saving black and white alike. Upon his return, he was spat upon by his white peers. A culmination of events came together into one tired decision for Rosa to board the bus that fateful day, where she vowed she would never be demeaned again.

That night, 5,000 people gathered to support Park's lonely act of courage, and Martin Luther King, Jr., addressed the crowd. His extraversion and charisma combined with her introversion and quiet strength— this winning combination set alight fires of protest across the southern United States. That very night, activists voted to boycott city buses to honor Rosa Parks and protest her imprisonment. The boycott lasted 381 days. People carpooled; some walked miles to work. An unjust society and wearisome circumstances called for change, and Parks' resolute stand sparked a revolt. Her own life and the collective life of the American people changed in that very moment.

In Park's chart, we find Uranus in early Aquarius widely conjunct Mercury, which is conjunct the Sun—forming a "rolling conjunction." This is where the proximity (here by sign) links the more distant Uranus into influence with the Sun through its relationship with Mercury. Her birth time is unknown, so we don't know the exact position of the Moon or Ascendant. The moon is most likely in Capricorn, but it may have moved into Aquarius already and could easily be within orb of Uranus, adding to the Aquarian mix of planets.

The revolutionary quality of the Sun-Mercury in Aquarius embodies the power of Uranus, the modern ruler of Aquarius. We find an individual who did not consider herself a rebel in an outward way. But when push came to shove, she did stand up to authority, or rather sat down! In a way it is this power that the quiet rebel has that allows the larger significance of her gesture to reverberate through her community. Those close to her likely knew that she would not have acted trivially or without provocation. This makes me think that the Moon is actually in late Capricorn—a serious self-image, a responsible person—and yet widely conjunct Uranus out of sign suggesting that when she does act, she is a conduit for the future.

Midlife Individuation

There is no one recipe for a successful midlife transition. In the following passage, Levinson identifies several approaches to which various researchers have given weight:

> "What are the most significant changes to be made in midlife individuation? Most investigators emphasize a single facet of the process. Erikson gives primary emphasis to Generativity vs. Stagnation as a stage of ego development in the middle years. According to Jaques, the central issue at midlife is coming to terms with one's own mortality; a man must learn now, more deeply than was possible before, that his own death is inevitable and that he and others are capable of great destructiveness. In her biographical study of Goya, Martha Wolfenstein proposes that the reworking of destructiveness was the basic process in his transformation, during his forties, from an excellent court painter to an artist able to deal with the universals of a human tragedy. Bernice Neugarten identifies the basic midlife change as a growing 'interiority': turning inwards to the self, decreasing the emphasis on assertiveness and mastery of the environment, enjoying the process of living more than the attainment of specific goals." [21]

Cicoria and Jung have given us examples of the tendency to turn within and, in that process, to discover new inner resources. This is surely a process that we could trace back throughout history. But in our modern age, our increased life spans have given us more time to engage in the process of individuation. Although there have been isolated instances of people living what would today be considered long lives, it was only in the 19th century that the average life span increased enough to provide one the opportunity to consistently explore the developmental potential of the Uranus cycle. [22]

There is cosmic timing at work with the discovery of the outer planets and our lengthened life spans. Even if ancient astrologers had knowledge of the outer planets, they wouldn't have been able to see them fully at work, as most people simply didn't live long enough. Today, most of us do.

Sigmund Freud

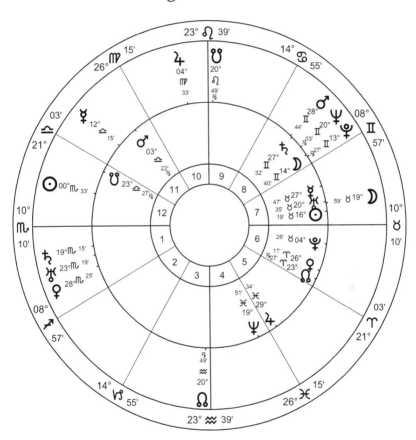

Sigmund Freud Bi-wheel
Inner: May 6, 1856. 6:30 p.m., Freiberg, Germany
Outer: October 23, 1896. 12:00 p.m. (no exact time), Vienna, Austria

Let's take a look at Freud's midlife transition. As the 20th century began, Freud published *The Interpretation of Dreams* in a limited edition of 600 books, for which he was paid the handsome sum of $209. Although the book's sales were underwhelming at the time, its publishing marked the start of the Depth Psychology movement.

We can trace the origins of this seminal work to the death of Freud's father, on October 23, 1896, an event that marked a shift his work. Throughout his 30s, in the period of development following the first Saturn Return, he spent much of his time developing his theories. This period was crucial and prepared him for the next step, the promise of which was revealed at his Uranus opposition, marked by the passing of his father. Instead of just thinking about his theories, he began to apply them and conducted the first known psychoanalytical analysis. He was both analyst and patient. We could make a joke about his Gemini Moon here! But the endeavor was utterly serious.

In the bi-wheel image above, we see Freud's natal chart as the inner wheel and the day of his father's passing as the outer wheel, at the time of his Uranus opposition.

Paul Vitz comments on the importance of this timing in Freud's development:

> "At the end of this decade of change from the university-science-biology world into his specialization in psychopathology, Freud was to start on his self-analysis, which took place roughly from 1896 to 1899. The death of Freud's father on October 23, 1896, was a most important event that apparently accelerated this analysis, for (among other things), it brought back the meaning of his father to him as a child. It also freed Freud to face his own attitudes toward his father in a way that would not have been possible if Jakob had still been living." [23]

We can draw a general observation here that an absent or overly tyrannical Saturn principle (sometimes literally enacted through the father) is the very thing that leads people into their individuation process (Uranus). In this manner, a Saturn retrograde, for example, which so often refers to an absent father or one who is aggressive and antagonistic, results in the individual having to dig deep within (retrograde motion) to find his inner authority (Saturn). This process naturally facilitates finding one's own way (Uranus).

Because it is so delicate a subject, it is a little-shared fact that alongside the feelings that arise with the loss of a parent or beloved figure, many consequently experience an unfolding of their own potential. The death of the parent may cause a shift away from identifying with the role of child within the family system to one of greater autonomy. Or it could be that such loss precipitates an inner search to replace what the parent figure represented in the unconscious. In so doing, the individual makes what was previously unconscious, more conscious. Jung saw this process as central to the task of individuation.

In others, the loss can constellate a deep depression if they resist this process—and its promise of greater autonomy—for fear of being overwhelmed by psychic chaos or because of an inner emptiness.

A paradox here is that the loss of a parent who was abusive, controlling, cold or fundamentally disappointing can be as problematic, or even more troubling, than the loss of a beloved figure. One might expect that the loss of an abusive figure would only be liberating. And it can be, when there is conscious work to support that. But all too often, the individual who struggled with the parent gains the possibility of freedom from the dysfunction, but is trapped by the archaic structures within the psyche that were *programmed by* that same dysfunction. Paradoxically, the seeming freedom can exacerbate one's awareness of how much past pain persists within; consequently, it can actually highlight the individual's involvement in perpetuating the dysfunction. The parent who was to blame may have passed, but the negative energy that still needs to blame someone lives on. And the only one left to blame is the self.

The Saturn Opposition with the Uranus Opposition

The Uranus opposition takes place around the same time as the second Saturn opposition. The Saturn and Uranus cycles intersect, just as they did when the individual was 21 years old. Therefore, right at this great moment of potential encapsulated within the metaphorical lightning strike of the Uranus cycle, Saturn calls on the individual to make or experience structural changes in the nature of her personal power and her relationship to others (opposition—the Libran aspect). When Tony Cicoria went through his amazing transformation, committing all he could to the spirit of music becoming alive within him, he also experienced sadness that his wife was unable to understand or relate to what was happening. This led to their divorce. His changes proved too much for her to grow with him.

For many people at the Uranus opposition, the Saturn opposition will mark the loss of a parent. While our increasing longevity means that this is changing somewhat, many will have lost a parent, if not both, by the Uranus opposition. For those who lose a parent during this transit, the individuation challenge will be in changing their relationship to their family of origin. Saturn symbolizes grief, and the Uranus opposition can involve a letting go of the past. Or, like Cicoria, we may be called on to surrender a partnership that isn't able to weather our profound transformation.

For others, the Uranus opposition will correspond to the dual task of following a new inspiration while taking on increased career commitments. That the Saturn opposition coincides so perfectly with the Uranus opposition speaks profoundly of the need to embody whatever creative or inspirational potential the lightning unleashes, through discipline and hard work, if its impact is to be sustained. Freud was all too aware of this, and he dedicated himself to his new path completely, without any guarantees that what he was doing would achieve the respect, recognition or fame that he would have liked.

Freud was always ambitious. Explicitly, he wanted to be renowned for something and had the support of his mother in this. But—unlike some with this kind of complex—Freud was prepared to put in decades of study and work to achieve his goal. We are often called on at this time to respond to the lightning strike with Saturnine dedication.

So Freud, free of the burden of his father's judgments about his chosen path, began to explore his psyche through his dreams, free associations and memories in the most detailed excavation of his subconscious motivations that he could manage. Remarkably, he did this on his own—though he did have a witness via a written correspondence with Wilhelm Fleiss. [24] While Freud greatly admired him, Fleiss was nowhere near Freud's intellectual equal. Moreover, he lived many miles away and theirs was only an epistolary connection. While his solo quest was bound to saturate his theoretical steps in his own bias, we have to admit that Freud had guts!

We can see from the bi-wheel that Freud's Uranus opposition had Uranus in Scorpio in the 1st house. So the very inspiration he was having was activating depth understanding (Scorpio) of his own instinctual (1st house) and sexual nature (Scorpio). He found the inspirational power of Uranus through his isolation and strength of will (transiting Uranus in the 1st house). That Freud had the kind of inner strength (Sun) and mental acuity (Mercury) to follow this process is indicated by his natal conjunction of Sun and Mercury with Uranus in Taurus. The Mercury-Uranus conjunction seems particularly apt as it links the deep memory (Uranus) with the linear mind and short-term memory (Mercury). Here we see Freud's capacity, under the stimulus of the Uranus opposition, to actually carry out a sustained investigation of his history—the past being mentally much more accessible to him than for the average person.

It would imbalance the scope of the current work to analyze Freudian theory and the way it evolved from this analysis. I have commented elsewhere (see my *Astrology and Soul Psychology* workshop) on the prior-life trauma signatures in his chart and what they, in part, refer to. What I intended to show here is the impact of the

Uranus opposition in releasing Freud's latent potential that—while transiting Saturn moved to oppose his natal Saturn in the three years following his father's death— prompted him to write his first major work. The Uranus opposition transit triggered his natal capacity for mental exploration of the unconscious mind (Mercury-Uranus), and the Saturn opposition transit represented the sheer dedication required to write for what was, at the time, very little reward.

The Love of Truth

This last point is a crucial one in the individuation challenge of the Uranus opposition. None of the subjects in the examples I have presented had a guaranteed happy ending. Often, they received no validating applause for their undertaking. That was not the point. Rosa Parks did not have the basic security of knowing she would survive the experience. Jung did not know if he would psychically survive. And Freud took a fairly major risk on that front himself; within polite Viennese society, no one would have known what was wrong with him had he undergone a breakdown during his inner exploratory process. Tony Cicoria had already survived a near-death experience but could not have known the toll it would ultimately take on his personal life.

A common thread in each of these examples is the dedication and commitment to one's unfolding individuation in the face of real obstacles and dissension—and a love of truth. Although Cicoria cared for his wife, his love of the music proved greater. Parks relied on her convictions in the face of life-diminishing legal and social blockages. Jung had to wrestle with his growing awareness that it was wrong for a brilliant young psychiatrist to continue to pretend that his mentor's restrictive views were his. These truths were all hard won. And perhaps miraculously, acted upon.

Despite how we might think of him given his preoccupation with sexuality, Freud was actually a conservative man (multiple planets in Taurus) and non-impulsive (Mars retrograde). He did not take the exploration of his personal demons lightly. And while his process was flawed, his courage and pioneering effort of will led to ground-breaking work that has had a lasting impact. In contrast with the faithful husband who waited patiently to marry his wife until he had satisfied her family that he could support her, Freud was a radical internal voyager because he believed in the truth of what he was doing. If he was dogmatic in the end, that was only because he cared so much about it that he wanted to see his vision carried out according to his ideal.

The guiding principle of the Uranus opposition applies to everyone. At midlife, the life energy quickens in the body and psyche and can be harnessed for good or for ill, depending on the evolutionary state and moral development of the Soul involved. This natural life energy is available to all of us. Some grasp the possibility and live brightly. Others, beset by fear and desiring to play safe, anxiously constrict around it, squeezing out all life.

The Uranus opposition presents each of us with this potential quickening of our life energy. What each individual makes of that opportunity is in part revealed in the potential described by the natal chart. But even more than that, the seed of potential is contained within one's consciousness and core orientation to life. Those who are willing, who can commit to the constructive possibility even amid hardship, experience the possibility for a super-charged effort into the new. Those who are stuck in a rut face a more challenging experience. Yet, even that holds promise, because it increases, through shock or struggle, the chance for the person to rise to something larger inside. In this manner, the Uranus opposition represents that most potentially expansive and radical of all life transits.

7

Astrology and Soul Psychology

As mentioned in the previous chapter, the word "psyche" has its origins in the Greek word for butterfly, and as mythologist Michael Meade points out, the word "psychology" is parallel to the phrase "butterfly thinking." This poetic etymological dimension breathes new life into a word that has come to have such academic and sterile connotations.

Our experience of clinical psychology has been skewed through the lens of pathology to our detriment. When we consider human development only from the viewpoint of *what has gone wrong*, we fundamentally limit that analysis and its usefulness both for individuals and for the collective.

James Hillman takes this insight further in his book *Suicide and the Soul* by showing how the shadow of the medical model has darkened psychology and reduced its capacity to handle meaning. If we take Freud at his most literal and mechanical, the psyche is merely a series of interlocking drives and mechanisms that automatically respond to certain internal and external pressures.

If we make the mistake of formulating a psychological astrology on the mechanistic worldview, we limit our options for transformation. Our lives are seen as a miniature version of a clockwork universe in which an impact event leads to a predictable series of individual responses. Our astrology becomes fatalistic and deterministic, limiting our sense of personal choice and free will.

By showing that Earth revolved around the Sun, the Copernican revolution brought a revelation that shattered the medieval mind-set, which had previously viewed heaven as a literal realm above us in the night sky. Instead of Earth being at the center, it became "just" another moving piece in a dance of objects around the sun.

Freud's contribution to the Copernican event is that his psychology, first emerging at the very turn of the 20th century, decentered the conception of the self. Instead of one's identity (Sun) being at the center of one's life (solar system), identity is revealed to arise out of a whole series of systems that are not only beyond the individual's control but quite possibly beyond his comprehension.

In *Cosmos and Psyche*, Richard Tarnas shows how Freud's thinking distorted the medieval understanding of the cosmos:

> *"For all the exalted numinosity of the Copernican birth, the new universe that eventually emerged into the light of common day was a spiritually empty vastness, impersonal, neutral, indifferent to human concerns, governed by random processes devoid of purpose or meaning... From seventeenth-century rationalism and empiricism to twentieth-century existentialism and astrophysics, human consciousness has found itself progressively emancipated and also progressively relativized, unrooted, inwardly isolated from the spiritually opaque world it seeks to comprehend. The soul knows no home in the modern cosmos."* [1]

In the late 19th century, huge public debates raged as various religious scholars attempted to dispute Darwin's incontrovertible evidence that the Earth was not actually six thousand years old, as calculated by the age of the patriarchs in the Old Testament. This debate still goes on in some quarters! So, we can imagine the intellectual turmoil that must have been common at the end of the 19th century as the edifice of Christian scholarship was submitted to such an acute deconstruction.

All progressive thinkers at this time were keen to throw in their lot with the victorious impetus of science and the breakthrough of rational thought from the confines of doctrinal enslavement. This is the milieu from which the pioneering work of depth psychology emerged and from which later figures such as Progoff and Hillman, among many others, have attempted to free psychology.

The Role of Astrology in Bringing Soul to Psychology

This book is allied with the greater cultural project of returning soul to psychology. When used in conjunction with astrology, depth psychology is a radical tool for insight and transformation, as evidenced both in my own life and in the lives of many of my clients and students. To this end I have spent considerable time researching the origins of psychology, the life and work of its founding fathers, as well as exploring the working method of a transformational astrology with many hundreds of students and clients. Not only does astrology benefit from this powerful re-imagining of psychology and its soul potential, astrology also plays a crucial part in the very formulation of such a return to soul within psychology.

Astrology Informs the Work of Jung and Assagioli

Both Jung and Assagioli studied with Freud at the peak of his powers and subsequently went on to develop their own visions of psychological practice.

As a person, Freud was considerably more generous and involved than his neutral scientific approach would indicate. He lent clients money, went out of his way to help those who were isolated or new in town by bringing them into his home and setting them up with social contacts. However, as a theoretician, Freud was obsessive in his insistence on the sexual component as central to his theories. He believed this to be a scientific given and a proven fact. And that became the foundation of his work. Ironically, this premise to which he clung so tightly is now largely discredited.

Still, at the time, the belief that the unconscious was the repository of unresolved sexual agitations from early life became the public motto of psychoanalysis and the dominant orthodoxy of the first half of the 20ᵗʰ century. For a psychoanalyst to stand against this view, as both Jung and Assagioli did, was to risk professional isolation and ridicule. Although Jung had already established a reputation, he did experience professional conflict through his decision to break with Freud. From the beginning, Assagioli recognized the limits of Psychoanalysis. He distinguished his approach from Freud's when he wrote: "Freud said, 'I am interested only in the basement of the human being.' Psychosynthesis is interested in the whole building."[2]

A little-known fact is that the study and practice of astrology played a critical part in the thinking, and crucially, the consulting practices of both Jung and Assagioli. The import of Jung's astrological studies has emerged in recent years through the work of Maggie Hyde and Richard Tarnas, among others. Astrology was no mere passing interest for Jung. He once wrote to the eminent figure Wolfgang Pauli explaining that he was not able to read the papers that the Nobel laureate physicist had recently sent because he was too busy studying astrology and synchronicity!

In 2012, I was blessed and honored to be allowed access to Assagioli's private archives in Florence for research purposes, along with my friend and colleague Keith Hackwood. While there, I made an astonishing discovery. There, among Assagioli's other papers, I found hundreds of detailed, hand-drawn horoscope charts. What has not been well known—until recently—is that Roberto Assagioli, the Italian doctor and psychoanalyst who founded the *Psychosynthesis* movement, was also an astrologer! And like Jung, he was not just a dilettante or amateur.

It is time consuming to calculate a chart from an ephemeris—something many modern astrologers may not have a real sense of, with the time-saving and more accurate computer programs that now do this work for us. That both men calculated hundreds, if not (in Assagioli's case) thousands of charts by hand, reveals the dedication both men had on a practical level of engagement.

However, to simply appreciate that Jung and Assagioli were serious students of astrology is to underestimate the significance of astrology in their professional lives: *they both used charts with clients.* In fact, while exploring Assagioli's archive, I learned that from the 1930s until the time of his death in 1974, he did not see a client without first drawing up a natal chart.

Furthermore, Assagioli became involved with Dane Rudhyar at a seminal time in the unfoldment of his astrological thinking. As the embodiment of a long epistolary friendship between the two men, Rudhyar went to Florence in 1936. Rudhyar's visit was coincidental with the publication of *The Astrology of Personality: A Reformulation of Astrological Concepts and Ideals, in Terms of Contemporary Psychology and Philosophy,* in which he first outlined his idea that the nodal axis of the Moon was key to evolution. Both Rudhyar and Assagioli were profoundly influenced by theosophy. And during this period, Rudhyar was weaving theosophical ideas with concepts from Indian astrology for the first time and sharing this work with Assagioli.

Rudhyar maintained contact with Assagioli throughout his life and also mentioned Assagioli a number of times in his later work. The longest period they ever spent together in person occurred just after the publication of *The Astrology of Personality* and during the first flowering of Assagioli's Psychosynthesis Institute in Florence. Sadly, this time was cut short, as it attracted the unwelcome attention of Mussolini, who regarded it as a negative pacifist influence. Nonetheless, their shared time held considerable significance for both the evolution of modern astrology and the direction of psychology.

Completely independently of each other, Carl Jung and Roberto Assagioli discovered and cultivated an in-depth relationship with astrology.

Eugen Bleuler, the man who coined the term "schizophrenia," was the director of a clinic in Switzerland called the Burgholzli. Bleuler was a forward-thinking man and one of the very first clinicians to try out Freud's ideas in a clinical setting. Bleuler invited the

brightest and best psychologists from around Europe, and for a period prior to the First World War, Assagioli and Jung found themselves as doctors in the same clinic—this clinic run by a progressive
man experimenting with Freud's ideas, but critically, not identified
with them.

I believe this was a crucial and formative period for both men.
Jung was in his early thirties and already had a reputation, whereas
Assagioli was considerably younger and was a precocious teenage
student who was in correspondence with Freud after studying him
in German. This would have been a powerful period for both men,
observing how theories of the psyche actually play out in individual
lives and supervised by a man who respected Freud, but only as one
voice among many. I believe that during this time both men for-
mulated a clear vision of psychology that was influenced—but not
weighed down—by Freud's doctrine.

Assagioli differentiates from Freud by recognizing the importance of the spiritual. He writes, "We accept the idea that spiritual
drives or spiritual urges are as real, basic and fundamental as sexual
and aggressive drives; they should not be reduced to sublimation or
pathological distortion of the sexual and aggressive components of
the personality - although in many neurotic cases such elements are,
of course, also present." [3]

At the time of their work together, it seems that Jung and Assagioli did not discuss astrology. In fact, at that point, it is likely
that neither man had any real interest in the subject. Later, in the
1930s, their burgeoning friendship was stopped in its tracks during the Eranos conferences, also in Switzerland, as Jung vehemently
rejected the theosophical influence on the conference. He refused
to attend until Alice Bailey and Dr. Assagioli (named as such by
Jung in a heavy-handed missive to the conference organizer) were
removed from the rostrum. Any chance they could get past this impasse was thwarted by the Second World War when Assagioli went
into hiding for years after his family home was sacked and his life
threatened by the Fascists.

Assagioli was always cordial later in life when talking about Jung and even wrote a pamphlet called *Jung and Psychosynthesis* because he felt that their approaches were so complementary. Jung himself was feverishly positive in the early days of their connection, writing to Freud: "I had the feeling that under it all there must be some quite special complex, a universal one having to do with the prospective tendencies in man. If there is a 'psychoanalysis' there must also be a 'psychosynthesis' which creates future events according to the same laws ..."[4]

The context of this letter is rather remarkable and reveals the profound intersection of ideas and potential among the three men at this point. For the above letter was sent after the now famous incident in which Freud and Jung were discussing the nature of occult forces and precognition in Freud's study and a loud retort came from the bookcase. Jung followed this perhaps innocuous event with the statement that he knew that it would happen, and he boldly asserted that it would happen again. Bemused, Freud rejected the notion as absurd, but even so, a few moments later the book case let out another loud noise!

Jung began this letter to Freud in a confessional tone: "When I left Vienna I was afflicted with some *sentiments d'incompletude* because of the last evening I spent with you." Here we can sense Jung struggling to deal with everything that the discussion represented, the key issues of what will break them apart a few years later. His lapse into French strangely both distances himself from it somewhat and, at the same time, emphasizes the issue.

Jung's use of the term psychosynthesis clearly indicates the influence of his colleague Assagioli (the letter is written from the Burgholzi during their time there together). One Jung biographer goes to great lengths to show the source of the term psychosynthesis, citing an obscure passage in Kant's *Critique of Pure Reason* on synthesis that Jung had marked, without making the connection to Assagioli. I'm intending to correct that mistake here. Until now, Assagioli's influence on Jung, proven by his use of this term, has gone unnoticed, along with the melting pot of ideas about psychology that the two men were experimenting with at the time. I hope that my efforts to correct the oversight here begin to filter into public discourse.

In *Memories, Dreams and Reflections,* Jung recounts how Freud was most adamant that together they must represent an unshakeable bulwark of the sexual theory, "against the black tide of mud of occultism." [5] Freud deeply feared that psychoanalysis, already perceived by many as a dangerous fringe subject, would be completely derailed by association with such subjects as parapsychology and occult or subtle forces. But Jung was already open-minded in these areas and became evermore earnest in his studies of them as his life progressed.

It says a lot about astrology's status in our culture that, until now, Jung's and Assagioli's interest in and use of astrology has been largely erased from history by mainstream historians and depth psychology proponents.

Both Assagioli and Jung were professional men of considerable integrity and spiritual power who were aware of the pioneering nature of their own work. Out of a sincere intention to help clients, they both utilized whatever methods they felt were of critical importance to personal growth. After experiencing the remarkable therapeutic power of astrology, neither could withhold it from their clients.

So when I say that the emergence of *soulful psychology* in the 20th century is built upon the foundation of astrology, I mean it quite literally.

A Profound Discovery

In that moment of profound significance in the summer of 2012, my colleague and I were led into the Assagioli archive by one of the many volunteers whose dedicated work has allowed what has remained hidden to finally see the light of day. On the first shelf of the room adjacent to the main study (which had been opened to a group for the very first time) I found a series of boxes marked with the words "Spiritual Astrology in English." Assagioli's writings on astrology include notes on multiple charts from his family members to major artistic, political and religious figures throughout the ages. That my friend and I were there for the first-ever opening of this part of the archive to witness a shelf full of Assagioli's astrological writings has a deep significance for me that is still sinking in.

Just the discovery that Assagioli was an astrologer at all was something of a revelation for me as the synthesis of astrology and psychotherapy has occupied such a central place in my life. Through no fault of my psychosynthesis trainers, my "situation" had been treated as an unusual one with all sorts of supervision implications. Dilemmas raised by my trainers and supervisors at that time remain key points of departure for many of the therapeutic issues I am exploring in the current work; to realize that I was not alone was of great personal significance.

More than this, the very man who created *psychosynthesis* was clearly a committed and professional astrologer! This is both a personal vindication of my path and a profound point about the origin and development of depth psychology. The two forms of depth psychology that really value the spiritual dimension of humanity emerged from two men who considered astrology a highly significant lens through which to explore both the cosmos and the human psyche. And I'll push the edges a little and proclaim them professional astrologers.

Holding Assagioli's detailed notated birth charts in hand, all in delicate ink on thin paper with only the perfect circle of the chart pre-imprinted, was moving. Underneath each of his charts is an assessment of the elemental balance and its hemispheric emphasis. These charts were collected alongside detailed typed essays on a spiritual astrology derived primarily from Alice Bailey's work *Esoteric Astrology*, which I had studied in my mid-twenties prior to training in Psychosynthesis. [6]

Assagioli's delicate fountain pen is inscribed over the thin transparency paper that he used so that he could draw a perfect circle each time for the charts that he calculated. There are whole boxes of files in which the charts of major philosophical, artistic and spiritual figures are studied with copious notes. This helped me realize that Assagioli had astrologically studied many of the figures who formed major sections of his work *Psychosynthesis: A Manual of Principles and Techniques*, meditating on them with the charts as guides.

If I was in danger of missing the significance presented in the Florentine archive, it was brought home to me again when I was teaching a workshop in Portland, Oregon, months later. In a previous reading, a client had recommended the Emmet Fox book *The Sermon on the Mount: The Key to Success in Life* after I had mentioned the Sermon in my workshop. I was in downtown Portland with a friend (who is also a psychotherapist) and we wandered into the huge Powell's bookstore with the loose goal of looking for the book. We were having a quick look at the astrology section, which curiously enough, is adjacent to the Christian book section. And I picked up an anthology in which I had an article when I noticed a nun standing next to me in full robes, hat, wimple and all. I did not think anything of it at first and went to the Christian book section where I found a copy of the Fox book.

My friend and I joined the queue to check out. Then the nun, now standing next to me in line, asked me what book I was getting. "*The Sermon on the Mount* by Emmet Fox," I said. Then I noticed that she was carrying a large tome and asked her what book she was getting. "The Bible, in Italian," she replied. "Oh, you speak Italian?" I inquired. "No," she said, and just before wandering away looked me in the eye and added, "I will just go wherever God sends me."

I was stunned. As much as anything, simply because the conversation had happened at all. I was glad my friend was there to corroborate this striking instance of synchronicity. It is the one and only time in my life that a nun (and one in full regalia) had ever spoken to me in any context whatsoever, never mind simply approaching me out of the blue. Then there is the detail that this had occurred at one of the very few times that the one and only book I was purchasing whose title would have been so perfect to share with a nun. It was only while walking down the street a little later that the significance of the Italian part of the conversation caught up with me.

Only a few weeks before that had I stepped into the archive of Roberto Assagioli and encountered material that—even at the time—had seemed of real significance. In fact, its importance led my friend and me, after hours of exhausting research, to pledge to write a book about this Italian doctor whose private life and study (not least, astrological) seemed to mirror a deep current of somewhat hidden thought and dialogue at the heart of the 20th century.

The significance of the discovery of the central importance of astrology to the thinking of both Roberto Assagioli and Carl Jung was forever underlined for me. So, too, was this message of going wherever the Divine wills one—even if one does not, initially, speak the language!

For Jung and Assagioli, the journey into astrology was mainly a private path into the unknown requiring them to learn a new language. Jung's family connections to psychism had interested him for a long time. His thesis explored such matters. Around the same period as his letter using the term psychosynthesis, Jung wrote to Freud:

"Occultism is another field we shall have to conquer—with the aid of the libido theory, it seems to me. At the moment I am looking into astrology, which seems indispensable for a proper understanding of mythology. There are strange and wondrous things in these lands of darkness . . .

Please don't worry about my wanderings in these infinitudes. I shall return laden with rich booty for our knowledge of the human psyche . . . For a while longer I must intoxicate myself on magic perfumes in order to fathom the secrets that lie hidden in the abysses of the unconscious." [7]

Jung uses a cautious tone here, and at this stage he is very careful to maintain his mentor's core concept.

Assagioli was also primarily isolated in his studies of astrology.

That both these psychologists who would go on to create international movements privately studied astrology in great depth is a matter of considerable consequence and could be regarded as a critical hidden component in the intellectual history of the 20ᵗʰ century. What emerges from this research is the central role that astrology played in the progressive movements of psychology in the 20ᵗʰ century. Coincident with the discovery of Pluto, advances in quantum physics and the splitting of the atom, is an increasing understanding of the unconscious as having a non-linear dimension of depth. Assagioli and Jung, both using astrology, made significant contributions toward this psychological shift. Their influence on Dane Rudhyar helped him become the translator of this depth into modern astrology.

Rudhyar's reference to Hindu occultism reveals both a theosophical influence (which links him to Assagioli) and his exploration of Hindu astrology, particularly in its focus on the nodes of the Moon. It is Rudhyar's synthesizing of these various elements in the context of the arising psychological framework that forms the foundation of modern psychological astrology. In fact, if we follow Rudhyar's Indian and theosophical influences most profoundly, we also find the basis of much of what is central to Evolutionary Astrology, presented as early as 1936 in a section of *Astrology of Personality* called *"Planetary Interweavings"*:

"If we should lie along the nodal axis we would look into the future facing North, and accept the past facing South. The North Node deals, therefore, with the work to be done, the new accomplishment, the new faculty to be developed; and if we are willing to *exert* ourselves in that direction, from it we shall receive power in abundance. The South Node represents the work that has been done, the well-known accomplishment, the routine performance already gone through many times."[8]

That the timing of this publication coincides with Rudhyar's visit to Assagioli reinforces the case for a cross-pollination having occurred between these two great syncretic thinkers. Assagioli introduced Rudhyar to the seeds of a transpersonal psychology almost completely free from the psychoanalytical model, and Rudhyar, through dialogue and looking at many charts together, could have shared his brilliant astrological thinking.

While perusing Assagioli's archives in Florence, I came across more evidence of Rudhyar's influence. In Assagioli's writing, we find two types of astrological thinking. One is derived from the Alice Bailey school of thought. Under the name the *Considerator*, he wrote many articles for esoteric journals in which large sections of the Bailey material is copiously regurgitated, large passages word for word. This is an aspect of his work that developed over time into a series of full Moon rituals and contemplative essays on collective spiritual impulses. At its best, this early writing conveys a sense of initiatory power through the esoteric rulerships and the twelve signs as symbolic of the Herculean journey to self-knowledge.

However, a second astrological voice arises in his writing from the very beginning of Assagioli's astrological studies in the 1930s. It is this astrological identity that I believe was consolidated by his lengthy discussions with Rudhyar. Most of Assagioli's handwritten charts involve hemisphere analysis, elemental balancing in the form of tables he drew below the chart circle, and notes on key historical figures in a psychological style free from the weight of the Bailey material. I believe that this astrological identity is in some crucial way his natural style, since he recorded his own charts in this manner right from the beginning.

There is evidence that during their visits, Rudhyar and Assagioli explored the charts of significant spiritual teachers and political figures and that those discussions formed the basis of many years of further study. This shared exploration informed Assagioli's writing on the major figures which then influenced the development of Psychosynthesis. In turn, their dialogue gave Rudhyar corroboration of his work developing the spiritual potential of astrology.

The precious nature of their meetings is highlighted by the calamitous events unfolding in central Europe at this time. That these conversations took place in Assagioli's family residence in the hills above Florence only a couple of years before this beautiful country house was ransacked and destroyed by Mussolini's Blackshirts adds a fragile quality to this historic meeting of minds. Soon after, Assagioli spent time in prison in solitary confinement and then much of the war on the run, living outdoors in the Italian Alps with a British paratrooper and members of the Italian resistance. The exposure of living rough exacerbated a congenital health condition in his only child, who died young only a few years after the war ended.

Rudhyar's and Assagioli's joint in-depth study of the natal charts of great artists, scientists and spiritual figures set a precedent for Psychosynthesis. This exploration of the great souls of humanity developed into a study of human potential that became the blueprint for *Psychosynthesis*. Assagioli thought of the term "Psychosynthesis" as describing the organic process of how we manifest our true potential. His study of natal charts provided the map for understanding that potential and developing his method. And so it is that astrology shaped the foundational principles of the first spiritual psychology. Just as understanding psychology can enrich astrology, and in particular the transformative power of the natal chart reading, so has psychology itself been shaped by astrology.

The Non-Pathological Vision of the Self

As this exploration of the work of Jung and Assagioli has shown, from early on within the analytic movement, counter to the direction that Freud adhered to, a *soul psychology* was being forged. Assagioli worked on a model of the human psyche that was non-pathological and that accepted the primary reality of the Self as the core potential within the human ego or "I." This is of great importance to the development of a therapeutic astrology.

Assagioli developed his own model of the psyche—the *Egg Diagram*. Both the birth chart and the *Egg Diagram* express a non-pathological model of the human being—one that can express the symbolism of a healthy self just as much as it can symbolize potential damage.

While searching through Assagioli's papers, I came across a photocopied drawing of the human aura from some sort of theosophical text. The aura was shaped like an egg, with various striations and forms within the ovoid shape. The day prior to visiting the archive, I was in the San Marco monastery looking at the frescoes of Fra Angelico—an amazing series of images that were painted into the still-wet plaster of the monk's cells. When the walls are cleaned, the painting shines forth anew, rather than being wiped away, so they still look fresh despite having been painted around 1440.

One of the frescoes in particular, *The Transfiguration,* shows Christ, his full energetic beauty revealed through an aura around him like a golden egg. The disciples below him are dazzled by his light and also have halos—just plain ones. Christ's halo has a red cross within it. The images are coded representations of the state of realization of the master and his disciples. Fra Angelico was painting a kind of spiritual tarot through the seminary so that people could experience the living truth of the revealed teachings.

Contemplating this, I had the intuition that Assagioli, a hermetic philosopher and Renaissance man (living in Florence, the birthplace of the Renaissance), stood where I stood and had seen the symbolism of the egg diagram revealed through the transfiguration (a named initiation within Alice Bailey's teachings). While in Assagioli's archive, I asked the helpful facilitator whether there was anywhere Assagioli especially liked in Florence, specifically "anywhere he might particularly like to sit and contemplate other than his study or garden?" She replied, "By the Frescoes of Fra Angelico in the San Marco."

My intuition had been right, and I had been open to the field from which one of the archetypal sources for the central image of the power of the human psyche had developed. The frescoes, truly remarkable in their power to arrest one and silence the sounds of the city, spiritually inspired Assagioli as he contemplated human potential. The spiritual essence of his work, his involvement in the core group of meditators with Bailey, is something that Assagioli kept quiet to let Psychosynthesis operate for all, even those without such specialized influences. It occurs to me that the "accidental" forced move of the archive, leading to more of it being revealed, is actually part of a need for Psychosynthesis, the original transpersonal psychotherapy, to emerge and engage the world explicitly on that level. I certainly feel that its core concepts can benefit astrologers with a spiritual or psychological awareness within their work.

Assagioli's Egg Diagram is the symbolic shape of the human aura and energy field as realized by the intuition and expressed by the visionary Christian mystic artist Angelico as the halo of the Soul. From that starting point, it becomes an extraordinarily elegant tool for understanding the potential of transpersonal psychotherapy. Transpersonal psychotherapy literally means, *beyond the personal*. This could relate to the collective of humanity; other sentient life; ecology; the spiritual realms; the place between lives (Bardo); other lifetimes; and identification with myths and archetypes. It is the level of psychology in which a karmic or spiritual astrology finds a true meeting place. It is no accident that the forms of psychology that offer sufficient multidimensional perspectives to become useful to astrologers—Jungian analysis and Psychosynthesis—were created by men who were astrologers themselves.

Let's explore Assagioli's *Egg Diagram* in more depth.

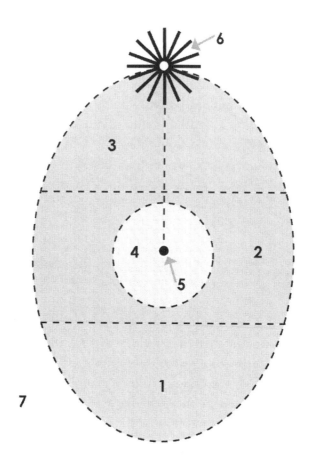

1. The Lower Unconscious
2. The Middle Unconscious
3. The Higher Unconscious
4. The Field of Consciousness
5. The Conscious self, or "I"
6. The Transpersonal Self
7. The Collective Unconscious

Fig. 1: Assagioli's Egg Diagram

Key Observations from the Egg Diagram

1, 2 and 3 - The Layers of the Unconscious

Here, Assagioli illustrates the unconscious as having a layered struc-ture of lower, middle and higher components. This has critical im-plications:

> *We are just as likely to repress or remain unconscious of our creativ-ity, power and inner beauty—in short, our true potential (repressed in the Higher Unconscious)—as we are to repress our shame, anger or inner pain (in the Lower Unconscious).*

This insight has tremendous power and potential benefit for ourselves and for our clients. A hallmark of humanistic and transper-sonal psychologies is that they address the future potential of the in-dividual (higher unconscious) as much as they explore the burden of the past (lower unconscious). This is of central importance when we are envisioning a psychologically mature astrology that can inspire as well as heal.

4 – The Present; the Conscious Field of Awareness

In the Egg Diagram, we see that our conscious awareness in the present moment is in a fluid state (represented by the uneven shape) that in the picture is relatively small compared to the vast nature of the whole field— the scope of unconscious material.

Assagioli saw this awareness as flexible; it could expand to po-tentially include all of the Egg (a state of *satori* or realization of complete awareness). Or it can be very small, completely identified with a minute area of awareness immediately around the ego (the experience of feeling stuck, or victimized by life).

As Eckhart Tolle's seminal work *The Power of Now* makes ex-plicit, the power we have to change our lives, or simply to experience them, to make them our own, comes from the present. Even the past and the future can only be experienced in the present as a memory, or as imagined possibility. The key to manifesting the power of the psyche is *the expansion of present awareness into the whole of the diagram*, the whole of our energy field or Soul.

5 – The Conscious self, or "I"

Sigmund Freud's concept of the ego is actually a product of the imagination of his first English translators. In the original German the ego was "*das ich*," literally, the "I."

The conscious self, or "I," is the nascent sense of identity that emerges during childhood as the infant learns to separate from the primary caregiver. Therefore, its primary nature, the bottom line of its awareness, is to form a separate sense of self.

Assagioli was very clear about the value of the "I." In his therapeutic work, he advocated that the work of synthesis was to begin by strengthening the conscious self, supporting the "I." This applies especially to many types of neurotic suffering or borderline personality issues that cause the individual to become lost in powerlessness, overwhelmed by chaotic unconscious forces or by the contingencies of life. The "I" is, after all, at the center of the diagram.

Yet, for all his supportive insight about the central "I," we see that it is placed within a much larger context of both personal and collective forces. It has a place *within* a much larger field of meaning.

The ego, or *conditioned self*, is symbolized in astrology by the Moon. The *core energy and purpose* of the current life is symbolized by the Sun. The Moon is the core conditioning of the current life, which fundamentally shapes the "I." The Sun is the primary energy utilized by the conditioned self.

The nodes of the Moon link the aspects of the unconscious together. In brief, the south node of the Moon represents the past nature of prior-life selves and natal/early childhood identity, expressed through the forms and identifications of the lower unconscious. The Moon represents the conditioned (through nationality, family, culture and education) self of the current life experienced more consciously as the point of awareness within the middle unconscious. The north node of the Moon represents the future intention to conscious evolution as expressed through the potential contained within the higher unconscious.

In contrast with Freud's ego concept, Assagioli's "I" is a more vital living component of our identity—an aspect of our real self. Freud's ego can be likened more to a mask of the "I" frozen into place through attachment to the personal self, and fear of loss. This marks Assagioli's contribution to a vision of human individuality that is non-pathological and supportive of more enlightened or realized states of consciousness through its capacity to be open to the energy of the Self.

6 – The Higher, or Deep, Self

At the crown of the Egg Diagram is the Higher Self. It is the symbol of the transpersonal center. Assagioli envisioned two primary forms of Psychosynthesis: personal and transpersonal.

Personal Psychosynthesis involves integrating the "I" with various sub-personalities—various parts of the personal self that may be occupying different strata of the unconscious. So personal Psychosynthesis involves experiencing the "I" as a conscious center of the three layers of the unconscious and feeling the possibility of the volition of the personal will, through the "I," to express creativity and service through self-expression. This would be to realize the "I" as a living personal essence, relatively free of identification with the ego in a Freudian sense.

Transpersonal Psychosynthesis involves the progressive realization that the "I" is actually a manifestation of the Self. This is symbolized by the line arising from the "I" to the Self or down from the Self to the "I." It is critical to understand that the energy here moves both ways. The personal self aspires to the truth of the Self. But actually, as one progresses on this path of understanding, one begins to experience more of the grace—that the Self is reaching down to the

"I." This is how Assagioli elegantly symbolized the spiritual experience of Self-realization.

Transpersonal Psychosynthesis, then, involves a contact with a nonlinear dimension of experience, corresponding to love in an impersonal sense, light (flooding the energy field or aura) and wisdom through that light permeating the different strata of the unconscious (making them conscious) and illuminating the real nature of the "I" as the Self. Here, as with the *Heart Sutra* in Buddhism, or the idea of the resurrection in Christianity, or the Atman of the Vedas, the very nature of the personal self is ultimately found to be opaque. The world of suffering, desire and attachment is actually the awakened world through the liberation of the self from those desires and attachments. Instead, the personal self, or "I," becomes only experienced within the light of the truth of the Self: an awakened awareness where, in its full form, the personal remains as a style, a gesture, rather than as a substantial entity.

Here we see the explicit spiritual realization that is inherent and fundamental to the insights of Psychosynthesis. This is the essence of Assagioli's teachings. His approach can be so useful when allied to a *Transformational* Astrology. This is the term that I find myself using more and more to express a vision of astrology that is the fusion of a democratic spiritual reality (for all) alongside a soul psychology. In essence, it is an expansion of the vision Rudhyar expressed through evolutionary astrology as it has been mediated by my work as a Psychosynthesis Therapist through a *Therapeutic Astrology*.

That explicit recognition of the power of psyche and the truth of Self-realization, alongside the elegance and sheer flexibility of the model, is what makes it so full of potential. For example, that flexibility can be found through the insight that the Self in the Egg Diagram is co-present in potential in the whole field, rather than just the top. If you look at the Egg Diagram and imagine that the star at the top (symbolic of the Self) is actually available in potential at every point in the Egg, we see that *real presence is everywhere*. The Self is radically present in every aspect of consciousness as simply the undifferentiated presence that lies behind all forms of consciousness.

I often use the term "deep self" instead of higher self to illustrate that this level of awareness is nonhierarchical. It is not a journey upwards per se—rather, a journey into the origins of awareness. Of course, consciousness enters the nonlinear and crosses the subject/object division at the point of the Self. In non-dual awareness, such ideas of higher or deeper self are merely poetic allusions to what is an indescribable experience within consciousness.

The Higher or Deep Self is represented emotionally and psychologically by Pluto—and in its mental aspect, as higher mind, by Uranus in the natal chart. Understanding the natal Pluto elucidates critical information regarding the core evolutionary intentions of the deep self, as underlying those of the conscious evolution (Moon and its nodal axis). This is the deep feeling of Soul (Pluto) as opposed to the feelings of the personality (the Moon, or "I").

7 – The Collective Unconscious

Note that all the lines in the Egg Diagram are dotted. This is key, for it indicates that all the boundaries within the energy field, while symbolically representative and therefore valuable, are ultimately permeable. They permit the exchange of energy and awareness between different states of consciousness.

The boundaries between different parts of the self, some seemingly conscious, others apparently unconscious, are permeable. What is now unconscious *could* become conscious. What is now conscious could yet slip into unconscious. This is a dynamic model of psyche, fluid and perpetually capable of evolution.

Just as the boundaries between different parts of the self (intra-psychic) are permeable, so are the boundaries between the self and others, the self and the world (inter-psychic). The individual energy field participates in the infinite field of consciousness which contains all of life. So the individual participates in the *knowing field* through the membrane of these permeable boundaries. Much as many amphibians, such as frogs, breathe through their skin (explaining why they are such sensitive indicators of airborne pollutants as their numbers are almost instantaneously impacted), so the individual psyche breathes through the collective field.

Jung saw the collective unconscious as the repository of the archetypes—the psychic realm where humans on both an individual and collective level find their fit amongst the many core templates of human experience. This overtly becomes a way of understanding astrological influence through the archetypes of the zodiac.

Assagioli's viewpoint is even more open. The *whole boundary* of the personal field is open to the transpersonal. We receive energy from the collective field, just as we emit ourselves in our true nature into that collective field.

We realize, then, that we are life, living itself in and through us. If the very nature of the personal field is permeable within the collective, then every time I suffer, or give in to my self-pity and my sense of victimization and powerlessness, so do I influence all around me, however subtly, through the permeable membrane of my psyche, my aura.

In the same vein, if I make a breakthrough and my energy is buoyed with the sheer magnetism of my dedication and commitment to self and other to serve—so the world responds to this act through the opening of my psyche to the world around me. The question of the meaning of an individual life is embodied in that recognition alone: I transform, the world around me is transformed (as I am part of the world around me). There is no separation.

The key symbol for this collective aspect of consciousness in astrology is Neptune—from this ultimate perspective of no separation, non-duality. In this space, "when two or more are gathered" becomes an invitation for the shared reality of spirit.

From the supplement to *A Course in Miracles*: "Who, then, is the therapist, and who is the patient? In the end, everyone is both. He who needs healing must heal. Physician, heal thyself. Each patient who comes to therapist offers him a chance to heal himself. He is therefore his therapist. And every therapist must learn to heal from each patient who comes to him. He thus becomes his patient. God does not know of separation ... " [9]

In this quote, we could substitute the word astrologer for that of therapist, and client for patient. From the perspective of Neptune as spirit or the *knowing field,* any idea of the empowered other giving wisdom or love is simply an expression of what another really *is.* So, all we can give to another is what he already is in truth.

More radically, for those uncomfortable with the language of *A Course in Miracles,* we can substitute the word "God" for the infinite field of reality. For by its nature, the infinite field knows of no separation between each life. The ultimate nature of the field is non-dual. We can see, then, that any healing or transformation that occurs through astrology or therapy is not caused by the therapist or astrologer, but rather is an expression of the unity of life itself.

Saying, Discovering, Revealing

A core dilemma I faced as both a psychotherapist and an astrologer—one that first emerged during my Psychosynthesis training—concerned two differing ideas regarding the ideal way to proceed within these distinct fields. In psychotherapy, the client ideally begins to discover her own truth and experience the power of insight leading her deeper into her own being. Alternatively, in astrology, the ideal seems to suggest that the astrologer reveals wonders to the passive client who merely has to show up for the appointment.

What I have found over time is that yes, all a client has to do is show up. But the quality of that showing up determines the quality of the reading. The client is actually bringing with him a resource that supersedes the birth chart itself: himself, and his innate knowing, alongside his memories, feelings and intuition. This respect for what the client brings to the reading helps dislodge the useless fantasy of the astrologer as a magician, producing meaning from out of the blue. That is not to say that exciting, or even life-changing,

information does not arise. It is just not useful to see it in that dualistic way, as a declaration of one to the other. This misses the way
the *knowing field* itself holds both people and allows insights to arise
from one or both of them.

David Hawkins writes: "Discovery of this field is simple, easy
and relaxed. The realization is a consequence of 'allowing' rather than
trying. It is surrendered to rather than acquired. As desire for, and
the ego's obsession with, control are relinquished, the field presents
itself for recognition." [10]

This seeming polarity between the self-discovery of the client in
her own terms and the apparent capacity of the astrologer, through
the natal chart, to articulate information about the client has simply
resolved itself the longer I have practiced both of these paths.

I have found that psychotherapy gains from the framework of
deeper meaning, the evolutionary journey of the Soul. I have found
that astrology readings benefit from turning toward the client and
her direct experience: her inner truth. What seem like two opposite
poles, when held together over time, have begun to blend and infuse
each other with extra meaning and power. I increasingly find the
whole idea of the astrologer disseminating information to the supplicant client distasteful.

The Two Extremes of Showing-Off or Over-Caring

In fact, in extremes this is an expression of what I have come to term,
in a derogatory sense, the *Magician Complex*. This is when, due to
an *inflation,* the astrologer overrides the client in order to show off
what the natal chart analysis can do to describe the client's experience. Over a conference dinner, an astrologer once expounded this
technique to me, describing how she would explicitly discourage her
clients from speaking for the first ten or so minutes of the reading in
order for them to reveal to the client her acute psychological analysis
of the client's personality. While I can understand that this is an attempt to establish a precedent of the insight of the astrologer, it also

smacks of ego inflation. As with all inflation, there is an underlying insecurity. Here, this person's technique appears to be more about trying to prove the validity of astrology—and therefore the astrologer—than it is about listening to the needs of the client or inquiring about her presenting issue or questions.

The other extreme, frequently seen in the counseling and psychotherapy worlds, is what I have come to see as the *Mother Complex*. This occurs when the counselor attempts to channel the entire expression of the therapeutic encounter through the filter of care: of being, or of appearing to be, caring. The danger here is of becoming bland and of never offering the client any form of detached understanding, objectivity or authority. Clients of mine who have experienced this kind of therapy before working with me usually say the same kind of thing. They report that initially, the feeling of being in a safe enough space to get whatever is was that they needed was healing. But when they had expressed what they needed to get "off their chest," they received no response, no meeting from the therapist, and an avoidance of the encounter. These clients invariably left therapy at that point. This could happen after one session or three months (in rare cases, even longer), depending on their level of attachment, need, and how pent-up they felt before beginning therapy.

Some clients have arrived for their very first session with me asking, "Are you the kind of therapist who never says anything?" These clients have become very frustrated by the silent type of care or excessive use of mirroring techniques. For example, if a client is angry, the counselor may say something like "I hear that you are angry." For most people, having what they are already feeling confirmed for them quickly becomes exasperating. Ironically, saying, "I hear that you are angry" over and over can lead to more anger. Furthermore, the danger of this fantasy of neutrality, or of "blanket care," is that it misses the pressing need of the client for the experience of the therapist or astrologer. As Owen Renik writes in *Practical Psychoanalysis for Therapists and Patients*, "The only thing an analyst really has to offer, and the only thing a patient can really use, is the analyst's account of his or her experience."[11]

Through this account, we also learn how the astrologer's personal experience can enhance the reading. So, in addition to allowing room for our clients to share as I've been advocating for throughout this book, we also need to allow room for our own presence in an authentic but uninflated way. It is key to know when it is time to share our life experience or our personal experience of astrology. When considering what to add and what to withhold, think in terms of what astrology done for you. Think about your understanding of specific aspects in your chart, and what insights have been beneficial to you. Have these insights ready to share if the opportunity presents itself.

When watching out for the pitfalls that might lead to an imbalance of these approaches, remember that the tendency is to lean towards the *magician complex,* since without some spark of meaning to share about the natal chart, a person is going to struggle to be a convincing astrologer. I am sure there are successful astrologers out there whose default mode is very similar to the *magician complex.* But that approach is incomplete—just as the mothering framework in counseling is also inherently limited, and therefore limiting of the client.

As the astrologer, it's important to consciously set the tone of the experience. If one forces an intellectual precision, that will be the dominant mode of relating. If one is primarily caring without offering much insight or authority, then that emotional tone will dominate.

There is a middle way of engaging with the other that is within the sacred bond of the *I-Thou* relationship and that allows the other to be himself—engaged in a process of self-discovery without shying away from the depth of meaning contained in the birth chart and within the psyche and of the Soul itself. It is this path in which you'll begin to experience a whole new degree of synthesis.

Chart Reading and the Knowing Field

In trusting the *knowing field*, one is able to follow the highest good as an intention within that field. Remember, the *knowing field* is the personal and transpersonal energy field which interconnects and interpenetrates every individual and envelops the counseling space. Holding a wordless and open stance in the awareness of the knowing field allows one to follow a structure for a reading that is not conditional. If we hold this level of trust, we can release any attachments to a certain astrological interpretation of the chart or a set list of questions. Both the client and the astrologer are then free to be real without scripting everything out beforehand. It's not that you don't prepare by studying the chart. It's that you cultivate openness during the reading.

This approach respects the central insights of the spiritual traditions: that underlying the perceived content of the mind, there lies a formless field of infinite context (called God, or luminous nature of Mind) from which we draw presence and meaning. In this way, certain mental projections and positions that we hold are revealed to be insubstantial, having no intrinsic or ultimate meaning. This approach aligns with core truths revealed through meditation:

"One benefit of meditation is the discovery that, intrinsically, the energy field of the mind is itself basically void of thoughts, feelings, and images, and that these activities actually occupy only about one percent of the total mind field . . . The undisciplined mind is attracted and glamorized by the active content of mind, with its kaleidoscopic parade of thoughts, images, and feelings because of the subtle narcissistic payoff of these activities. To silence the mind, it is necessary to notice the subtle, continuous payoffs, be willing to surrender these illusory gains, and instead identify with the mind as a silent energy field that is not limited to the personal self." [12]

This underlying energy, built of silence and not limited to the personal self, is the *knowing field*. And its universal presence supports every encounter, both therapeutic and astrological. The key to entering this field in the presence of another is to begin with sacred respect of the *I-Thou* encounter. From this place we can see our intellectual limitations and the pretensions of even our most well-rounded theoretical knowledge of astrology, or therapeutic healing. It is not that our ideas about healing or the meaning of the birth chart have no value or meaning, but rather they are revealed to be fundamentally less special than we may have thought. Instead, the luminous nature of reality begins to shine through that with which we have begun to drop identification.

The curious and profound realization that begins to occur as one develops an increasing trust in the *knowing field* is that life itself starts to reveal answers to the questions being asked. It is as if an aspect of the presence that cares about the sentient life within it spontaneously responds to what is occurring in the reading, and one can increasingly surrender to what occurs, knowing that one is being held.

In this presence, we are led to the point of the natal chart or the person's life experience that needs focus. When the client speaks about her life a certain phrase might stand out; against the backdrop of the field, it emits a frequency or turns a certain color (these are metaphorical statements to evoke the paradoxical combination of subtlety and underscoring that occurs simultaneously), revealing another dimension to what the client is saying. Perhaps there is a resonance with her childhood or a link to another part of what she had recounted previously. With experience, the capacity to hear the psychological age of the part of the individual speaking becomes ever more lucid.

Another dimension revealed is that of the karmic picture, or what seems to emerge from the previous experience of the soul. I have long been sensitive to an energetic condition in myself—a strange shiver or electricity through my crown and down the back of my head, neck and shoulders—that alerts me when a client's words seem to echo within the many mansions of the soul's memory. With practice and sensitivity, you will develop your own ways of recogniz-

ing and picking up these kinds of subtle layers of energetic communication from the field.

The Intention of the Reading

Again, preparation is still important. But we must not impose too
much structure. You might consider starting your session with a
question that engages the client's participation from the very beginning, like, "How can I help today?" With this simple question, you're
conveying your respect for the client's input and experience while
stating your intention to be of service.

Enter a reading prepared to discuss a few key points about the
chart; then, be open to simply be with that person and see what
emerges. In that openness, the natal chart exists like a map, a guide
that is there should you need it. As the territory is complex, often
you will, though not as often as you might expect. Don't bury your
head in the map and miss the amazing view right in front of you.

Many people prepare for readings by spending a lot of time,
with considerable anxiety. I find this time is better spent memorizing the chart. By doing this, you can hold the chart in mind while
maintaining eye contact with the person in front of you. If more
analysis is required, you can do it during the reading. If a question
involves checking the progressions and transit activity for a certain
month or year, modern computing makes that quick and easy.

Even if your memory struggles to hold the entire chart, you can
learn to remember only its crucial parts. For example, if you're using
my method—memorizing just the Pluto placement, the nodes of
the Moon and anything in a fourth harmonic relationship to those
placements will give tremendous insight when held lightly in the
mind's eye.

Different Readings for Different People

With this open approach, you'll find every session is different. You might do one reading in which you carefully explain the whole structure of the individual's chart and relate it to his past experience. In the next reading you may only speak for ten minutes as the client needs to share powerful events. Then you only use her chart to help her accept and process what happened. The next reading might just focus on one primary question which we use the chart to contemplate. These are three readings, all different in structure, not just because they are different charts, but because they are different people with different needs.

And again, remember your audience. You'll take a different approach with a student of astrology and someone who does not have much interest in astrological methods. With the former, you may draw illustrative structures on his chart printout and engage him in reading the chart with you to facilitate a combination of personal growth and astrological insight. With the other, you may not even use explicit astrological terminology. The key is to always remain open to the authentic needs of the one who has come to you for a reading.

This of course means that while the basic natal pattern remains the same, a person could come for a reading with you one year and come again a year or two later, and each reading will develop in accord with the person's development. This is a beautiful living web of interconnectedness between the astrologer, the client, the natal chart and life itself through the *knowing field,* of which the natal chart is simply a symbolic representation.

The natal chart is, in essence, the symbolic potential encapsulated in a moment of space-time through the correspondence between the micro- and macrocosmic worlds ("As above, so below," as the great hermetic maxim puts it). This symbolic potential becomes actualized through the consciousness of the individual—which is the deciding factor par excellence. This process could be compared to the concept of *entelechy* put forward by Aristotle where, when the conditions are right, the potential of life emerges into the actual, as that is its nature. When people are given the right conditions for their true potential to be understood and supported, then, quite naturally, it begins to manifest.

The Therapeutic Value of the Client's Experience

Nothing ought to override the consciousness of the individual. Astrology will lead us astray the moment we begin to feel that the strange sets of symbols the chart contains somehow give us greater access to the soul of the other than the individual herself. No one knows the client more than she does. As we've been exploring, it is hubris (or an over-active *magician complex*) to think otherwise. Although that does not mean we cannot gain insights from the chart that might surprise or shock the client; that is not the same thing. What I am referring to is an inner humility before the '*Thou*' of the client rather than a systematic arrogance towards the '*it*' (Buber) of the client that over identification or confidence in the nature of astrology can bring about.

This is a complex point and worth elucidating clearly. One critical component is that the astrologer is being encouraged to bow to the deep self of the client, not his neurotic, distracted or false self. Distinguishing between the two is paramount. This is why there is a never-ending stream of therapeutic literature and why quality counseling and therapy trainings take so long. To develop the capacity to distinguish between the layers of the psyche and how they present within the multiplicity of human character and expression relates to the essence of therapeutic wisdom. While training and study can prepare the ground for this capacity, fundamentally, it is a quality that cannot be taught. It arises instead from a combination of self-insight and experience.

Even with considerable self-insight and experience, a near constant attention and radical humility before the other must be maintained in one's therapeutic work. This is *sadhana*, this is one's practice. There is no perfection within that practice. Even the most experienced therapist or therapeutic astrologer will make mistakes.

Yet experience and self-knowledge will minimize them, or at least reveal how honest and speedy acknowledgment of the mistake might itself lead to greater capacity for depth within the relationship.

Experience and acclaim comes with their own trappings. As we gain more confidence in our methods of practice, we might also become more attached to those methods. Mistakes serve to keep us humble and engaged with the real in this context. The mistake may not actually be theoretical or technical, but rather an expression of how to adapt one's technical expertise into the lived experience of the client.

From the perspective of the client, it is not good enough to have mastered a technique that one simply displays unchanged in reading after reading. The danger is that such a method is used to bludgeon into submission the reality of the client's subjective experience. In the face of any evidence from the client that conflicts with our approach, we might find ourselves taking the position that our years of expertise make it true for her, and that she has simply not realized this yet. Even if there were a modicum of truth to such an insight, the situation calls for effective counseling skills united with a fundamental respect for the subjective reality of the client. Sometimes the technical capacity of the professional astrologer can be used as a defense against the deeper form of engagement with the client I advocate for in these pages.

Conversely, many a skillful student, yet inexperienced practitioner, becomes overly concerned, to the point of distraction, with doing a good job. Here the super-ego, with all its potential for inner tyranny, can come into play. And these kinds of astrologers become lost in endless preparation of the chart, as if it were possible to predict the reality of clients to whom they haven't even spoken yet. Never mind that the student astrologer who spends 6-8 hours preparing for a 90-minute reading could never become professional, as she would never have enough time to see her clients!

Clearly, many astrologers are not therapists, and yet have devoted considerable time and energy becoming expert in a field that is sufficiently complex that one could devote one's entire lifetime to its study and not hope to comprehend it all. We might rightly say that such a lifetime of study is worthwhile in its own right. But one of the core aims of this book is to raise awareness about the client's point of view in an astrological reading. For those whose natal chart readings focus on the development of the potential of the client, or character analysis, or even predictive ruminations on the individual's calling or self-expression, the reality of the counseling aspect of the work will be raised even higher, especially for the client.

People invest great expense in and project great meaning onto the natal chart reading. They would not do this if they did not reasonably expect to gain information or guidance as to the meaning, purpose or direction of their lives. In that context, they might reasonably expect the astrologer to have some considered degree of expertise in dealing with people and in negotiating multiple perspectives, including conflict and its resolution, different paradigms in relationships, a working definition of maturation, perspectives on potential careers and so on.

If the practitioner is offering some form of coaching or psychological astrology, she might reasonably expect to add to that list an understanding of developmental psychology, the impact of early childhood experience on adult relationships, and the nature of unconscious structures including defensive patterns. If the astrologer is offering a spiritual or karmic perspective, then it might be reasonable for the client to expect an understanding of the different spiritual traditions of the world and the astrologer's take on karma and the evolutionary journey of the soul.

If astrology is to achieve the professional standing and respect to which many who practice it aspire, then surely, astrologers themselves need to explore the interface between astrology and the existing traditions of the world—philosophy, religion, depth psychology, the arts and sciences. The danger is that astrology draws on a potpourri of New Age perspectives on spirituality and quantum physics and a relatively superficial understanding of Jung for validation of its insights. In this case, astrology cannot help but be positioned as a New Age phenomenon.

I make these points not because I am invested in critiquing the astrological community. I am in fact interested in astrology gaining respect as the multidimensional transformational tool that I experience it to be at its best. So, because I see so much potential in it, I ask more from it. In a culture such as my own in the United Kingdom, in which a concept of reason that increasingly takes the form of scientism is king, astrology is denigrated as an intellectual cul-de-sac or parlor game. Or worse, it is seen as the very epitome of delusional thinking. In this environment, the only academic validity toward which astrology can aspire is as an object of cultural anthropology in which it is studied as part of the evolution of beliefs from "primitive" cultures through to the modern day astronomical world. Even when, within this paradigm, astrology is studied sincerely and the great tradition from Babylonian times through the Egyptian and Hellenistic worlds is explored and validated, the danger becomes that astrology is venerated as a prized antique within a collection. What is in danger of being lost is the living potential of astrology; the understanding of the birth chart that might utterly transform an individual's life, right now.

Astrology's real potential is so inspirational. I have witnessed first-hand astrology's actualized potential to illuminate, with the light of the soul, the living experience of what it means to be a human being. It has been my intention here to make the case for the conscious application of therapeutic awareness within the natal reading in order to enrich the experience for both the client and astrologer, enhancing our perception of the soulful encounter, and acknowledging the process with the respect and awe it deserves.

Endnotes

Introduction

1. Christina Rose, *Astrological Counselling: A basic guide to astrological themes in person to person relationships* (Wellingborough, Northants: Aquarian Press, 1982), 15.

2. Ibid, 23.

3. Deniz Ertan, *Dane Rudhyar: His Music, Thought and Art* (Rochester, NY: University of Rochester Press, 2009), 31. A picture shows him crossing out a sentence of the New Grove dictionary of music which said he was a Theosophist and describes him as having "a grasp of theosophy without a sense of obligation to the theosophical movement."

Chapter 1

1. Quoted by Christina Rose as the inscription to *Astrological Counselling* (Northants, UK: Aquarian Press, 1982).

2. Letter to Louise Dorothea of Meiningen, duchess of Saxe-Gotha Madame (30 January 1762).

3. James Hillman, *The Myth of Analysis* (London: Routledge and Paul, 1960), 122-3.

4. James Hillman, *Healing Fiction* (Barrytown, NY: Station Hill Press, 1983).

5. Wolfgang Giegerich, *What is Soul?* (New Orleans, LA: Spring Publications, 2012), 16.

6. Ira Progoff, *The Symbolic and the Real* (London: Conventure, 1963).

7. 19 billion dollars in a recent account by Irving Kirsch, *The Emperor's New Drugs* (London, Bodley Head, 2009), 1.

8. Thomas Szasz, "Curing the Therapeutic State: Thomas Szasz interviewed by Jacob Sullum," July 2000, Reason.com. Retrieved June 2015 from:

http://reason.com/archives/2000/07/01/curing-the-therapeutic-state-t

9. Mark Epstein, "The Trauma of Being Alive" (New York: New York Times, 2013).   http://www.nytimes.com/2013/08/04/opinion/sunday/the-trauma-of-being-alive.html

10. Sigmund Freud, *New Introductory Lectures on Psychoanalysis* (London: Hogarth Press and the Institute of Psycho-analysis, 1964), 74.

11. Patrick Curry, *Astrology, Science and Culture* (Oxford: Berg, 2003), 15.

12. Plotinus, *The Six Enneads* (Chicago : Encyclopædia Britannica, 1955) Tractate 2:3.

13. Patrick Curry, *Astrology, Science and Culture* (Oxford: Berg, 2003), 16.

14. Ibid, 12.

15. Richard Dawkins, *The Selfish Gene* (Oxford: Oxford University Press, 1976).

16. Karen Horney, *Neurosis and Human Growth* (New York: Norton, 1950), 18.

17. Retrieved 2/14/2014: http://www.reuters.com/article/2011/09/04/us-europe-mental-illness-idUSTRE7832JJ20110904.

18. See Aldous Huxley, *The Perennial Philosophy* (London: Harper & Brothers, 1945).

19. Paramahansa Yogananda *Autobiography of a Yogi* (Los Angeles, CA: Self-Realization Fellowship, 1946), 188.

Chapter 2

1. James Hollis, *Creating a Life: Finding Your Individual Path* (Toronto: Inner City Books, 2001), 18-19. Reproduced in full with the kind permission of the author – though I have changed the word patient to client throughout – to reflect my non-psychoanalytic orientation (i.e., I call the people I work with clients, not patients) and to emphasize the link to astrology.

2. Jung in Mario Jacoby, *Individuation and Narcissism: the Psychology of Self in Jung and Kohut* (London; New York: Routledge, 1990), 100-101.

3. Mario Jacoby, *The Analytic Encounter: Transference and Human Relationship* (Toronto: Inner City Books, 1984), 44. Kohut quoted by Jacoby, 43

4. Donald Kalsched, *Unlocking the Secrets of the Wounded Psyche: the Miraculous Survival System that is also a Prison*; interview with Dabiela Sieff (West Sussex England: Caduceus), vols 69 and 70.

5. Ibid.

6. Richard Rohr, *Immortal Diamond* (San Francisco: Jossey-Bass, 2013), 62.

Have -
Lib *

Power vs. Force   **Chapter 3**

1. David R. Hawkins, *Transcending the Levels of Consciousness* (Sedona: Veritas, 2006), 186.

2. Brene Brown, "The Power of Vulnerability," Ted Talks, http://www.ted.com/talks/brene_brown_on_vulnerability?language=en

3. Gregg Levoy, *Callings: Finding and Following an Authentic Life* (New York: Harmony Books, 1997)

4. Ernest Becker, *The Denial of Death (New York: Free Press, 1973), 89.*

5. I have found that in person readings are superior in many ways. Readings over the phone or by Skype are very close to that but it takes a certain expertise with this format to compensate for the lack of capacity to read body language and to generate the same degree of presence. Taped and written readings, can be very limited as this removes the client's capacity to feedback and to co-create the reading with the astrologer. Taking time to gather more detailed information from the client over email can circumvent some of this limitation, but readings in which the client can communicate in real time are preferable. For the most profound experience of a reading to occur, both client and astrologer collaborate together to find the most relevant way to explore the symbolism of the natal chart within the individual life.

6. Brene Brown, "The Power of Vulnerability," Ted Talks, http://www.ted.com/talks/brene_brown_on_vulnerability?language=en

7. Richard Rohr, *Immortal Diamond (San Francisco: Jossey-Bass, 2013), 126 (quotation)*

8. The emptiness of sunyata is critically different from personal emptiness; things are shown to be devoid of inherent existence because they are all of one taste, they all manifest from the same consciousness.

9. Donald Kalsched, *The Inner World of Trauma: Archetypal Defences of the Spirit* (New York: Routledge, 1996), 5.

10. All Wales Psychotherapy Network Annual Conference, Abergavenny, June 1, 2012. The theme was trauma. Keynote speaker Remy Aquarone. Aquarone's talk: "Dissociation in Transition" - from hysteria and the use of hypnosis to Freud's model of Fantasy and the Oedipus complex and finally back to Janet's structural dissociation of the personality - with a focus on clinical work and multidisciplinary team working.

11. Paramahansa Yogananda, *Autobiography of a Yogi* (Los Angeles: Self-Realization Fellowship, 1971), 188-9 (quote from guru Sri Yukteswar).

12. Ted Hughes; William Scammell, *Winter Pollen: Occasional Prose* (New York: Picador USA, 1995), xiii. (from the Introduction by William Scammell)

13. Erica Jong, *Ordinary Miracles: New Pomes* (New York: New American Library, 1983), poem *Only One Story*.http://www.ericajong.com/poems/thereisonlyonestory.htm

14. Veronica Goodchild, *Eros and Chaos: the Sacred Mysteries and Dark Shadows of Love* (York Beach, Me: Nicolas-Hays: Distributed to the trade by Weiser books, 2001), 3.

15. Ibid, 130. Quoting Jung.

16. *Supplements to A Course in Miracles: Psychotherapy* (New York: Viking: Foundation for Inner Peace, 1996), 7.

Chapter 4

1. Donald Winnicott, *The Maturational Processes and the Facilitating Environment* (London: Hogarth; 1965), 30.

2. James Hollis, *Under Saturn's Shadow: the Wounding and Healing of Men* (Toronto, Canada: Inner City Books, 1994), 27.

3. Morris Berman interview podcast, "Dark Ages America," January 2015. http://whatnowsolutions.org/morris-berman-dark-ages-america/

4. A.H. Almaas, *The Point of Existence: Transformations of Narcissism in Self-Realization* (Boston: Shambala, 2001), 318.

5. Ibid.

6. Sigmund Freud, *An Outline of Psychoanalysis* (New York: W.W. Norton, 1969), 89.

7. Jacques Barzun, *From Dawn to Decadence: 500 years of Western Cultural Life: 1500 to the Present (New York: Harper Collins, 2000)*, 552.

8. Faramerz Dabhoiwala, *The Origins of Sex: A History Of The First Sexual Revolution (New York: Oxford University Press, 2012)*, 1.

9. Sigmund Freud, *An Outline of Psychoanalysis (New York: W.W. Norton, 1969)*, 95.

10. Donald Kalsched *The Inner World of Trauma: Archetypal Defenses of the Spirit (New York: Routledge, 1996)*, 5.

11. Ibid.

Chapter 5

1. Dane Rudhyar, *Planetary Octaves and Rulership*, retrieved from Khaldea.com on 2/14/2015: http://www.khaldea.com/rudhyar/astroarticles/planetaryoctaves.php

2. Ira Progoff, *The Symbolic and the Real* (London: Coventure, 1963), 50.

3. Martin Buber, *I and Thou* (New York: Scribner, 1958), 81.

4. Dr. David Hawkins, *Transcending the Levels of Consciousness: the Stairway to Enlightenment* (Sedona: Veritas, 2006), 99.

5. To learn more, I recommend two great books illuminating this process of projecting our value onto other people written by Jungian analyst Robert Johnson: *Inner Gold,* (Koa Books 2010), and *The Psychology of Romantic Love* (Arkana, 1990). A great book about the way the individual is conditioned by the early environment is *The Pearl Beyond Price: the Integration of Personality into Being* by A H Almaas (Shambhala Publications Inc 1996).

6. Dr. David Hawkins, *The Eye of the I: From Which Nothing is Hidden* (Sedona: Veritas, 2002), 6.

7. Ibid, 7.

Chapter 6

1. Dane Rudhyar, *The Lunation Cycle* (Sante Fe: Aurora,1967), 1.

2. Retrograde motion is not "real" motion of the planets, but is created by the earth's orbit and its influence on the apparent motion of a planet when seen from Earth. Retrograde planets do not actually change their orbit; the only change is a perceptual one from the geocentric observation, when the position of the planet in relationship to the orbit of the earth around the Sun creates an apparent backward motion.

3. Ken Wilbur, *Integral Psychology* (Boston: Shambhala, 2000), 93.

4. Colin Wilson , *A Criminal History of Mankind* (New York: Putnam, 1984), 137.

5. Jacques Lusseyran, *And There Was Light* (Boston: Little, Brown, 1963), 8.

6. Ibid, 10.

7. Ibid, 10.

8. As many have, few as clearly as Ernst Becker in the *Denial of Death and The Problem of Evil.*

9. Daniel J. Levinson, *The Seasons of a Man's Life (New York: Random House, 1978), 134-5.*

10. See *Healing the Soul*, p154-5.

11. Quoted in William Fraser, *Words on Wellington*, 1889

12. Daniel J. Levinson, *The Seasons of a Man's Life* (New York: Random House, 1978), 250. Quoting James Baldwin, from his review of Elia Kazan's *The Arrangement.*

13. Ibid, 191.

14. Ibid, Preface X-XI. As an aside, it comes as no surprise to astrologers that Levinson naturally identified the life transitions he calls the "Age Thirty Transition" and "Midlife Transition" because they correspond to the timing of two classic astrological life markers: the Saturn Return and Uranus opposition. Facts like these present astrologers with an opportunity to educate the public about astrological validity.

15. Ibid, 248.

16. Oliver Sacks, *Musicophilia* (London: Picador; 2008), 4.

17. Ibid, 3. Event occurred in 1994. See also New York Times book review: http://www.nytimes.com/2007/10/28/books/review/Gottlieb-t.html?_r=0 and New Yorker article "A Bolt From the Blue": http://www.newyorker.com/ magazine/2007/07/23/a-bolt-from-the-blue. His probable birth chart is January 29, 1952 in New York – from personal internet source - http://suite101.com/article/who-is-drtony-cicoria-ndes-a51732 - Uranus is 12 degrees past opposition, with Neptune and conjunct his Mercury, south node ruler – a wider orb that I have found significant and began to work with after considering Richard Tarnas' work on historical analysis in *Cosmos and Psyche*.

18. Oliver Sacks, *Musicophillia* (London:Picador, 2008), 6.

19. Ervin Laszlo, *Science and the Akashic Field* (Rochester, VT: Inner Traditions, 2004), 49.

20. Ibid, 116 (italics mine).

21. Daniel J. Levinson, *The Seasons of a Man's Life* (New York: Random House, 1978), 196.

22. Professor Christopher Dye, *The Times of Our Lives: a History of Longevity* (Gresham College) - http://www.gresham.ac.uk/lectures-and-events/the-times-of-our-lives-a-history-of-longevity

23. Paul Vitz, *Sigmund Freud's Christian Unconscious* (New York: Guildford Press, 1988), 71.

24. Ibid, 71.

Chapter 7

1. Richard Tarnas, *Cosmos and Psyche* (New York: Viking, 2006), 28.

2. Firman and Gila, *Psychosynthesis: A Psychology of the Spirit* (Albany: State University of New York Press, 2002), 19.

3. Roberto Assagioli, *Psychosynthesis: A Manual of Principles and Technique* (New York: Viking Press, 1965), 194.

4. Carl Jung in a letter to Sigmund Freud, Burgholzli-Zurich, April 2, 1909, *The Freud/Jung Letters*, abridged version (London: Penguin, 1991.), 143.

5. Carl Jung, *Memories, Dreams and Reflections* (New York: Pantheon, 1963), 150.

6. A more accessible presentation of Bailey's work can be found in Alan Oken's *Soul-Centered Astrology* and Errol Weiner's *Transpersonal Astrology*.

7. *The Freud/Jung Letters*, the abridged version (London: Penguin, 1991), 223.

8. Dane Rudhyar, *The Astrology of Personality: a Re-formulation of Astrological Concepts and Ideals, in Terms of Contemporary Psychology and Philosophy* (Sante Fe: Aurora 1991), 258.

9. *Supplements to A Course In Miracles* (New York: Viking Penguin, 1996), 29.

10. Dr David Hawkins, *I:Reality and Subjectivity* (Sedona: Veritas, 2003), 308.

11. Ibid, 50.

12. Dr. David Hawkins, *Reality, Spirituality and Modern Man* (Sedona: Veritas, 2008), 297.

Selected Bibliography

For further reading on counseling dynamics:

General

A. H. Almaas, *Diamond Heart – Book One: Elements of the Real in Man* (Boulder, Co; Shamabhala Publications Inc, 1996)

A. H. Almaas, *Diamond Heart – Book Three: Being & the Meaning of Life* (Boulder, Co; Shamabhala Publications Inc, 1996)

Steve Biddulph, *Manhood: An action plan for changing men's lives* (Sydney: Finch, 1995)

Ernst Becker, *The Denial of Death* (New York: Free Press, 1973)

Robert Bly, William C. Book, *A Little Book on the Human Shadow* (San Francisco: Harper & Row, 1988)

John Bradshaw, *On the Family: A New Way of Creating Solid Self-Esteem* (Deerfield Beach, Florida: Health Communications, 1996)

Joseph Campbell, *Thou Art That: Transforming Religious Metaphor* (Novato, CA: New World Library, 2001)

Lionel Corbett, *The Sacred Cauldron: Psychotherapy as a Spiritual Practice* (Wilmette, Illinois: Chiron, 2001)

Mihaly Csikzentmihalyi, *Flow: the Psychology of Optimal Experience* (New York: Harper & Row, 1990)

Clarissa Pinkola Estés, *Women Who Run With Wolves: Myths & Stories of the Wild Woman Archetype* (New York; Ballantine Books, 1992)

Viktor Frankl, *Man's Search For Meaning: An Introduction to Logotherapy* (New York; Simon & Schuster, 1959)

John Geiger, *The Third Man Factor: Surviving the Impossible* (New York: Weinstein, 2009)

David R. Hawkins, *Letting Go: The Pathway of Surrender* (Carlsbad, CA: Hay House, 2013)

Bert Hellinger, Gabriele Ten Hovel, *Acknowledging What Is: Conversations with Bert Hellinger* (Phoenix, AZ: Zeig, Tucker, 1999)

James Hillman, *The Soul's Code: In Search of Character and Calling* (New York: Random House, 1996) —*H?*

James Hillman & Michael Ventura, *We've Had a Hundred Years of Psychotherapy And the World's Getting Worse* (San Francisco, Calif; Harper San Francisco, 1993)

James Hollis, *The Middle Passage: From Misery to Meaning in Midlife* (Toronto: Inner City Books, 1983)

Aldous Huxley, *The Doors of Perception* (New York; Harper & Brothers, 1954)

Stephen Jenkinson, *Die Wise: A Manifesto for Sanity & Soul* (Berkley, California: North Atlantic Books, 2015)

Robert A. Johnson, *Inner Gold: Understanding Psychological Projection* (Hawaii, Koa Books, 2008)

C. G. Jung, *Memories, Dreams, Reflections* (New York: Pantheon, 1963)

Gary Lachman, *A Secret History of Consciousness* (Great Barrington, MA: Lindisfarne, 2003) *LIB* *Revolutionaries of the Soul - Lachman*

R.D. Laing, *The Divided Self: An Existential Study in Sanity & Madness* (Harmandsworth, Middlesex; Baltimore: Penguin Books, 1965)

Peter Levine, *Walking the Tiger: Healing Trauma: The Innate Capacity to Transform Overwhelming Experiences* (Berkley, CA: North Atlantic Books, 1997)

Gregg Levoy, *Callings: Finding and Following an Authentic Life* (New York: Harmony, 1997)

Alice Miller, *The Drama of Being a Child and the Search for the True Self* (London: Virago, 1987)

The Outsider - Colin Wilson — *LIB*

Sylvia Brinton Perera, *Descent to the Goddess: A Way of Initiation for Women* (Toronto: Inner City Books, 1981)

Owen Renik, *Practical Psychoanalysis for Therapists and Patients* (New York: Other Press, 2006)

Richard Rohr, *Immortal Diamond: The Search for Our True Self* (San Francisco, CA: Jossey-Bass, 2013)

Peter Rutter, *Sex in the Forbidden Zone: Where Men in Power – Therapists, Doctors, Clergy, Teachers, and Others – Betray Women's Trust* (LA; Tarcher, NY: Distributed by St Martins Press, 1989)

Meredith Sabini, *The Earth has a Soul: The Nature Writings of C G Jung* (Berkley, CA: North Atlantic, 2002)

Robert Sardello, *Love and the Soul: Creating a Future for Earth* (New York: Harper Collins, 1995)

Phillip Shepherd, *New Self, New World: Recovering Our Senses in the Twenty-First Century* (Berkley, CA: North Atlantic Books, 2010)

Alan Watts, *The Book; On the Taboo Against Knowing Who You Are* (New York; Pantheon Books, 1966)

Robert Whitaker, *Anatomy of an Epidemic: Magic Bullets, Psychiatric Drugs and the Astonishing Rise of Mental Illness in America* (New York: Crown Publishers, 2010)

Irvin D. Yalom, *Love's Executioner and Other Tales of Psychotherapy* (New York: Basic Books, 1989)

Professional Counseling Interest

A. H. Almaas, *The Pearl Beyond Price: integration of personality into being, an object relations approach* (Berkley, CA: Diamond Books, 1988)

A. H. Almaas, *The Point of Existence: Transformations of Narcissism in Self-Realization* (Boston: Shambhala, 2001)

Roberto Assagioli, *Psychosynthesis – A Manual of Principles & Techniques* (New York; Hobbs, Dorman, 1965)

Roberto Assagioli, *The Act of Will* (New York; Viking Press, 1973)

Roberto Assagioli, *Transpersonal Development – The Dimension Beyond Psychosynthesis* (London; Aquarian Press, 1993)

Richard P. Bentall, *Madness Explained: Psychosis and Human Nature* (London; New York: Routledge, 1992)

Eric Berne, *The Games People Play – The Psychology of Human Relationships* (New York; Grove Press, 1964)

Jerome S. Bernstein, *Living in the Borderland: The Evolution of Consciousness and the* ↙ *Challenge of Healing Trauma* (London; New York: Routledge, 2005)

Jean Shinoda Bolen, *The Ring of Power: The Abandoned Child, The Authoritarian Father, and the Disempowered Feminine: a Jungian Understanding of Wagner's Ring Cycle* (San Francisco: Harper, 1992)

Stephen Harrod Buhner, *Ensouling Language* (Rochester, Vt; Inner Traditions, ↙ 2010)

Martin Büber, *I and Thou* (New York; Scribner, 1958)

Patrick Casement, *On Learning From the Patient* (London; New York: Tavistock, ↙ 1985)

Lionel Corbett, *The Religious Function of the Psyche* (London; New York: Routledge, 1996)

John Firman & Ann Gila, *Psychosynthesis: A Psychology of the Spirit* (New York: ↙ State University of New York Press, 2002)

John Firman & Ann Gila, *The Primal Wound: A Transpersonal View of Trauma, Addiction, and Growth* (New York; State University of New York Press, 1997)

Sigmund Freud, *An Outline of Psychoanalysis* (New York: Norton, 1949)

Stanislav Grof, *The Future of Psychology: Lessons from Modern Consciousness Research* ↙ (Albany, NY: State of New York University Press, 2000)

Onno Van Der Hart, E. R. S. Nigenhuis, Kathy Steele, *The Haunted Self: Structural Disassociation and the Treatment of Chronic Traumatization* (New York: Norton, ↙ 2006)

Bert Hellinger, Gunthard Weber, Hunter Beaumont, *Love's Hidden Symmetry: What Makes Love Work in Relationships* (Phoenix, AZ: Zeig, Tucker, 1998)

⋇ James Hillman, *The Thought of the Heart and the Soul of the World* (New York; Spring Publications, 1998)

⋇ James Hillman, *Healing Fiction* (Barrytown, New York: Station Hill Press, 1983)

James Hillman, *Re-visioning Psychology* (New York: Harper & Row, 1975)

Karen Horney, *Neurosis and Human Growth: The Struggle Toward Self-Realization* (New York: Norton, 1991 new ed)

⋇ Mario Jacoby, *Individuation and Narcissism: The Psychology of the Self in Jung and Kohut* (London; New York: Routledge, 1990)

Carl Gustav Jung, *The Collected Works of C. G. Jung – Bollingen Series 1-20* (London; Routledge & Kean Paul, 1953-1979)

Carl Gustav Jung, *The Undiscovered Self* (Boston, Ma; Little, Brown, 1958)

Donald Kalsched, *The Inner World of Trauma, Archetypal Defenses of the Personal Spirit* (London; New York: Routledge, 1996)

Donal Kalsched, *Trauma and the Soul: A Psycho-Spiritual Approach to Human Development and its Interruption* (London; New York: Routledge, 2013)

Irving Kirsch, *The Emperor's New Drugs: Exploding the Antidepressant Myth* (New York: Basic Books, 2010)

Carolyn Myss, *Sacred Contracts: Awakening Your Divine Potential* (New York; Harmony Books, 2001)

Will Parfitt, *The Elements of Psychosynthesis* (Dorset; Element Books, 1990)

⋇ Will Parfitt (editor), *Psychosynthesis: New Perspectives & Creative Research – The Best of the Synthesist Journal* (Glastonbury; PS Avalon, 2009)

⋇ Bill Plotkin, *Soulcraft – Crossing into the Mysteries of Nature & Psyche* (Novato, Calif; New World Library, 2003)

John J. Prendergast, Peter G. Fenner, Sheila Krystal, *The Sacred Mirror: Non-Dual Wisdom and Psychotherapy* (St Paul, MN: Omega Books, 2003)

Ira Progoff, *The Death and Rebirth of Psychology: An Integrative Evaluation of Freud, Adler, Jung and Rank and the Impact of Their Culminating Insights on Modern Man* (New York: Julian Press, 1956)

Ira Progoff, *The Symbolic and the Real: A New Psychological Approach to the Fuller Experience of Human Existence* (New York: Julian, 1963)

Robert Romanyshyn, *The Wounded Researcher: Research with Soul in Mind* (New Orleans, La; Spring Journal Books, 2007)

Nathan Schwartz-Salant, *The Black Nightgown: The Fusional Complex and the Unlived Life* (Wilmette, Illinois: Chiron, 2007)

Nathan Schwartz-Salant, *The Borderline Personality: Vision and Healing* (Wilmette, Illinois: Chiron, 1989)

Paul Shepard, *Nature & Madness* (Athens, Ga; University of Georgia Press, 1982)

David J. Wallin, *Attachment in Psychotherapy* (New York: Guildford Press, 2007)

John Welwood, *Toward a Psychology of Awakening: Buddhism, Psychotherapy and the Path of Personal and Spiritual Transformation* (Boston: Shambhala, 2000)

Ken Wilber, *Integral Psychology: Consciousness, Spirit, Psychology, Therapy* (Boston: Shambhala, 2000)

Donald W. Winnicott, *The Maturational Process and the Facilitating Environment: Studies in the Theory of Emotional Development* (New York: International Universities Press, 1965)

About the Author

Mark Jones is a licensed Psychosynthesis Therapist and astrologer from Bristol, UK. Educated at the Universities of Warwick and Manchester and with the Synthesis organization in Bristol, Mark is internationally known for his work in the field of Evolutionary Astrology. With over a decade of experience as a therapist and astrologer, Mark specializes in past-life analysis and on-going psychological counseling. Mark is a graduate of Noel Tyl's Masters astrology program and is a certified Evolutionary Astrologer.

Mark teaches and lectures in the U.S. annually. His teaching schedule is available online at www.plutoschool.com.

In early 2011 Mark unveiled his online Pluto School of Evolutionary Astrology. His school features at-your-convenience downloadable lessons, mp3 audio workshops, and video downloads.

Contact the author for information about workshops, private readings and counseling.

Mark can be reached at markjones@plutoschool.com.

Learn Astrology with Mark Jones

Study couseling astrology with Mark Jones. Mark's complete *Foundation Course in Evolutionary Astrology* is now offered online at: www.plutoschool.com. Enrolled students can study at their own pace, with instant access to online course materials.

The Foundation Course consists of 12 modules which teach students how to give an evolutionary-style astrology reading based on the concepts Mark presents in *Healing the Soul*. Classes include written and audio material, as well as self-tests and recommendations for additional study. At the end of the course, students are eligible to pursue certification in Evolutionary Astrology with Mark Jones.

Mark is also available to all students for private tutorials. Learn more and enroll today: http://www.plutoschool.com/about-pluto-school

Counseling Skills for Astrologers Course

New in 2015! Take the next step in your studies and enhance your readings with Mark's *Counseling Skills for Astrologers Course*. Designed to help students integrate the concepts presented in *The Soul Speaks*, this course is offered as a series of self-study modules. Presented in audio and pdf format for instant download.

Live Webinars

Mark is proud to offer live webinars at AstrologyUniversity.com. Stop by today for the full schedule of upcoming live events and pre-recorded courses available for instant download.

Made in the USA
Middletown, DE
12 September 2015